BLEEDING
ORANGE

BLEEDING ORANGE

Fifty Years of Blind Referees, Screaming Fans, Beasts of the East, and Syracuse Basketball

JIM BOEHEIM

WITH JACK McCALLUM

HARPER

An Imprint of HarperCollins*Publishers*

HarperCollins books may be purchased for educational, business, or sales promotional use. For information, please e-mail the Special Markets Department at SPsales@harpercollins.com.

All photographs are courtesy of Syracuse University Athletic Communications unless otherwise noted.

FIRST EDITION

Designed by Renato Stanisic

Library of Congress Cataloging-in-Publication Data has been applied for.

ISBN: 978-0-06-231664-6

14 15 16 17 18 OV/RRD 10 9 8 7 6 5 4 3 2 1

I will never be an old man. To me, old age is always 15 years older than I am.

—Francis Bacon

In Europe and America, orange is commonly associated with
amusement, the unconventional, extroverts, fire, activity, danger,
taste and aroma, the autumn season and Protestantism.

—Wikipedia (They forgot Syracuse basketball.)

CONTENTS

BLEEDING
ORANGE

PROLOGUE

No one is leaving. There are 35,000 people in the Carrier Dome, the scoreboard clock reads 00:00, and no one is leaving. Normally, the end of a game initiates a full-scale dash to the parking lots surrounding the Dome. Only so many ways out of our building and so many ways home.

But no dash tonight. Tonight we beat Duke. And no one is going anywhere. In fact, they're standing.

Within hours, our 91–89 overtime win will be rewound as an ESPN "Instant Classic," and I have no argument with that. There's a long way to go in this season, but this night had the feel of living history.

Yet as a coach, you can never celebrate for very long. There is always the next game, always another test right around the corner. Your decisions are endlessly debated, especially the ones that may have cost you a win, the ones that make your guts roil for days. But . . .

What you get in return—sometimes—is beyond calculation. This is one of those times. So as I start to walk off the court, I stop and stare up at the crowd, soak in the noise, bask in the moment, something I don't usually do. Since this is one of those special days, I want to share something small and sincere with the fans who stuck around to show how much the win meant to them.

I'll stand here a minute and maybe figure out what I'm feeling. Scribble some stray notes in my head. I've been doing it all season, from the first day of practice until now—the first time I've attempted to chronicle my life in coaching and my life at Syracuse.

So I wave to the crowd, turning around like a governor at a political rally. It's a small gesture, but they respond in kind.

"Mom's crying," Jamie, my daughter, tells me when I get to the pressroom.

"Why?" I ask.

"Because she never saw you stop and wave like that," she tells me. "She never saw you so happy."

IT'S EXTREMELY HARD for those of us in sports to use the F-word.

No, not *that* one.

I'm talking about "fear." It is with me most of the time. It was with me when I first stepped onto the Syracuse campus 50 years ago, an unknown, unsculpted walk-on, the hick from Lyons, New York. And it's with me now as I contemplate the 2014–15 season, one with many unknowns, like all seasons. It's with me as I look back on the most recent season of consummate highs and soul-crushing lows, two solid months of being ranked either number one or number two before a bitter disappointment in the 2014 NCAA tournament.

I have a fear of failing every day. You would think that the more tests you've passed—and I've passed more than a few during six decades of playing, coaching, watching and loving this game—the more it would go away. But it doesn't. It's not so simple as calling fear a "motivating factor." I'd be motivated to succeed even if I didn't have the fear. I wish I didn't have it. But it goes back a long way, back to my first days at Syracuse.

I'm 17 years old, a walk-on at a time in college basketball when there are 20 scholarship players. I'm in a regular dorm with a non-basketball-playing roommate from Philadelphia, while the recruited players all live together in athletic housing, a team even away from the court. Me? I can't even get a locker. I'm racked with doubt. Will I make it? Will I have to transfer to a smaller school? Will I have to crawl back to Lyons, where a lot of people believed I wouldn't make it in the first place?

I'm not claiming that my experience was—is—unique. Actors experience stage fright, writers get blocked, teachers lie awake at night and composers—well, I haven't known too many happy composers. Most athletes, too, experience fear to one degree or another, even the superstars. LeBron James knew he was a great player, probably from the time he was ten years old, but he had a fear that he wasn't going to win a championship. You're not immune to fear just because you're great.

But what do you do with that fear? Do you get paralyzed by it? Run from it? Or do you treat it as *part of the process*, something you have to overcome to move from point A to point B? That's what you have to do. You overcome fear by going out every day and performing, understanding that, just as fear is natural, so is the idea that you can overcome it.

Fear shouldn't hurt or hinder. My players should have a fear of taking a test, a fear of failing to do the things they need to do to stay in school and be productive members of this team. If you don't have that kind of fear, you start taking things for granted.

The fear I experience as a coach is much worse than what I felt as a player. Believing that you're prepared is not necessarily a remedy for alleviating fear. When I got the Syracuse head job in 1976, I felt I was ready. But the first time I sat down as the head man, I wondered, *Am I ever going to win one game?* And still, now that I'm inching toward 1,000 wins—a goal I don't know that I'll be able to reach—I wonder, *Will I ever win another?*

As a coach, you're responsible for everybody. If you have a

supersize ego, you can blame failure on the players, but in point of fact it's your job to get your charges to do the right things. That doubles or triples the fear factor. Every day you wake up, you're worrying about a whole bunch of people, not just yourself.

If you look at it logically (though it's difficult to look at anything in sports logically), 40 years of doing anything should make you better at it, and that should help allay the fear. The writer Malcolm Gladwell says that 10,000 hours of practice is "the magic number of greatness," and I've logged many more hours than that as a coach. What you might lose in energy as you get older is outweighed by what you learn with experience, the skills you developed that hardly seemed important once upon a time. I delegate responsibility more now, for example, and I believe that helps both the players (since I'm not the one in their face all the time) and my assistant coaches (who become better at their jobs and buy into the fact that they are important). I think I have a better handle on which plays will work at which points in the game. I'm not sure why. One answer is that, without even knowing it, your brain cycles through dozens of past situations in a split second, enabling you to seize upon one: *Okay, this will be best*. Of course, you're not always going to be right. But you'd better be right more than you're wrong.

One thing that experience doesn't bring you, though, is peace of mind. You don't get happy with winning; you just get sad with losing. My wife, Juli, says that losing for me is like "a temporary death," and I suspect that is true for most coaches. That is the curse of coaching. Losing crushes you.

SO WHY AM I still here? Why am I still putting myself through the fear and the anxiety as I get ready to turn 70 in November 2014, when I will be starting my 45th year as a coach at Syracuse University, the last 39 as the head man?

Well, first of all, I believe that I'm as good as I've ever been at my job. As an assistant coach for the U.S. national team in two Olympic cycles, with a third coming up, I've had the opportunity to work with some of the best players in the world—LeBron James, Kevin Durant, Kobe Bryant, Chris Paul—and alongside the guy who might be the best coach in the world, Mike Krzyzewski (whom I am always delighted to beat, by the way). That has made me better.

I have three outstanding assistant coaches—Mike Hopkins, Adrian Autry and Gerry McNamara, all of whom played for me, a history that enables us to communicate in a kind of Orange short-hand. We have one way of doing things, and that's the Syracuse way. Those three guys have made me better.

We know what kind of players we want at Syracuse, and we're getting a lot of them. Our fan support continues to be the best in the country. Our entry into a new conference, the Atlantic Coast Conference, has energized me with the challenge of matching wits (if you'll allow that "wits" enter into coaching) with men like Krzyzewski, Roy Williams and Rick Pitino. All of that competition and support has made me better.

Also, I do not get misty-eyed for the good old days when the players were much more fundamentally sound than they are now. I don't know how many times I've heard those comments, and they're just not true. Many fans equate the increased athleticism of today's game with a disappearance of fundamental basketball, and those people are either ill-informed or making judgments based primarily on race.

Just because today's game might look *different* doesn't mean that players don't know how to play. The two indictments brought most often against contemporary basketball are that ballhandling is sloppy and defense is casual. Both complaints are nonsense. My 2013–14 team turned the ball over about nine times a game, compared with about 16 times a game when I was playing. And there is no comparison between the defenses of today and yesterday—today's are much more sophisticated.

Now, I won't tell you that today's college game is *better* than it used to be, and let me see if I can make that distinction clear. It is beyond obvious that individual teams were better when the best players stayed for four years, players like our Derrick Coleman. We had Derrick, Sherman Douglas and Stevie Thompson on the same team, all of whom stayed for four years, and there were many programs with just as good a veteran core. The John Wooden UCLA teams with Lew Alcindor and Bill Walton would still dominate today, because their personnel was so superior.

But what wasn't around three or four decades ago were the Butlers, the George Masons, the VCUs, the Gonzagas. Almost anybody can beat you today, because there are so many more good players and coaches. If I were an economist, I'd put it this way: From a micro perspective, the game is not as good as it used to be; the best teams aren't as good as the best teams back then. But from a macro perspective, when you assess the entire landscape of college basketball, it is so much richer now. There is much more breadth and depth to the game. The weight training and physical preparation of players today far surpasses that of even a generation ago. And though a lot of traditionalists don't want to hear it, much of that growth has to do with AAU basketball and the nationwide competition that it spawns. My two sons are playing in AAU tournaments against nationally ranked kids in their age group; when I was their age, I didn't know the names of the players in the next county, let alone have the chance to play against Indiana's Mr. Basketball.

But anyway, here's the reality of college basketball: To a large extent, the quality of the game doesn't matter to its long-term success. College basketball will *always* be popular. The essence of our sport is fans caring about *their team*, no matter what. Syracuse followers, even our older ones, do not spend much time, believe it or not, pining for

Pearl Washington and Derrick Coleman and reminiscing about the old days. They are happy with C. J. Fair, Jerami Grant, Tyler Ennis and Trevor Cooney, with this added proviso: *as long as we're competitive.* The bond between school and fan is what sells college basketball, what makes it great, what makes loyalty the key ingredient in a major program. That's a big reason why I'm still here.

Another factor in my longevity: I know what I need to do to get ready. One of the secrets about staying in the game this long is getting enough rest during the season. If I'm physically tired, I don't make good decisions, so I build in time to relax, at home and on the road.

Now, I'd be lying if I said that I enjoy all aspects of coaching as much as I used to. Practices, for example, might be a little harder for me to participate in to the degree that I used to. I'm not quite like Pitino, who I'm quite sure will be coaching as long as he draws breath, because Rick loves it all—practices, workouts, games, travel, even the media circus.

But, surprisingly, one of the things that usually drives coaches out of the business doesn't bother me: I honestly enjoy recruiting. With the help of my assistants, we've streamlined the process, and it's fun evaluating talent. Especially when you're right.

Syracuse is where I belong. It's in my bones. I went to a barbershop on Marshall Street in my freshman year and got my locks cut by a young man named Duke Drumm. Fifty years later, he's still the only one who has worked on what now passes for my hair. I don't embrace change; there are enough variables in coaching to make every day seem different.

I was interviewed for the Ohio State job in 1987, but I knew within about five minutes that I wouldn't take it if it was offered. And I never thought seriously about the NBA, which to a college coach wasn't much of a lure back then anyway. Had I wanted to make that move, the right time would've been in 1996, after we got to the NCAA championship game against Kentucky. But losing that game only made me want to stay more, to see if I could get a title. And when we won in 2003, it only made me want another one.

As Carmelo Anthony has progressed in the pros, I admit I've thought about joining him in the NBA, however briefly. But it was too late by then. I was known as a zone coach, and the pros aren't looking for that. Plus, I would've started as an assistant, and I'm too accustomed to being in charge.

There have been some difficult periods, times of doubt, defeat, disappointment and even disillusionment. As this book is being written, I'm dealing with an ongoing NCAA investigation, which is wearing on me. But one thing has never been hard: staying at Syracuse. Judging by how frequently some of my fellow coaches have moved around in their careers, it seems almost antiquated to have stayed in one place. But not for me—not for the Man Who Never Left. And when you've been around as long as I have, you do have one advantage: Most of your critics have either given up or died off.

Plus, it's amazing how clear the view is from one fixed point.

Let me show it to you.

1

A LONER ARRIVES ON CAMPUS

Contrary to popular belief, being the son of a mortician does not make you weird or obsessed with death or anything like that. In my case, all that being the son of a mortician meant was that I didn't want to be a mortician. Neither did my sister Barbara, seven years my junior.

My great-grandfather started the Boeheim Funeral Home in Lyons, New York, in the mid-1800s, not because he had some perverse death fixation but because he made caskets at his furniture store and figured it was a canny expansion, the business of dying being invulnerable to market forces. The family sold it, but our name lives on in the Boeheim-Pusateri Funeral Home, which is still there on William Street, almost directly across from the elementary school. I'm not sure why they left "Boeheim" on there. My oldest friend, Tony Santelli, says it's because Boeheim is still a pretty good name around Lyons. I hope that's the case. If we have a bunch of losing seasons . . . well, I don't want to think about that.

We thought of ourselves as from "upstate New York." Our sense of geography was pretty simple: Buffalo constituted western New York, Albany was eastern New York, and we were in the middle. Lyons was a great place to grow up, a kind of *Leave It to Beaver* town with a little more of an edge. The Boeheims were German in an

Italian neighborhood, but honestly, it's not like my family celebrated their cultural heritage much. My favorite food ran to spaghetti and meatballs, not sauerbraten.

The Lyons I grew up in had a population of about 5,000, but we didn't think of it as particularly small. It seemed just right. There were probably 70 of us who went from kindergarten through high school together. Everyone looked out for his neighbor, and nobody locked his door. On weekend mornings when I had trouble getting out of bed—which was most weekend mornings—Tony would stroll in the back door, pass through the kitchen (with a view of the cold bodies in the embalming room off the other side) and run right up the stairs to my bedroom to wake me up.

The New York Central Railroad came through there (still does), and Erie Canal Lock number 56 is nearby, so there were plenty of jobs. Parker Hannifin had two plants there, and the Hickok belt company had one. I grew up in a prosperous Lyons, which is not the case today. You know how we're always talking about the disappearing middle class? Lyons could be held up as a model. Tony and I first met because our parents belonged to a country club—not an exclusive one, but one that drew mainly from a middle class that no longer exists.

My father, Jim, was a straight-shooting kind of guy, a solid businessman. The line I always fall back on is that my father had a good side but managed to keep it pretty well hidden. Maybe that's partly because he lived much of his life with the slug from a .22 lodged in his spine, the result of his brother having accidentally shot him when they were young. The doctors at the time didn't want to take a chance on removing it. As a result, one of his legs was shorter than the other and he had a kind of limp.

My father was a hunter and a fisherman, and much of our time together was spent going on bass trips and pheasant hunting. As I got older, I would fish alone, sometimes at midnight. The solitude never bothered me, and, no, I don't think it had anything to do with the solitude forever present in the embalming room. It's just the way I was. We did golf together, but we would rarely finish nine holes before one of us stomped off in anger. It was the same with any sport or game—table tennis, Monopoly, horseshoes. We both took losing very, very hard. Sister Barb has a word she uses to describe what happened when my father and I faced off in anything: "fiasco."

I inherited more of my athletic ability from my mother, Janet, who was a good golfer and had played basketball in high school. She was probably responsible for my growing to six foot three, too, since she was five-eight, fairly tall for a woman in those days.

Despite how competitive my father was, and how much he resisted praising me, he and my mother attended every single high school and college game I played. When they couldn't get there for road games, the radio play-by-play was on in our house. My sister remembers my father, who might've been entertaining guests or conducting a business meeting in the living room, saying to her about every two minutes, "Barbara, could you go check the score?"

There was only one person in the world who nailed a basket up in our backyard and added lights so I could shoot at any time: James Boeheim Sr.

I owe my parents a major debt for something else: my memory. They were national-class duplicate bridge players who traveled all over for tournaments, though I'm not sure opponents were always glad to see my father. If you dropped the wrong card, he was the kind of guy who said, "You made that same mistake five years ago." That gets old in a hurry.

Like many kids, I worked in the family business, and it didn't seem unusual to me that that involved picking up bodies. Somebody had to do it. The Boeheim hearse also pinch-hit as the town ambulance, so I occasionally went on runs to the hospital as well.

One time, when I was 15 or 16, a woman delivered a baby when I was along for a ride.

But for me, it was never about undertaking or obstetrics. It was always about basketball. I was one of those kids shoveling snow off the driveway, which was spacious, since it had to accommodate the hearse and funeral parking. By the time I was five, I was already shooting a pair of socks through a flowerpot I put on the wall in the living room. When I was in third grade, I was already an avid fan of Lyons High, a wide-eyed kid who thought that Kenny Chalker, the team star, was the greatest player in the known world. When I was a freshman and sophomore at Lyons High, I refereed the high school intramural games, which provided one of my nicknames—"Sid," after Sid Borgia, the best-known NBA ref at the time. The other nickname was "Heimer," after, of course, my last name.

I went to Rochester Royals games from time to time—about 50 miles away—but I grew up loving the Boston Celtics, probably because they were the dominant NBA team. I have a vivid memory of watching Bill Russell, who came late to the Celtics because of his participation in the 1956 Olympics, blocking what seemed to be every shot in one of his first games. I would've been 12 then. If there was a game on, I watched it. For some odd reason, the game of the week often featured Memphis or Bradley, the Missouri Valley Conference having magically figured out a way to infiltrate eastern TV screens.

Fortunately, I was in the right town to chase my hoop dreams. Would I have ended up as a player or coach had I been born somewhere else? Did my desire to pursue basketball come from being born in a basketball town? Was there some kind of hoops osmosis that blew like a wind through Lyons at that time? Or did I have it from birth and Lyons only helped mold me? It's impossible to say.

What I do know is that a man named Dick Blackwell, the coach at Lyons High School, unquestionably turned me into a better basketball player than I would've been. He took a bunch of us when we were in sixth grade and started training us. We worked out every Saturday morning at the high school. We had undefeated teams when I was in seventh and eighth grade and again when I was a freshman at Lyons High. The sophomores won the JV championship without me, since Coach Blackwell had elevated me to varsity. In my junior and senior years, we lost only three games, with largely the same group that Coach Blackwell had put together six years earlier.

I was the classic gym rat. Often we practiced at night, at seven o'clock, so I would stay after school, watching the JVs, jumping rope, shooting hoops and (more or less, but mostly less) doing my homework.

Coach Blackwell was a little guy, maybe five-six, but he had been a paratrooper, and we called him Blackie behind his back. Far behind his back. To say that Coach Blackwell—to this day I can't bring myself to call him by his first name—was a disciplinarian would be a vast understatement. We could fast-break, but only if we had numbers, and only if we could do it in control. He was organized and demanding, every practice moment orchestrated, no horseplay tolerated. You came out in certain spots for warm-ups and you had better be in those spots. The day after a game, he would have all the stats—shots, rebounds, steals—updated by the morning. He had to review the game film to do it; throw in the fact that he didn't have a computer and it must've taken him hours.

Of course, you tend to romanticize and exaggerate what happened to you when you were young, but I believe to this day that Coach Blackwell would've been successful at any level.

Still, like most kids, I thought I knew everything, so we clashed here and there. He caught me running in gym class once, and I didn't start the next game, because I had broken a rule. Later in life, I was much less disciplined than Coach Blackwell in my coaching approach, much less on the throttle every minute like he was.

But I picked up some of his organizational skills, and he influenced me deeply, especially in how to approach getting the best out of yourself.

We were a Class B school, but we played up a division and beat everybody. In my senior year, the 1961–62 season, we averaged 72 points a game and gave up 38. In one game against the second-best team in our league, Canandaigua, we got off to a 40–8 lead in the first quarter. I had 22 points. Coach Blackwell never wanted us to humiliate a team, so the starters didn't play much the rest of the game.

There was no state tournament then, just sectionals, and in my senior year we lost in double overtime in the finals, a game that people still talk about around Lyons . . . in the same tone they use to describe funerals. The game was at the Rochester War Memorial, in front of over 10,000, and I doubt they've had that big a crowd since. East Rochester beat us 58–57, a defeat so wrenching I've never been able to forget it. Over the years, I've been asked numerous times about my most disappointing defeat, and most figure I will say the 1987 NCAA championship loss to Indiana. I don't. I say the East Rochester game. My years at Syracuse might compel me to follow up with "Okay, I guess 1987." But when I have a basketball nightmare, which I do from time to time, it's almost always about East Rochester 58, Lyons 57. I'm a little torn up right now just remembering it.

I was a good high school player. I averaged about 17 a game and finished with over a thousand points for my career. I was named the outstanding player of that sectional final, even though we lost. I could run all day, I was a student of the game, and I could shoot. But though I was the best player in Section V, I was still barely sought after by college coaches, even by the modest standards of recruiting in the early 1960s.

Maybe it was my physical appearance—six foot three, 150 pounds. Or maybe it was the glasses that gave me a non-jockish look. I've worn glasses since the third grade. Like most kids, I resisted them initially because I was embarrassed. I remember taking off my glasses, stashing them in my desk and asking a classmate to read the board—not a strategy destined for long-term success. Eventually I gave up, put them on and kept them on. They're on right now, because they're rarely off.

Later, as a sophomore in college, I tried contact lenses, but they never worked for me. I felt more comfortable in glasses and never cared much about the nerdy vibe they might've given off. One time during a freshman game, I was guarding a guy closely and he knocked off my glasses and warned, "Don't guard me like that." I went to the locker room, got them taped up and went back and guarded him the same way.

One thing is for sure: I needed them. Without glasses, I could barely see the *E* on the eye chart. But, strangely, I never had a vision problem in sports. Neither do I remember being called Four Eyes, although I'm sure it happened. When you have bad eyes, it helps to have bad hearing, too. I suppose the most lasting effect of the glasses was that they gave me an identity. You throw in a bad sport coat, like the ones I wore in the '70s and '80s, and I became a caricaturist's dream.

BACK THEN, WE didn't think as much about college as kids do now. Nor did high school coaches spend much time cultivating the attention of college coaches. These days, it can be practically a full-time occupation . . . unless the AAU coach does it. Dick Blackwell, in any case, didn't feel that it was in his job description to get Jim Boeheim into college. And I didn't start thinking seriously about going to school until my senior year, which might seem strange to you, considering that my alternative was continuing in the family business. Perhaps it would've been different if UCLA or Kentucky had wanted me, but they didn't.

But I knew that I wanted to play somewhere. I had played games at the University of Rochester, about 45 minutes away, and had watched the Royals. They were good. And they were close to home.

Colgate had shown a real interest in me, though. I liked that. I remember that feeling sometimes when I recruit players today. Colgate was about an hour and a half away, and I ended up sending in my $100 deposit, because I figured that was my best opportunity to play at a solid program.

Soon after that, though, unbeknownst to me, the coach of nearby Sodus High called up the new leader of the Orangemen, Fred Lewis, to say he knew about a player. Bill Nelson had been a soccer All-American at Syracuse and had played basketball, too. After he got off the phone with Lewis, he called Dick Blackwell and suggested that I take a visit to the Hill. The drive from Lyons to Syracuse is about an hour, but I got lost 20 times before I finally arrived at the old Archbold Gymnasium on campus, on the same ground that's covered now by the Carrier Dome.

I didn't have much of any connection to Syracuse. My dad went there for a year before mortuary school, but that meant nothing. I had attended Dolph Schayes's basketball camp as a high school freshman, but that wasn't a significant lure. 'Cuse had won the national championship in football in 1959, and running backs like Jim Brown and Ernie Davis were legendary, but it's not as if they were calling me up to come play wide receiver.

The basketball team, by comparison, was not particularly compelling—except as a case study in losing. From late in the 1960–61 season until almost the end of 1961–62, the Orange had lost 27 straight games. Rochester was better, and Colgate at that time was *much* better, having just graduated a certified legend named Bob Duffy, a fantastic player who was drafted into the NBA after scoring 1,500 career points.

But Syracuse had its own selling points, not the least of which was that it gave athletic scholarships; Colgate did not. Also, Fred Lewis was a fast-break advocate who had been a huge success at Southern Mississippi. Fred was a great salesman. He had pledged to rebuild the program so that it rivaled King Football, a promise so optimistic it bordered on the absurd.

Fred actually had a report on me when I showed up, which made me feel good. Rich Duffy, a sophomore guard and Bob Duffy's younger brother, showed me around. He told me that a phenomenal athlete named Dave Bing had visited campus the week before and was probably coming. The name didn't mean anything to me. The days when the best high school players were known throughout the land were still far off.

When I met with Coach Lewis, he told me, "Look, I don't have a scholarship for you, but if you come here and do well, you can earn one." It turns out he told two other guys the same thing, one of them being Don Martin, who would go on to be my attorney.

So the opportunity to play at a big school presented itself, and I accepted the challenge. Nobody was particularly enthusiastic about my chances, including Dick Blackwell, who doubted I could play at that level, even given Syracuse's dire times. As for me, I didn't know if I could make the team or not. Only that I wanted to try. And I sure as hell didn't know that once I hit the Hill, I would never leave.

THE RECEPTION I got when I arrived on campus was incredible. Fred Lewis was there with outstretched arms, cheerleaders shouted my name, the scoreboard read BOEHEIM . . . Okay, not really. Nobody—and I mean *nobody*—was waiting for James Arthur Boeheim.

It took me 15 hours to register for classes. I walked back and forth between my dorm and the new Manley Field House, where registration was taking place, a dozen times. I got lost, I didn't have enough money, I didn't have the right forms, this course was closed, this course didn't exist, and on and on. You name it, I screwed it up. If you had told me then that I'd still be here in 2014, I would've said you were crazy.

Throughout most of my freshman year I was pretty much a loner—few friends, zero dates. There was a dorm for the players, but walk-ons were in with the rest of the student body. My roomie was a guy named Lee Hammer, who went to bed at nine o'clock. He claimed to be a rated squash player, but I played him one night and beat him like a drum, proving either that I was in great shape or that squash rankings needed some work.

I wasn't entirely unconfident about my chances on the basketball court, but when you arrive as a walk-on it's like you have a scarlet letter on your chest, a giant *W*. There were some good players here—Frank Nicoletti, Norm Goldsmith, Rex Trobridge, Dick Ableman and a particularly zany but talented guy named Fran Pinchot. They weren't all more skilled than me, but they were all more physical.

And then there was this other freshman, this guy who seemed to be from another planet.

"Mom," I said when I called home, "there's a guy here named Bing, and there is no way I am *close* to being as good as he is."

"Well," my practical-minded mother said, "I guess that means you'll have to be better than all the *other* guys."

2

THE "B&B" SHOW

ave Bing came to Syracuse from Washington, D.C., largely
because he was recruited by Ernie Davis and John Mackey,
two icons of Syracuse football. They gave the school gravi-
tas, a national identity. Had Syracuse not been a national football
power in the early 1960s, there's a lot else in its history that would
have been different, too.

The basketball team was composed mostly of white players, but
Ernie told Dave, when he escorted him around campus for his official visit, that it was a comfortable place for African Americans and
that he could make a big difference to the program. That was more
than obvious, because the program stunk.

If Bing, one of the nation's top recruits in 1962, hadn't decided
upon Syracuse—a school, remember, that had 4–19 and 2–22 records in the two seasons before he arrived—then our rise to promi-
nence would have been a lot slower, assuming it would've happened
at all.

The first time I played against him was in a pickup game before
our freshman season started. I literally could not get a shot off
against him. Gerry McNamara, my assistant who helped us win a
national championship in 2003, describes the first time he scrimmaged against Carmelo Anthony as a "holy shit" moment. That's

what this was for me, and that's when I made that phone call home to my mother.

Dave was just that good, fundamentally sound and way more athletic than everyone else. But it wasn't just that. He had come from an old-school household where his parents made him hit the books, go to church, say *yes sir, no sir*—that kind of thing. Dave was a fun-loving guy, but those lessons had sunk in. He never lorded his talent over anyone else. He was one of the best leaders I ever saw. If you couldn't follow Dave Bing into battle, you couldn't follow anyone.

Word got around quickly about our freshman team, which carried the unfortunate name of the Tangerines. There was a buzz around school anyway, with the basketball games moving to Manley Field House, and the fans had heard that we had blown out the varsity by 40 points in scrimmages. A couple of years later, it was a national story when a big center named Lew Alcindor led his freshman team over the UCLA varsity, the defending national champions. To an extent, that's what happened here. Had freshmen been eligible to play, we probably could've replaced the entire varsity, and Dave would've been, without question, the team's best player and probably its captain. As a freshman.

Our tip-off was before the varsity game, five o'clock or so, and by the time we got rolling, there would be thousands of fans in Manley, most of whom promptly left after we played. I'll never forget, early in his first game, when Dave made a steal and dunked with two hands. The place went nuts. Dunking wasn't exactly a novelty, but it was by no means as regular as it is in today's game—and, incredibly, Dave had never dunked in practice, at least not that I remember. We stood there with our mouths open, like the fans. (A couple of years later, the NCAA banned the dunk for a while; this was the so-called Alcindor Rule.)

Dave was unique for his time, as athletic as anybody today. I compare him to Oklahoma City's Russell Westbrook, whom I have coached on the Olympic U.S. national team. Dave glided by people effortlessly. He could shoot. He slid between screens so quickly that he never even brushed a defender. And he worked hard.

Years later, after I had become an assistant coach at Syracuse, I would conjure up the example of Dave as a player and make it work for me. I used to tell Dennis DuVal, who was a great player here from 1970 to 1974, "Look, I saw what made Dave great, and I can give those lessons to you." Dennis didn't buy it at first, but then he did, and he became an All-American. No, that didn't happen purely because he "modeled" himself after Bing; that's too simple. But he says today that the lessons of Bing had a galvanizing effect.

Dave and I didn't begin as close friends. He treated everyone with the same respect. I was hardly special, not even a starter at first. But more than anyone, I figured out how to play with Dave.

He was listed as a 3 at the time, but he was a small forward in the same way that LeBron James is a small forward. He was going to get the ball wherever and whenever we needed him to get it. And when he did, he was going to get doubled and tripled, so I found open spots and he found me, because, as talented as he was, Dave was also unselfish. I was a good shooter, and I could run all day. Though I was a backcourt player, usually the 2 guard, throughout my college career I almost never dribbled, because I didn't have to. I was usually open.

So though no one called this the B&B Show, Dave and I gradually began to share a chemistry that would only grow stronger.

That doesn't mean I was on a slam-dunk course to be a good player. A friend of mine who was a year older said to me, in all seriousness, "You know, you were decent as a freshman, but why are you trying so hard? You're never going to play beyond that." Fortunately, not everyone saw it that way, particularly the freshman coach, Morris Osborne, who advocated for me to get that last scholarship, which I did. When I found out over the summer, I felt like I belonged, that I had followed my mother's instruction and proven myself as good as anyone except Bing.

IF YOU WANT to know how different things were back then, consider that I didn't even know who my roommate was going to be for sophomore year. But when I walked into the dorm, there was Bing's stuff on the other bed. For whatever reason, Fred Lewis had decided that we would be roomies. Until I happened to be at the same party as a girl named Juli Greene three decades later, it was probably the luckiest thing that ever happened to me.

Without Dave, I was just another guy—another guy who tried to stay away from the football players when they were in the locker room. They would beat your ass and throw you in the shower. In the dining hall, they would reach down and literally take the steak off your plate. "Hey, thanks, Jim."

But they never really messed with me, because I was usually with Dave, and he was every bit the BMOC that they were. To the football players, I was the Roommate, the White Guy Who Played with Dave. I angled to walk across campus with him so girls would talk to me, too. It rarely happened that way, but I lived in perpetual hope.

Being Dave's roommate gave you a cool quotient that, let's face it, I didn't have otherwise. I had had one girlfriend in high school. I didn't know who Marvin Gaye was. I didn't know what Motown was, except maybe a town named after a Moe I hadn't heard of. I knew who Chubby Checker was and had maybe done the Twist, awkwardly, sometime in high school. I dressed like a rube.

So Dave introduced me to music and culture I had never experienced. He came to Syracuse—it seemed at the time anyway—as almost a fully formed human being, whereas I was still a kid in many ways, "the hick from Lyons," as Sam Penceal, our point guard, called me. I threw my clothes into a jumble on my side of the room and took them home to be washed; Dave didn't have many clothes, but he kept them neat and orderly, everything in its place, an army regimen to his daily routine.

Still, there was only so much Dave could do, and despite my social evolution I never tried to be fake black. I couldn't have pulled it off anyway. I tried to remain my own person, and that was someone who never went to parties, never pledged a fraternity, never aspired to be the smoothest dude in the room. But just being around Dave gave me confidence, opened up the world beyond Lyons, New York. For all the enviable skills he would later demonstrate—as an NBA superstar, a successful businessman, and the mayor of Detroit—the even-handed way he dealt with people was his greatest strength.

NOT ALL OF my Syracuse teammates were as well-adjusted as Dave. We had a fascinating character named Fran Pinchot, a six-three forward who could score but was always on the verge of self-destructing. Almost from the start of freshman year, we had a bet on when he would do exactly that. He rarely went to class, ran the football betting pools on campus and all in all was the kind of guy who would have felt right at home in *Animal House*.

A couple of nights before our first freshman game, Fran drove onto the grass of a dorm and let about ten people out of the car he was driving, the college version of a circus clown show. The campus police spotted him, and off they went in pursuit, sirens wailing. Instead of pulling over, Fran elected to outrun them. He had no license or registration. They chased him all around campus before he went off the road, crashed into a house and broke his leg.

"Coach, I'm going to straighten out," Fran promised Fred Lewis when they met.

"Maybe that will be the case," said Fred, who by then had done the background checks, academic and automotive, "but not at Syracuse."

Flash-forward one year. We're in Miami playing in the Hurricane Classic. I remember it well, because Dave had convinced Coach Lewis to take along a big kid named Bob Murray, who rarely played, and Bob had a big second half in one game to help us win the tournament. We're sitting on the bench before the opening tip and along comes Fran Pinchot. "Hey, guys, let's go," he says. "I got a hundred on you."

We won the tournament, the final game against a Miami team that had Rick Barry. You take your motivational messages wherever you can get them.

As for Fran Pinchot, he became a high school basketball coach and then a professional poker player. Perfect.

As a student, I might have been better than Fran, but I was hardly in line for a Rhodes Scholarship. I was good in history (and would later earn a master's degree), but I was average in everything else. The only thing that saved me was that I had a great memory—my parents' bridge memory—so I'd let everything go and then cram 12 straight hours for a test. It worked, but as a studying model I don't recommend it, and these days I tell my kids not to do it that way.

As far as basketball goes, I couldn't have asked for more. I was a walk-on who got a scholarship and ended up rooming and playing with a guy who was later voted one of the top 50 NBA players of all time.

With Dave as our leader, we just kept getting better. We played a 2-1-2 offense and got the ball to Bing on the wing. We ran and pressed as much as we could. Nobody could guard him. In my opinion, he was the best player on the court in every game.

All right, with one exception. Against Cornell one season, I scored the first 8 points and 13 of the next 16. Even more than usual, they were doubling Dave and losing me. Dave still finished with 23 points and 31 rebounds. I had 25 points and they gave me the most valuable player award, probably because they were sick of handing out hardware to Bing.

That was the only time I got the best of Dave, outside of when I invited him home and sent him to "get the dessert" from the embalming room. As the butt of many of his practical jokes, it was nice to put one over on him.

We went 17–8 as sophomores and lost to NYU (which had All-American Happy Hairston and Barry Kramer) in the NIT. As juniors, we went 13–10, but eight of those losses came before early January. We went 11–2 to finish the season, but in those days that wasn't nearly enough to make either the NCAA or the NIT. We peaked as seniors, going 22–6 and beating a real good Davidson team in the NCAA East Regional before losing 91–81 to a great Duke team that had Bob Verga, Jack Marin and Steve Vacendak.

A footnote to that tournament: That was the *Glory Road* championship year—Texas Western, with college basketball's first all-black starting five, beat all-white Kentucky. As far as I'm concerned, the Wildcats shouldn't have reached the Final Four. The only reason they beat Duke was that Verga had the flu and couldn't play. And I'm almost positive that Duke would've beaten Texas Western and there would have been no *Glory Road*. Still, it was better for college basketball that Don Haskins's great team won it all.

It was a good movie, too.

A couple of my best memories involve Bill Bradley, who came to Princeton a year before Dave and I got to Syracuse. So by the time we played them for the first time, in Miami in that Hurricane Classic, we had already heard the legend surrounding "Dollar Bill." I wanted to see for myself, so after our practice I hung around. It was a big facility, and at first I couldn't figure out who Bill Bradley was. Then I spotted this unobtrusive guy in full sweats, carefully laying down tape on the floor. He gets a manager to rebound for him and starts from ten feet. All swishes. Then he moves to another taped spot, and another and another, and all the while nothing but net.

"Well," I deduced, "that's Bradley."

In that first game against him, we played a box-and-one, the typical way to defend Princeton: Sam Penceal on Bill. They're beating us most of the game, largely because of Bradley, but he fouls out and we go on to win 76–71. So, suddenly, Sam Penceal becomes a "Bradley Stopper." We knew it was nonsense, but the tag stuck.

The next year, we play them in the ECAC Holiday Festival at Madison Square Garden, which was a big deal back then. We put the Bradley Stopper on him again, Bill gets 37, and they crush us, 79–69.

In terms of being a complete player, I would take Bing over Bradley, simply because Dave was a better rebounder and defender. But Bill was an immortal college player, a true student of the game and a fierce competitor. I was privileged to play against him.

But basketball moments are not the first thing I think of with those guys. Dave and Bill knew each other a little bit, and after the Holiday Festival game was over, Dave took me to meet Bradley. There we were in the bowels of the old Madison Square Garden on Eighth Avenue, the three of us, just talking. All right, they talked; I listened. The previous summer, Bill had interned for a congressman in Washington, D.C., and Dave invited him to his local playground. Bill had gone over there and gotten the predictable response: What does this straight-looking white guy expect is going to happen here? He's going to dominate in *our* house? Then the unexpected happens. Bradley and Bing run textbook pick-and-rolls and back-doors and they crush everybody, an experience I would replicate later with Dave on that same playground.

Still, as cool as it was to watch Bill and Dave playing together, it isn't the basketball that lingers so much as their sheer *presence*. I couldn't have articulated it at the time—and still have trouble now—but even back then, I knew I was in the company of two extraordinary men who would go on to do extraordinary things.

A COACH'S NOTES I

From my office window, I have a great view of the activity below on the courts of the Carmelo K. Anthony Basketball Center, which we refer to simply as "Melo." Practices these days resemble a three-ring circus: activity all over the place, loud music and a general air of excitement. I can't help but compare it to my practices in Manley Field House 50 years ago—no bells and whistles, except for what the coaches were blowing. Now we have so many managers that our managers have managers, and all of them stay busy. Every player has his own ball retriever. Dave Bing? Still the greatest player in Syracuse history? He had to fetch his own shots, unless I was throwing them back to him.

But this is how it should be. Practice time has gotten much more efficient than it was when 20 guys were jammed onto a single court. You couldn't get much done in the old days because there was too much standing around.

It's loud down there, too, and frankly, I don't love the music. I leave that choice to the players, but all noise stops when I blow the whistle for the official beginning of practice. I suppose James

Naismith had a whistle; it's still the coach's most efficient tool (and thank God technology hasn't yet rendered it obsolete).

Today, the 27th of September, is the earliest start ever for practices, which traditionally began on October 15. But the NCAA has passed a new bylaw to allow teams to practice 30 times in 42 days, starting on September 27 and stretching to November 7, the day before you can play the first official game. That is a long time to spend with your team, and I honestly don't know if I'd still be coaching without the Melo Center. It's as good as any facility in the country and also serves as a valuable recruiting tool. Obviously, we have Carmelo Anthony, among some other generous backers, to thank for it. And Juli Boeheim.

I started thinking about a new facility years ago. I had visited a few around the NBA, the one in San Antonio and those of both the Nets and the Knicks, to get an idea of how they were put together. We got a proposal of $18 million and, as with most things built on college campuses, we were looking for a gift to jump-start construction. If you donate a couple of bucks, a college will name an appetizer after you in the student union.

This needed more than that. We got started with a generous $2 million gift from Joyce Hergenhan, a loyal Syracuse fan and alum who has season tickets, even though she lives in Fairfield, Connecticut. From there our thoughts turned to Carmelo, who was by then a well-compensated NBA superstar. The responsibility to ask him fell to me, but on the appointed day, I just couldn't do it. I've had to put the arm on many a donor over the years, but it was impossible to pull the trigger with Carmelo, and my wife read it on my face.

"You didn't ask him, did you?" Juli said, already knowing the answer.

"I just didn't feel comfortable," I replied.

So Juli picked up the ball and took it to the hoop. She suggested $3 million. Carmelo pondered it for a few days, talked to his people and eventually said yes. It's still one of the biggest gifts ever made by a pro player to his college, particularly a player who stayed only one year. (Albeit a championship one.) Sure, superstars like Carmelo make a lot of money, but they have a lot of people pulling on them, too.

It's one of the best investments this program ever made. (The one-year investment in Carmelo back in 2002 worked out pretty well also.) Two courts, side baskets, a big training room, offices that overlook the court . . . all in all a long way from Manley, where the dirt football field met the basketball court. This facility would've cost $40 or $50 million in New York City, so don't let anyone tell you there are no advantages to being situated in the sticks.

We opened it on September 24, 2009, with Carmelo on hand to take the first shot. He settled behind the three-point line and received a pass from Gerry McNamara, his teammate on the 2003 championship team. "Make it," I instructed. He did. Now that's some great coaching right there.

THIS SEASON, WE got off to an even earlier start by playing four August games in Canada, which is permitted under NCAA rules. If that sounds like an easy summer stroll, it wasn't. Carleton University is a Canadian power and gave us all we could handle before we won 69–65.

We're ranked eighth or ninth in most preseason polls, which seems about right. There are two reasons we're in the top ten: We made the Final Four last season (which shouldn't matter but does), and we have one of the top returning players in the country in senior C. J. Fair (which should matter and does). While some coaches like to be ranked low, either to diminish expectations or so opponents will get overconfident, I'd rather start high and have people believe you're good. Why not? If people think you're bad, they think they can beat you. Now, if you really *are* bad, that's a problem.

C.J. is a reliable scorer, and we're high on a freshman guard named Tyler Ennis, who played on the Canadian junior national team and doesn't do anything that makes your eyes pop out except win. When we were recruiting him, we noticed that his high school and AAU teams almost never lost. He's mature beyond his years, but our inexperience in the backcourt is our major concern. Our frontcourt should be pretty solid, particularly on defense.

I like to have a good idea of what we have going into the season. It's one thing to stand in front of your team and proclaim that every starting position is open, and quite another to make that the reality. You lose credibility if you declare open competition when everyone knows your mind is basically made up on most of the starters. And mine is.

My philosophy has never been to stack up on McDonald's All-Americans, even if I could. We've had about 20 in 35 years, compared with 60 or 70 in some of the other top programs. That can be a meaningless designation anyway—Tyler came in as only the fourth or fifth best high school point guard in the country, and I think he'll be as good as any of them.

There have been years when we've had a ten-deep rotation, but that is rare. Still, we now turn down players we would've been glad to take ten years ago. I've been here for so long that recruits and parents know there's little danger of my not being around all four years. Plus, I have three assistants who all played for me. When you come to Syracuse, you become part of a family whose roots go back several generations. How many of our rivals can say that?

We'll test our inexperience early by going to the Maui Invitational, around Thanksgiving. I have a theory that tough competition will help you if you're good, but if you're not, it will only hurt you. Despite the fact that people say you can *learn by losing*, the way I see it is that if you lose a bunch of games big, what you're learning is how to lose big.

I think we'll weather it, though. We have a good talented start-ing five in Fair, DaJuan Coleman and Rakeem Christmas up front, with Ennis and redshirt sophomore Trevor Cooney in the back-court. Off the bench we have Baye Moussa Keita, maybe our best interior defender, and Jerami Grant, our best athlete. By the middle of the season, Grant might be starting.

Critics love to talk about our "easy" schedule, as if we're the only team that plays weaker opponents early in the season, but we're not doing it simply to fatten our record. For example, if we play Colgate at home, which we usually do, and will do again this season, we make about $400,000 and Colgate makes about $90,000. If we were to play that game at Colgate, we make nothing and they make about $30,000. Some schools pay for their athletic programs by playing these road games against bigger schools . . . and sometimes they even win them.

The advent of early-season tournaments has automatically toughened your average schedule anyway. We played Kansas in Kansas City one year. We've played Florida early, Memphis early, North Carolina early. This year we'll face good teams—Baylor, Cal, Dayton, Gonzaga, Minnesota—in Maui. And the bottom line is: Since 1979, we've played in a tough Big East Conference, and now we'll have to adjust to the ACC. That's weeks and weeks of diffi-cult games in the heart of your season. In terms of helping your team, you need only four or five good games before your conference schedule begins; you don't need to beat yourself up with eight physi-cally draining games because the conference will be tough enough.

Our schedule going forward will always be challenging. We'll have an ACC/Big Ten game, not to mention independent games against some of our traditional opponents we're no longer play-ing in the conference: Syracuse–St. John's, Syracuse–Villanova, Syracuse–UConn and, of course, Syracuse–Georgetown, will go on . . . just not all in the same year.

3

MY SPOT ON THE BENCH

I sometimes think what a different course my life would've taken had I not become a pretty good player at Syracuse. Maybe I would've gotten discouraged with basketball and given it up. My best guess is that I would've returned to Lyons to run the family business.

That may sound strange, given my reluctance to become a mortician. But I think I would've been entirely capable of just *settling* for something, though I would have delegated the embalming to someone else. Without basketball, I think I would've drifted, and the funeral home in Lyons was my most likely landing place. Besides that . . . who knows?

When I graduated in 1966, the only thing I knew for sure was that I wanted my life to be about basketball. I wanted to play or coach. But was I good enough for the pros? To be sure, the NBA would involve more than getting the ball to Bing, heading for an open spot and waiting for a return pass. Coaching was a strong possibility, but I didn't want to do it unless I was certain I was finished as a player.

Then there was the Vietnam War.

So I enrolled in graduate school and became one of the country's most reluctant history scholars. At that time you could make a hundred bucks or so playing in this semi-pro weekend circuit around Syracuse. I played for a team called A.L. George out of Binghamton. It wasn't the NBA, but it was good, competitive basketball. I was averaging about 35 a game, and we had made it to the finals of a tournament in Auburn, New York, when I got a call from Dave asking me to give him a ride.

"I didn't even know you were playing," I said.

"Well, somebody called and said they'd give me a hundred bucks to play," Dave said. "So I guess that means I'm playing against you."

We agree on the ride up that we won't guard each other. I have like 25 points in the first half, so Dave's coach makes him guard me, and of course I start feeling like he's getting all the calls from this old ref who's just trying to keep up.

"Look, he doesn't need your help," I tell the guy. "That's Dave Bing."

Eventually the ref gets tired of my whining, so he thumbs me out of the game, and I say, "Look, pal, I'm not leaving. Everybody wants to see the end of this." He doesn't really have the energy to argue, so I stay. I end up with 49 and Bing has 46 and probably about a hundred rebounds, yet they beat us by a couple of points. For a long time after that, Dave and I would say it was one of the best games we were ever involved in.

I hope the fans who were there in the small Auburn gym that night appreciated that little piece of basketball history. I think they did—the place seated about 800, and I've had at least 2,000 people tell me they were there.

Not long after that, Dave, the second pick in the 1966 draft, was averaging 20 points a game and winning Rookie of the Year honors with the Detroit Pistons.

Al Bianchi, an ex–Syracuse Nationals player with whom I had an acquaintance through Dolph Schayes's camp, arranged a tryout for me with the Chicago Bulls. Jerry Colangelo, who would later supervise the Olympic team on which I was an assistant coach, was the Bulls' young general manager. Look, anybody who was ever cut from anything says they were "the last cut," but that's my story and I'm sticking with it. I played well enough to make the team. Problem was, the guy I was showing up, Dave Schellhase, was a six-three guard out of Purdue who had been a first-round draft pick and had a no-cut clause in his contract. Guess what: They didn't cut him. The way I learned my fate was simple: I looked at the board and my name wasn't there. So I shrugged, got in my car, drove back to Syracuse and—reluctantly—picked up my history textbooks.*

I then began playing for the Scranton Miners of the old Eastern Professional Basketball League (which became the Eastern Basketball Association, which itself served as a precursor to the Continental Basketball League). Paul Seymour was my coach in Scranton that first season, and, after he got the head job with the Detroit Pistons, he asked me to come up and try out. Paul was a great guy. He had played and coached with the Syracuse Nats, then become the coach of the St. Louis Hawks, a really strong franchise. But the Hawks had fired Paul because he wanted to start Cleo Hill, a black player, and his stars—Bob Pettit, Cliff Hagan and Clyde Lovellette—were against it.

Paul wanted me to be his fourth guard behind Bing, Jimmy Walker and Howie Komives. Paul was all but handing me a spot, and having Dave there would make me feel comfortable. But I knew in my heart that I wouldn't play much, because those guys were all better than me—*way* better than me, even Komives. It wouldn't be a long-term future plan. It was a little sad, but I passed it up, and that was that as far as the NBA went. Somehow the league managed to survive without me.

---

* As for Dave Schellhase, he played exactly 73 games over two seasons. I guarantee that, out of pure stubbornness, I would've lasted longer than that.

I can't help but think that, had I taken that fourth guard spot, I would've played for a few unproductive years and discovered that I was more cut out for coaching. So I would've become an NBA assistant and eventually a head coach. Which means that, while I might be richer, I also would have gotten fired at least twice.

Back at Syracuse, several things kept me going. I was a resident adviser, so I was eligible to play intramural football. I was the quarterback and ran a spread offense that couldn't be stopped. Three years, three championships. One of my advisees was Tom Coughlin, who was a star football player and later coach of the New York Giants. Funny that Tom never called me when he was looking for a QB pre–Eli Manning.

I kept on playing in the Eastern League, and it's a wonder it didn't kill me. Not the basketball—the driving. It's about a two-hour drive from Syracuse to Scranton, but not in a whiteout, which is typical during the winter in these parts. I remember one night the drive took me five hours. The visibility was so bad that I was driving about five miles an hour and opening the car door every few feet just to see the road. But I never had an accident.

One year, I was also teaching junior high history in Syracuse, and I would drag into school exhausted from driving and playing two games on the weekend. They gave me 27 of the worst kids. Fortunately, a young student from India knew the material better than I did, and I assigned him the responsibility of teaching much of the course work—a valuable lesson in delegation of authority.

IN 1969, THREE years after graduation, I arrived at my destiny. Roy Danforth, who by then had taken over for Fred Lewis, hired me as a graduate assistant. I say "hired," but I didn't get paid. However, I did get $2,000 for coaching golf, which, if not the easiest job in

America, is certainly among the top ten. We had good teams, and in 1972 Roy made me his full-time assistant with the varsity.

It was a great time to be in Syracuse. Fred had a couple of tough seasons after the B&B show ended—okay, after Bing left—but Roy, who was a bit of a showman, began to lift the program. He was a man of infinite energy. He could stay out all night and still be at school by 8:00 A.M.—though almost never in his own office. He was all over the place, visiting every coach and secretary, socializing and schmoozing.

Like Roy, Manley Field House was an outsize personality, one of the toughest stops in the country for visiting teams. The basketball court was on one side, and on the other was dirt where the football team practiced indoors. The dirt came right up to the court, and there was a two- or three-foot drop. When the football team was in there, the dust would just start flying, and it was like you were playing a *Friday Night Lights* game in West Texas.

Manley had old wooden bleachers on one side and permanent seating in both end zones. They could shoehorn about 9,500 people in there, and the advantage to the home team was clear: noise. To this day it remains one of the loudest places I've ever been in. When students realized they could distract the other team, it got even more earsplitting. And so "the Zoo" was born.

When I look back, those years in the early '70s represented the last gasp of the "Old Syracuse." Manley was a big part of it, and so was the football coach, Ben Schwartzwalder, who had been on campus since 1949. He was known, among other things, for being absentminded; he once showed up in his pajama bottoms to coach a morning practice.

My locker was next to his in the coaches' locker room, which was about half the size of my office today in Melo. We had these old Universal weight machines, and Ben put one in his office so he could work out. He was fanatical about golf and used to hit balls into a cage at Manley. He was a good player who usually shot around 80, yet he played to a 22 handicap. I went out with him once, shot a 71 to his 79, and lost every dollar in my wallet because I was giving up a stroke per hole.

"Jim," he would tell me, "I have that handicap because I need an edge. Those other coaches are damn cheaters."

I thought better of alerting him to the irony of that statement.

My most vivid memory of Ben is watching him come in after a scrimmage in the Syracuse winter, flapping his arms, blowing on his hands and brushing snow off his coat.

"BOEHEIM!" he would shout. "How was it in here today? Nice and warm?"

"Real toasty, Coach," I'd say.

"Ah, you pantywaist pussies," he'd say, slapping me on the back.

Schwartzwalder retired after the 1973 season, his legacy somewhat tarnished by a couple of racial incidents. There's no doubt that Ben belonged to an older generation with a few antiquated ideas. Without a doubt, he made impolitic comments. From my perspective, though, the old-school paratrooper was a tough son of a bitch to *everyone*, and a lot of character went out of Syracuse when he left.

SYRACUSE'S NEXT BIG basketball moment after the Bing years occurred in 1975, when, against all odds, we made it to the Final Four. "Roy's Runts" they called us, because we weren't particularly big. Our center and best player, Rudy Hackett, was only six foot nine.

We were probably a better team in the two previous years, when Dennis DuVal, one of the more forgotten stars in Syracuse history, was in our backcourt. But things fell right for us that season, and we got a big win against North Carolina in the NCAA tournament, which brought us one win from the Final Four. North Carolina was a great team, with Mitch Kupchak, Phil Ford and Tom LaGarde, while we were described as "a mid-major," which, quite honestly, was accurate. To this day, I'm not sure how we did it. After we beat the Tar Heels, Hackett had a monster game against Kansas State, and there we were, matched up against Kentucky.

We wouldn't even have gotten to that North Carolina game, incidentally, without the assistance of Kobe Bryant's dad, Jellybean Bryant, La Salle's star player. We played the Explorers in the East Region—in Philadelphia, of all places, his hometown—and Jellybean missed a point-blank layup that helped us win in overtime.

We weren't at Kentucky's level yet, though, and our Cinderella run ended with a 95–79 defeat, which was followed by a loss to Louisville in the meaningless consolation game they played back then. One of my best memories of that time was sitting behind John Wooden, the storied UCLA coach. We had the honor of being in the Final Four the year of his last NCAA title, which was his eighth in nine years and his tenth in twelve years, a record that remains implausible if it weren't there in black and white.

We had a good season in 1975–76, even though we lost in the first round of the NCAA tournament. But our improbable run the previous year had made Roy a hot commodity in the coaching community, and, sure enough, he accepted a job at Tulane after the '76 season. Tulane was moving into the Superdome, and lots of promises were made to Roy about how the program was going to become big-time, on a par with the UCLAs, Kentuckys, North Carolinas, et al. If coaches only had a dime for every time they heard that.

Roy took some heat for leaving, because there was also the feeling that he knew he was taking the job weeks before he informed Syracuse. He had been a delegate for Henry "Scoop" Jackson (not to be mistaken for Scoop Jardine, who played for me 30 years later) and wanted to stay long enough to cast a vote in the New York State primaries. Whatever—everyone at Syracuse owes Roy a debt for what he did for this program, not to mention how much he enlivened the campus social network.

The question now was: Would Syracuse promote Roy's 31-year-old assistant?

Or would they go outside to get someone with head-coaching experience?

The way I saw it, there was only one correct decision.

TO AN EXTENT, I had some leverage. At that time, the University of Rochester was looking for a coach and I had the inside track for the job. On a Wednesday in early April, about three weeks after the season ended, I interviewed for the position. I walked away thinking that it was mine for the taking. They were Division II then but were talking about moving up, which I obviously would've advocated for.

I knew what I really wanted, though. I wanted my alma mater. Two days after the Rochester interview, I went in to talk to Syracuse. Five other people were in the room: athletic director Les Dye, board chairman David Bennett, trustee Carroll Coyne, a college vice president named Mel Mounts, and the person who mattered the most, Cliff Winters. Cliff's official title was vice chancellor for administrative operations, but it could've been the Guy Who Ran Syracuse. His word was the one that mattered. Cliff was Thomas Cromwell, the voice behind the throne.

I knew that Mounts was against me for sure, and I wasn't certain about anyone else.

"We want to open up the job for four weeks," I was told. Among the coaches they wanted to interview was Frank Layden, who had coached Calvin Murphy at Niagara. If the job had been for stand-up comedian, clearly Frank had the edge, but that's not what it was about. So I took a deep breath and said . . .

"No. Either I'm getting the job or I'm going to Rochester."

There was a moment of stunned silence.

In truth, I was mad, and I only grew more incensed as I started enumerating my arguments. That tends to be my M.O. Here's what I said:

I played here. I put in the 2-3 zone that Roy used to so much success. I recruited the players who got us to the Final Four and worked with them every day. I operated on the lowest recruiting budget ever; I drove my Oldsmobile Starfire everywhere—Washington, Philly, New York—and always returned the same night, listening to Pete Franklin out of Cleveland and whatever ball games I could pick up to stay awake.

I had more reasons: Roy recommended me for the job. The players want me. National Letter of Intent Day is right around the corner, and I'm the guy recruiting Roosevelt Bouie, who is the player we need to take us to the next level. If I leave, Roosevelt may go to St. Bonaventure. Rosie did not like Roy—he had let that be known—but he liked me. Go figure.

All of my arguments had the virtue of being true.

It was a gamble, but this much I know: At the time, I *never* considered that I couldn't do the job. It wasn't about making idle threats; it was about pursuing something I knew I could do. I had played the game at a high level but wasn't by nature a high-level player. I *thought* the game, though, and that's one of the best qualities a coach can have.

I was told to wait outside, but it didn't take long for Cliff to find me. And on April 3, 1976, I was named the eighth basketball coach in Syracuse history.

At this writing, there has not been a ninth.

4

THE HONEYMOON'S OVER

The local newspaper's announcement that I had gotten the job included a pronunciation guide for my last name. *BAY-hime*. These days, if the head job went to a former player who had already been around the program for 14 years, anyone interested in that story would know how to pronounce his name. But there wasn't nearly as much publicity and attention given to matters back then, so a lot of people still mispronounced the first syllable of my name as *BO*, with a long *O*. Later, when we were in the Big East, P. J. Carlesimo always referred to me as "Bo," and St. John's coach Lou Carnesecca used to greet me with "BO-heim, BO-heim," grabbing my hand. I assume he actually knew the pronunciation, but with Louie you could never really be sure.

After getting the job, I had three immediate orders of business:

- Lock up Bouie, a big center. Roosevelt was a dominant high school player, but he was a kid from a small upstate New York town, Kendall, and he didn't want the bright lights. It was St. Bonaventure or us, because he was also close to Jim Satalin, who coached there. I was confident we could get him. Syracuse had more bright lights than St. Bonaventure, but they weren't all that bright.

- Sign a skinny kid out of Cincinnati named Louis Orr.
- Hire another assistant to join Bernie Fine, a former Syracuse manager whom I had already hired.

All of it had to be done quickly.

Rick Pitino was already in my sights for that second assistant's job. He was a young guy, 25, who had been an assistant at the University of Hawaii. I always told him that he had to put an entire ocean between his first and second jobs. Also, he was going to have to make the transition from Hawaii weather to Syracuse weather, which wouldn't have been a problem for me, but I'm not everybody. Rick, a great camp clinician, was out of that tradition of fast-talking East Coast guys who worked the circuit, thought fast on their feet and knew how to motivate.

I had gotten the job on a Friday, and on Sunday I drove to New York to convince Rick to come to Syracuse. The problem was, Rick had just gotten married and was preparing to leave on his honeymoon. A more patient and considerate man might've given him a day or two, but I was neither back then, and our two key recruits waited in the balance. So . . .

"Rick, this is Jim Boeheim," I said in a phone call to the newlyweds' room at the old Americana hotel. "We need to talk."

"That's great, Jim, but I just got married, so I can't do it today, and I'm leaving on my honeymoon tomorrow," Rick said.

"It *has* to be right now," I told him. What I didn't say at the time was, "And you *won't* be going on your honeymoon if I have anything to say about it."

Reluctantly, Rick came down. The former Joanne Minardi stayed upstairs. They were doing what all newlyweds do, and by that I mean counting the envelopes of cash they had received at the reception.

We sat and talked for two or three hours. The bellboy came

down every 45 minutes or so, telling him, "Your wife wants you." Rick was obviously torn. He wanted to be with Joanne, too, but he also wanted the job.

I'm making $25,000, so I tell Rick that his salary is $13,000. He says he wants $15,000. So I say, "Well, I can get you a couple thousand more from the camp." So we agree somewhere around $17,000. These days, the gap between head coach and assistant is a lot more than that.

"Here's the final thing," I tell Rick. "You gotta come tomorrow."

"I'm going to Puerto Rico on my honeymoon," he tells me.

"No, you're not," I say. "You're going to Cincinnati to sign Louis Orr. I have to work on Roosevelt Bouie."

"Oh, my wife's gonna love this," he said.

Actually, that wasn't the worst of it. They came to Syracuse, Rick and I took off recruiting, and Joanne was stuck living in a house with my three roommates, who included Tom Green, the Syracuse freshman coach at the time, who would go on to coach Fairleigh Dickinson for 26 years. They also included a bartender and a guy who bet on the ponies. On the plus side, it wasn't winter.

If anyone deserved the national championships that Rick later won at Kentucky and Louisville, it was Joanne. When Juli and I were honeymooning in Bermuda, the phone rang in our suite at about 5:00 A.M. Woozily, I answered.

"It's Joanne Pitino," she said. "I've waited years to get you back."

NOBODY KNEW MUCH about Louis Orr when we first started recruiting him. I had gotten a call about him from Ron Grinker, an agent known for his honesty, which made him unusual.

"Jim, you don't know me," said Ron, "but I have a player who I think would be good for you. He will be a pro, I can tell you that right now. He's six-eight, six-nine, but a little skinny."

"Okay," I told Ron. "I'll come out and see him."

Ron takes me to Xavier, which is the other school recruiting Louis. I'm basically sneaking around in their gym while he works out. And when Ron said "skinny," he wasn't kidding. Louis was the skinniest kid I ever saw, maybe 160 pounds—and believe me, I *knew* skinny. But I liked him. So we bring Louis in for a visit, he likes us and he verbally commits.

But it still remained for Rick, the newlywed, to sign him. That happened to be right after Louis went off for 32 points in an all-star game against the Russian junior national team. Now a lot of coaches knew about Louis Orr.

So Rick introduces himself to Louis's dad, and the man says, "I'm sorry, Coach Pitino, but it doesn't look good for Louis to come to Syracuse now."

Rick is almost ready to faint when Mr. Orr slaps him on the back and says, "Nah, I'm just bustin' you. Louis is coming."

All in all, Rick had some kind of honeymoon weekend.

As a recruiter, the young Rick Pitino was prone to overstatement. He came to me once and said, "I have a kid in New Jersey. He's the best guard ever." And I said: "Rick, I played with Dave Bing. He's better than Dave Bing?" Rick agreed that it was probably an exaggeration.

On another trip, we went to Nashua, New Hampshire, to see a kid named Rich Shrigley, whom Rick was high on. Shrigley was a decent prospect, maybe six foot five. Rick tells me that he'll handle all the talking, because he knows *everything* about Rich Shrigley. It was different in those days. We'd make 15, 18, sometimes 20 home visits, and in most cases you didn't come equipped with the reams of printouts you have now. That call I got from Ron Grinker about a six-nine NBA prospect that nobody knows about? I'd hang up the phone these days, because it would likely be a hoax.

Anyway, at the Shrigley house, Rick launches into his spiel, which goes something like this:

"Coach Boeheim's not the kind of guy to say this, but he will get you drafted. You will be in the first or second round . . ."

Okay, Rick, rein it in a little.

" . . . And if you don't make it, Coach Boeheim will get you a job for thirty, forty thousand dollars . . ."

Okay, Rick, rein it in a lot.

" . . . And you will see playing time at Syracuse, because Coach Boeheim doesn't overrecruit. It's not like at North Carolina State and other places where they bring in a bunch of guys and they don't play and nobody is happy and . . ."

At this point, Mrs. Shrigley interrupts and says, "Excuse me, Coach. Are you talking about my brother's school?"

It turned out that the extensive dossier Rick had on young Shrigley did not include the fact that his uncle was Norm Sloan, the coach at N.C. State.

We stayed in the Shrigley house for another half hour or so—among the most awkward 30 minutes in recruiting history—and later, on the drive back, we had to pull the car over several times because we were laughing so hard.

"Come to think of it," Rick said, "Mrs. Shrigley did look a helluva lot like Norm Sloan."

Postscript: Rich Shrigley didn't go to Syracuse or N.C. State. He went to Boston College.

It's hard to reconcile the image of Rick we have now—always up off the bench, always talking, always in the middle of everything—with what he was like as an assistant. He rarely said anything back then during games, a true assistant, working hard with the players, doing a lot of stuff we probably wouldn't do now. Like the brick drill, in which players did slides while holding bricks straight out.

Rick would get them out there early, and sometimes the real practices would seem easy compared with the pre-practices.

Drills like those are rarely part of today's game, which puts an emphasis on individual workouts. They're done in the morning or early afternoon, between classes, when assistant coaches can give players one-on-one attention. Under NCAA rules, we're allowed 20 hours per week to practice with our team in the preseason. So if we have six two-hour practices, that leaves as much as eight hours for individual workouts.

I'm sure that some of our past players would've been better served with individual workouts. Tony "Red" Bruin comes to mind. He was a talented player who never lived up to expectations. Leo Rautins, who played with Tony in the early '80s, once said, "Red was the kind of player who wanted to be driven to the gym. And Boeheim doesn't drive guys to the gym." With scheduled workouts away from the grind of regular practice, maybe it would've been different for Red.

Plus, individual workouts help a kid prepare for his pro future, if he has one. Any coach who has been around for a long time will invariably get criticized for not adequately getting his kids ready for the NBA. Dean Smith and John Thompson heard it, and so have I. But I never considered that you couldn't be both a coach who wins in college and one who prepares his best players to be pros. We worked on getting Michael Carter-Williams to be stronger and to become a better shooter, which ended up helping him and us. We worked hard on C. J. Fair's ballhandling, which helped us and should help him if he finds an NBA home. I guarantee you this: If I have a bunch of future pros on my roster, I will have a great Syracuse team.

But a coach can do only so much. Holding him responsible for what awaits a player later in his career is foolish. So if Dean didn't prepare some players well for the NBA, does that mean he deserves credit for Michael Jordan? Jack Leaman was an excellent coach at

UMass, but I doubt that his tutelage was responsible for the success of Julius Erving. Did Bill Hodges make Larry Bird into a legend? Did Jud Heathcote transform Magic Johnson into an all-time great? Vast generalizations that people make about coaches are usually way off-base.

Now, bringing in kids to work alone in the morning does seem more "professional." But it's also more efficient, a much better use of a player's time. And the individual workouts enable you to spend less time in the teamwide afternoon practices. You've already built a foundation.

But back in the '70s we went at it hard, partly because we wanted a running team, partly because we were intense as coaches, and partly because that's the way most everybody did it.

In the preseason, we did ballhandling drills around the track, which included crab-walking. We had prescribed times for running the mile. We made the players run a hill near campus called Skytop. We devised a full-court layup drill, in which you had to make 120 in three minutes. The next day it was 123. Then it was 126. We did two-on-one defensive drills in which the "one" didn't get off defense until he made a stop. There were no chairs in the gym; players didn't sit down, and neither did coaches.

Roosevelt Bouie tells the story—frankly, I don't remember it—that he missed an intrasquad scrimmage once because he overslept. If it happened, it was the *only* time, because Rosie remains one of the hardest-working players I ever coached. Anyway, he claims I said to him, "Oh, by the way, you owe me an hour and a half of running—but I'll let you break it up into half-hour sessions over the next three days." According to Rosie, I sat there on a chair reading a newspaper—which does sound like me—while for three straight days he ran for a half hour steady after full practices. On the third day he said, "Good night, Coach," and collapsed in exhaustion after I left.

These days we can make it tough on players with running drills, but not like in those days of yore. We stopped the Skytop run, the timed mile and dribbling crabwalks. We still do the layup drill, but now we shoot for 120 in four minutes. We can't reach the numbers we did years ago—back in Rosie's day we could sometimes get to 130—because we have more walk-ons who are not quite as skilled athletically. We still don't sit down at practice, but there is a chair for me, the consequence of bad knees, spells of plantar fasciitis and age.

All in all, though, we probably do as much aerobic work and conditioning as we ever did, except that it's more sophisticated, conducted with trainers and strength coaches who know what they're doing. Players are in better shape now because they work at it year-round. You know what constituted a commonplace summer "workout" for Pearl Washington? Going horseback riding in up-state New York. (More on Pearl later—the basketball player, not the equestrian.)

So while it's true that players are much less likely to "run through a wall for you," which is what we used to say about the gutsy kids in the old days, it's also true that they're much more knowledgeable about what they have to do to get themselves ready. They understand the seriousness of preparation at a much younger age.

Still, that first team of mine, 1976–77, set a template for hard work and dedication that has, for the most part, continued at Syracuse. Rick was a big part of that. I owe him a debt, and he owes me one for giving him a shot, even if I did interrupt his wedding weekend. We've done a little verbal sniping at each other over the years—that happens when you're in competitive situations—and he stayed only two seasons before getting the head job at Boston University, but we will always have a bond from that first team.

When he was here, Rick used to say, "Oh, Jim will be at Syracuse forever." I don't know whether he just tossed off the line or if he really believed it. But after my first season, I certainly thought

I would. Collectively, that team became known as the Bouie and Louie Show, or the Louie and Bouie Show, whichever you prefer. Those two were great players and good guys. And the whole team was like that. They went to class, graduated on time, worked hard and played hard.

Man, I thought, *this coaching thing is easy.*

Then I got Derrick Coleman and Rony Seikaly.

Man, I was about learn, *this coaching thing is hard.*

A COACH'S NOTES II

It's the day after Thanksgiving and here we are in Melo, just hours after flying back across an ocean and a continent from Maui, the tournament trophy in our hands. We played extremely well. Trevor Cooney shot the lights out, Tyler Ennis played like a fifth-year senior instead of a 19-year-old freshman, and our 2-3 zone defense caused problems with every team we beat—Minnesota, Cal and Baylor in the final.

But now it's time to go to work, with Indiana due at the Dome in four days. Playing a tough nonconference team after getting back from a long trip is generally not the way I like to do things. In the past, we've noticed a deadness in our step after an early-season road tournament. But it can't be helped—it's the Big Ten/ACC Challenge.

The team is in front of me, and when we're all together like this, it is *my team*. That is the way my coaching philosophy has evolved.

If you watch the interaction of our team on a daily basis, you will see how integral to our success my assistants are. They're in tune with the Syracuse way, they know what I want to accomplish, and they're all in terrific basketball shape. Gerry McNamara sometimes gets up 500 three-pointers a day, and he can still outshoot anybody on our team, and probably most players in college basketball.

It's become a little like a football system with position coaches. The assistants conduct the individual workouts with our players—Mike Hopkins with the bigs, Adrian Autry with the forwards, Gerry with the guards. They scout the opponents, each one assigned to a specific team. They brief me on particulars, though chances are I'll know a lot of it anyway, because I watch a lot of basketball.

They are also the ones to talk to the players about off-the-court matters. If a player is having trouble with his girlfriend, my assistants are far more likely to know about it than I am. I don't even want to know about it, unless it becomes a Problem.

When I was an assistant, I was a hugger like Mike. (Okay, maybe not at that level, because Hop is a serious hugger.) The players told me their problems and I dispensed advice. The fact that I knew so much about the players when I was an assistant helped me get the head job in 1976.

But players, by and large, would rather stay away from me, and I can't afford to have a close relationship with one player and not the rest. Naturally, I might respect one player more than another—that's just human nature—but I do everything possible not to let that show.

It is important, though, that my guys understand that I haven't forgotten what it was like to be a player. I don't expect them to conjure up in their mind's eye a vision of a bespectacled Boeheim in high white Converse. But there are constants in this game throughout the generations. As a player, for example, I never liked doing wind sprints, never saw the point of them, as long as you ran hard at other spots during practice. So we don't do many wind sprints.

But it's important that my role as CEO of the program is understood. Marty Headd, a guard who played here in the 1970s and one of the toughest kids we ever had, was once asked by a reporter whether he had a good relationship with me. Marty looked at the guy strangely and said, "What's the difference? He's not my friend. He's my coach."

So here's the way I do it here: I coach the whole team. I don't coach individual skills. When I whistle the team together before practice, I do all the talking. When we're together watching film, I do all the talking. When we're in the locker room before a game, I do all the talking.

Now, on the bench during a game, it changes a little bit. I do *most* of the talking, although my assistants are free to give me input, as long as it doesn't come in massive volume. They might say, "Trevor looks a little tired," something along that line. They also give instructions and directions to their position guys, either off to the side, when I'm finished talking, or as the players leave the huddle. I don't meet with my assistants before the timeout huddle forms like most coaches do. It wastes time, and I know what I'm going to say. At halftime, I do all the talking. After the game, I do all the talking, all the screaming and all the lecturing.

The way I look at it, a head coach at a major program is paid a lot of money to make decisions, and if you can't make those decisions, you had better get out of the business.

Some decisions, of course, are easier than others, though what those are vary from coach to coach. How much video to watch, for example, is not a hard decision for me. The answer is: not much. We probably watch less film than any team in the country. If guys are making a mistake, I feel it makes more sense to show them what they did wrong on the court. Now, there are times when video is valuable. Once in a while, when a player is not getting back on defense but insists that he is, you can fire up the proof.

Steve Spurrier told me once that, though his assistants watch a lot of film, he doesn't watch any at all. His philosophy is: We're going to run our stuff, and let's see if you can stop it. I don't completely buy into that, but I lean in that direction.

What video I do watch at home, by the way, is on VHS. I get both a DVD and a VHS cassette, and I usually go old school. (Tell you the truth, I wish we still had film, with that old whirring projector.)

Here's another decision that's not hard for me: whether to take a player out when he gets into early foul trouble. I generally leave a starter in when he gets two fouls in the first half, and that goes against standard philosophy. But I've seen coaches take good players out in the first half after they collect their second foul, and by the time they get into the locker room, a ten-point lead has become a four-point deficit. Plus, staying out of foul trouble is part of the reason we play zone, as I'll explain.

Here's another reason: If a player knows he will be yanked after getting his second foul, he stops playing hard after getting his first. Had I given Derrick Coleman a quick hook, he might as well have had a lounge chair out there for all the defense he'd be playing after getting one foul.

What are the hard decisions? Well, for me, there are two: When should you really try to take control of a game as a coach? And who do you go to when you need a big shot down the stretch?

Our offense is structured with multiple plays, ranging between 12 and 15. Some games, we might run only three or four of them if they're producing results. Throughout the game, you have to give your point guard room to make his own decisions. You have to let the game flow. But at some point—I see it as about six minutes left in a close game—a coach has to take over the game, start making the play calls and stressing the importance of each possession.

Now, who takes the big shot in close games? That's a difficult one. Sometimes it might seem obvious, like when you have a player such as Pearl Washington or Carmelo Anthony. But even that isn't a sure thing. Pearl wasn't our best percentage shooter, and Carmelo had McNamara. If you run a motion offense, the shots just come out of your regular stuff, but we don't run much of that. I've found that the wrong guy shoots too much in a motion offense.

So is it the player who's got the hot hand that night? The player who is being guarded by their weakest defender or by the guy who has four fouls? The player who's made the most clutch shots for you? The player who *wants* it the most?

There's no easy answer, particularly when you have a balanced team, as was the 2012–13 team that made it to the Final Four. We had Michael Carter-Williams, who could make plays going to the basket. We had James Southerland, who was our most reliable outside shooter. We had Brandon Triche, who had started since he was a freshman and was accustomed to pressure. And we had C. J. Fair, who in some respects was our most versatile offensive player, even though he was usually our fourth option.

There is never an easy answer, but over the years, if you've gotten the ball to the wrong person too often, then you've lost a lot of games.

What you hope for as a head coach, though, is that decisions about who takes the last shot are the *hardest* ones you have to make. Because every year, something happens off the court that you have to work out, and if you do that without anyone knowing about it, you've earned your money. The off-court decisions can drive you out of coaching a lot sooner than the on-court ones. I've had a few of those.

5

WHEN ORANGEMEN PLAYED
AT MANLEY

My first victory as a head coach came in an exhibition against the Chilean national team. I ran out on the court before the game like a young colt, charged up, ready to take on the world. It was around my 32nd birthday, but I felt like I was a 13-year-old kid. I learned quickly, though, that it's best to not only conserve your energy but also to not get too high or too low about anything. The peaks and valleys are what take it out of you.

Our first official game was against Harvard, in the Tip-Off Classic in Springfield, Massachusetts, November 26, 1976. We had a good team, with smart players, and all I instructed them to do was fully execute our set offense, a brilliant strategy that produced a one-point lead at halftime. So in the second half I junked the plays and ordered them to loosen up, and we won 75–48. Valuable lesson learned early: Adapt if you have to, and don't be so structured, particularly if your talent is superior to theirs.

We lost to West Virginia 83–78 in the finals of the tournament, and, after a win over Colgate, we had to go on the road against Louisville and Boston College, three days apart. I know the tendency is to overemphasize events that happen to you when you're young, but these were important games. They would to a certain extent define our team and demonstrate whether the confidence that I had shown, and the faith the administration had shown in me, were justified.

Seventh-ranked Louisville had Wesley Cox and a fabulous freshman named Darrell Griffith. We were probably 15-point underdogs, but we won 76–75. When I think back on my career, it was one of the best wins I ever had; behind Griffith, a.k.a. Dr. Dunkenstein, Louisville would win the NCAA championship three years later. After we beat Boston College, easily, we were on our way.

In many ways, that first season was a dream. Bouie and Louie were smart and dedicated, even as freshmen. To this day, when Jimmy Satalin sees Roosevelt, he says, "Rosie, you broke my heart when you didn't come to St. Bonnie's." One player can be extremely important to a program, and who knows what could've happened with the Bonnies had they gotten Bouie?

We had two experienced senior guards in Jimmy "Bug" Williams and Larry Kelley. Rosie, Dale Shackleford and Marty Byrnes were all terrific rebounders. I brought Louis off the bench, but he still averaged almost ten points and seven rebounds. Plus, I could go as deep as 12 players, which was necessary, because we pressured all over the place and asked our guys to go full tilt on defense on every possession. In many ways, my teams now are polar opposites from that first one; these days, my formula is more like seven rotation players and an eighth who can give me minutes here and there.

I was in an extremely good political position for a young coach. Jake Crouthamel was coming in as athletic director, and he was already a powerful guy around campus and would remain in charge until 2005. He had been a halfback/defensive back at Dartmouth and the first player ever to sign with the Dallas Cowboys. (He was traded before he played there.) He had been a coach at his alma mater before coming here.

All that is to say that Jake was the ultimate Football Guy. He went to practice, he drew up plays, he lived and breathed football, and he didn't care much about basketball. Later, when we were in Philadelphia one year for the Big East games, all the athletic directors went to the game except for Jake, who went out to dinner. He came to our NCAA tournament games only because he had to.

Now, if you have an A.D. who doesn't care much about your sport, it can be a bad thing. But Jake cared about results and was smart enough to know that a winning program is good for the whole department. So I could more or less do my own thing, increase the recruiting budget here and there without prior approval, and, as long as we won, I wouldn't have to worry too much.

Third, I loved our conference, the Eastern College Athletic Conference. After all these years of Big East wars with Georgetown and UConn, it sounds anachronistic to bring up St. Bonaventure, but the Bonnies were a monster rivalry. We didn't like them, they didn't like us. And though we held a 23–3 lifetime advantage over them, they were never a pushover. In this dream first season, one of our four losses was a 91–84 defeat to the Bonnies.

The ECAC had been the home of Calvin Murphy, still one of the most memorable college players in history. He was at Niagara from 1966–67 to 1969–70, and in those four seasons he averaged— wait for it—48.9 (in freshman games), 38.2, 32.4 and 29.4. Murphy's teams beat us five times in seven games. In the 1967–68 season, he got 50 against us, and the next year, having apparently spotted further weaknesses in our defense, he went for 68. As I looked on from my assistant's spot, I was completely flummoxed. We prepared for him, had planned to double him, but he just split our guys and got off a jumper before the other three could come. Or, if they kept him from splitting, he simply went around them. And when he shot his jumper, his feet were level with the defender's chest. You could foul him, but he made every damn free throw. Calvin Murphy was the hardest small guard—*ever*—to play against, and that includes Allen Iverson.

Finally, we had Manley Field House, our sixth man. It was first used as a basketball facility in my freshman year, 1962, so it felt like home to me. To visiting teams it felt like jail. Students began lining up for tickets ten hours before the game and maybe—just maybe— they had drunk some beer. They barked at the opposition and threw dog biscuits. The Zoo, the Kennel . . . take your pick. Both were unnerving to opponents.

There's always a fine line between school spirit and going off the deep end, and at Manley the only lines they cared about were drawn on the court. But any coach will tell you that his favorite home arena has one prevailing characteristic: He wins there. So to me, Manley Field House was the beating heart of Syracuse athletics. I was a happy young coach.

WE GOT BACK at St. Bonnie's with an 85–72 win in the ECAC play-offs, then beat Old Dominion to win the ECAC Upstate-Southern championship. Rolls off the tongue, doesn't it? With a name like that, you can begin to see some of the identity issues the ECAC had. And then it was on to the NCAAs, where, in the Mideast Region in Baton Rouge, we upset Tennessee 93–88 in overtime. Yes, we had Bouie and Louie, but no one had come up with that name yet. Tennessee, however, had the Bernie and Ernie Show—Bernard King and Ernie Grunfeld—and *everyone* knew them. Both were first-team All-Americans and future pros.

But we beat them. Three of our guys fouled out in regulation, and two of theirs did also—Bernie and Ernie. So as much as anything, it was our depth that won the day. I was able to reach down into the bench and get five points in overtime from Billy Drew, a junior swingman.

We got run out by UNC-Charlotte in the regional finals, but that wasn't as embarrassing a loss as it might've seemed. They had an outstanding player named Cedric "Cornbread" Maxwell, who would go on to be a dominant NBA player.

The Louie and Bouie Show almost got derailed before it really got rolling. Just before the 1977–78 season, Louis's father died after surgery for lung cancer. I got a call from Ron Grinker, who told me that Louis had gone home and was thinking about staying there, probably transferring to Xavier. It was nothing against Syracuse; he was just distraught about losing his father. I flew out there and told Louis, "Look, I think the best place for you is Syracuse. This will be your home."

When you're a coach, charged with both handling young men and trying to win games, you have to look into the mirror from time to time and decide whether you're saying something to help the player or just trying to help yourself. Yes, we would be a better team with Louis Orr. But I truly believed that the best option for him, both for the present and for his future as an NBA player, would be to stay at Syracuse. I believed it with all my heart. I had just lost my mother, at age 58, to leukemia, and I talked to Louis about that. Eventually, with the help of his family and Grinker, Louis decided to stay. He says to this day that it was the best decision for him, and it certainly was good for us. Gale Catlett, who was coaching at Cincinnati when Louis was in high school, would always shake his head when Louis torched West Virginia, where Gale ended up coaching. Like a lot of others, he had failed to see much potential in this string bean of a kid.

IN MY SECOND year, we invited Michigan State, which had a freshman guard named Earvin "Magic" Johnson, to play in the first Carrier Classic. Their coach, Jud Heathcote, spoke at a dinner before the banquet, and when he stood up everybody was expecting the predictable platitudes. *Nice to be here. Thanks for inviting us.* But Jud says, "I can't believe we're here. I didn't want to come down here and play." It was an indelible moment in the history of the rubber-chicken circuit. I wondered then if I would ever reach the point where I could say exactly what was on my mind. Turns out I did, though I was usually slightly more diplomatic than Jud.

We beat Michigan State 75–67 in the championship final, and Marty Byrnes had a big game, with 17 points. He just dominated inside. But because Magic had gotten so much preseason hype—much of which he deserved, of course—the writers gave him the MVP in a losing cause. He wasn't even the best player on his team in that tournament—Greg Kelser and Jay Vincent had both played better than Magic.

So after the game I went ballistic. I threw a rolled-up program at the local writer who had voted for Magic. I was beside myself. I still remember the Michigan State sports information director looking at me in confusion and saying, "Wait a minute. Didn't you win the game?" It didn't matter to me. I guess it was the feeling of being disrespected. I've always hung on to that. But even the Michigan State coach agreed with me. "I always think the MVP trophy should go to a player from the winning team," said Jud, the guy who didn't want to be here. More to the point, the MVP himself agreed with me. "I didn't expect it," said Magic. "I was surprised a guy from Syracuse didn't win it."

The next day, a local writer ripped me for showing no class, and some say that it marked the point when my relationship with the local press turned rocky. I see it as something else. To me, it marked the moment when it became clear that I would stand up for my players, in any and all circumstances, if I believed they were being shortchanged.

Our team began to develop a personality, a tough, spirited ethos that was typified by a player like Marty Headd. Before one game, I mentioned that it was going to be a dogfight and all of a sudden Marty goes, "Bow wow *wow!*" Everybody thought he was crazy. During a game at St. Bonaventure in 1979, Marty was in fact as sick as a dog but was playing really well. He kept throwing up into a towel on the bench, and I kept putting him back in (with his blessing of course) with two instructions: Don't stop making jump shots, and don't start vomiting on the court. He listened to both orders, though after the game he was severely dehydrated.

People always tell me that I identify with guys like Marty Headd. You never lose that walk-on mentality, I suppose, the idea that you had to work your butt off to earn respect and therefore you gravitate to those kinds of kids. But don't take that too far. Most coaches, including me, would rather have immense talent. Talent, more than anything, turns you into a genius.

I was learning to utilize a player's strength, figure out what he does best and put him in that position to succeed. If a player can't do something, then don't ask him to do it and then wonder later why he couldn't do it. He couldn't do it because he *can't* do it. One of the guys I always thought put his players in the right spot was Lou Carnesecca. When you played St. John's, they didn't do a lot that was complex, but at the end of the shot clock, you could bet that Walter Berry or Chris Mullin would have the ball.

I was learning, too, that I could juggle defenses. I always had that zone in my head—we played it in high school under Coach Blackwell, though it was more of a 1-2-2 than a 2-3—but we used a lot of man-to-man, too, in those early years. It was all good—the team, the fan base, the arena, the conference.

Except I was beginning to hear some disturbing news. First, we would be moving out of Manley to a giant dome that was being built on campus. Why would we do that? What could be better than Manley? Why would we move to something that looks like a futuristic greenhouse?

And there was a movement afoot to join a new basketball conference called the Big East. Why would we do that? What could be better than Syracuse–St. Bonnie's?

6

BEASTS OF THE EAST

f someone asked you to name the best college basketball coaches in history, who would you take? John Wooden, for sure. Mike Krzyzewski probably. Adolph Rupp? Hank Iba? Dean Smith?

How about college players? Lew Alcindor, for sure. Maybe Oscar Robertson? Jerry West? Pete Maravich?

How about basketball executives, a more obscure category? The average fan probably couldn't name more than a couple. But any of us who were around at the dawn of the Big East would have one candidate to be carved into rock before all others.

Dave Gavitt.

None of us who eventually made our names in that conference— John Thompson, Lou Carnesecca, Jim Calhoun, Rollie Massimino, Rick Pitino, P. J. Carlesimo, Gary Williams, me—could've gotten there without Dave.

While I was toiling happily away (well, as happily as I ever toil) in the ECAC, Dave, the athletic director at Providence College, was thinking about something else. Something big.

Everybody in our world knew Dave, who would've been the Olympic coach in 1980 if not for the boycott against the Soviet Union. I had scouted his teams at Providence when they had Marvin "Bad News" Barnes and Ernie DiGregorio. Before he went from the bench to the boardroom, he had led Providence to eight straight NCAA tournaments and one Final Four.

Dave was a Big Thinker, and Dave thought that basketball in the East was getting the short end of the stick in terms of attention and NCAA bids.

He was correct. The major programs were in the far West (UCLA), in the middle of the country (Kentucky and Kansas), and down south in the ACC. When I came to Syracuse as a student in 1962, it had been eight years since an eastern team had won the NCAA title—that was Tom Gola's La Salle team—and not another would win until 1984: Patrick Ewing's Georgetown team, which by then was in Dave's new conference.

Dave wanted the automatic bid to the NCAA tournament that would eventually go to the conference champion, and he knew that several other teams in a strong conference would invariably get at-large bids. He saw the allure of the Boston–New York–Washington television market, and he thought he could get a fledgling TV network interested in broadcasting our games: a humble operation that went by four little letters that was just getting off the ground in Bristol, Connecticut.

Our TV "exposure" in the ECAC had amounted to one "Game of the Week," which was broadcast mostly on regional affiliates, and at less frequency than the name implied. The biggest thing about it was that Marv Albert did the play-by-play. It was your one big shot for television, and you got your team all dressed up like you were going to the prom. But that game—and we played in some good ones—never caught hold of a national audience.

You can't overstate how important television was in Dave's thinking. At the time, St. Bonaventure, for example, was as good a program as, say, Seton Hall. But, being in western New York State, it didn't have a metro New York connection; Dave knew that would be critical in the long run, that programs would be built because of the television exposure.

The ECAC's main problem was that it was confusing—teams scattered all over the place like small island nations. In fact, it really wasn't even a league, more like an umbrella organization. There were 232 schools in the ECAC, all of them with different goals, different budgets and different leadership. It was a microcosm of the NCAA. Danny Schayes was one of the smartest players I ever had at Syracuse, and he told me once that even he couldn't name all the major programs in the conference. Lou Carnesecca, who would become one of my beloved rivals in this new Gavitt conference, used to say that he'd mention the letters *ECAC* to coaches from the West and the South and they would think he was talking about some obscure government agency.

Plus, the NCAA had passed a rule that a conference team had to play every other team in its conference. Dave didn't like that. His interest was getting Providence to the NCAA tournament, not fostering a rivalry with, say, Norfolk, Virginia–based Old Dominion, with which we shared an inexplicable connection as members of the Southern Division of the ECAC.

Dave thought the solution would be a "super conference" of eastern schools, which would be called the Big East. It would help raise the profile of eastern basketball, simply by getting more bids to the tournament. The way Gavitt had it figured, 38 ECAC teams scrambled around each year for three at-large tournament bids, like a pack of dogs fighting over a pork chop.

Beyond the fact that his brain worked at a level above almost everyone else's, Dave was a diplomat. That combination of brains and personality doesn't come along often. His great strength was getting people to do things they didn't want to do, then getting them to believe that they had thought of them. He was a masterful politician primarily because he pretended he wasn't a politician. Jim Calhoun put it this way: "Dave led us by the hand, and we didn't even know we were being led."

It takes a lot of arm-twisting to get a league organized. There are ancient alliances between schools that have to be broken. Not only are there differences in motivation and direction between institutions, but there are diverse agendas *within* institutions. What an athletic director views as beneficial might be at odds with what his coach thinks. Which was the case at Syracuse: I could not see the benefit of joining the Big East, which would include two schools, Georgetown and St. John's, that we were already playing in ECAC competition, and a couple of others, UConn and Boston College, that we played once in a while.

But Dave worked it all out, primarily because he had built relationships with so many people. From the beginning, Providence was in, obviously, because Dave was there. St. John's came along early, because Dave had bent Lou Carnesecca's ear about it during a flight back from Italy, which Dave had taken precisely for ear-bending purposes. Seton Hall wanted to go with St. John's; they were more or less partner schools. Boston College fit the profile, too—Catholic, small, except that, like Syracuse, they had a first-rate football program. That didn't seem important at the time.

Georgetown signed on. They had been one of the first three schools at the first Big East meeting, back in May of 1978. John Thompson had a lot of power at Georgetown and had played for Dave at Providence. He really liked Dave, and Guys That John Really Liked constituted a relatively small club. There is no way that John would've ever signed off had Dave not been at the helm. John Toner, who was a powerful A.D. at Connecticut, was one of Dave's friends, so UConn was in as well.

My boss, Jake Crouthamel, had been a fraternity brother of Dave's at Dartmouth and, like everyone else, trusted him. So that was that. Rutgers, which had made the Final Four with a great team in 1976, decided against joining and stayed with the Eastern Eight, which later formed the foundation of the Atlantic 10. I'm sure now that Rutgers later regretted not joining.

And so, on May 31, 1979, the Big East was officially born with Syracuse, Boston College, Connecticut, Georgetown, Providence, Seton Hall and St. John's. Villanova came aboard the next season, and Pitt the season after that.

I doubt that even Dave, the visionary who died in 2011, foresaw the heights we would hit.

SO, YES, HISTORY will put me down as being "anti–Big East" in the beginning. But it was more that I was just "pro–status quo," which is natural for a coach who is having success. Here was John Thompson's response about going into the Big East: "I thought they were crazy."

Plus, something else was going on at around this time. I was being told that we were moving from the friendly confines of Manley to the Carrier Dome, a behemoth structure that was being erected, primarily as a venue for football, on the site of Archbold Gymnasium, a beloved campus spot for old-time players like me. The way I saw it, they were tearing down a piece of history. Going from Manley to the Dome would be like going from a comfortable elementary school gym where you knew every bump on the floor to Madison Square Garden, where you couldn't even find your way to the locker room. (Later, of course, MSG would feel like a second home.)

I mean, how much change can one man take? Coaches like comfort. When you have a winning program like we did at the time, you want to hold on to it, because you get evaluated by winning, not by leaping into the great unknown. You throw a coach a Big Idea and he cringes, unless he can figure out how it adds up to wins. That's why you don't let coaches make all the decisions. (Only the most important ones.)

So I didn't like it and kept pestering Cliff Winters (the guy who hired me) with questions about this mysterious dome. Will we be able to practice when we need to? What if the football team has to use it? What if it's too cold? What if our jump shooters can't hit anything because of their depth perception in the great big space? I had a theory (which I maintain to this day) that only big-time players make shots in large arenas. If we could take a recruit of uncertain talent and have him take shots in a big building, we would have a better idea if he could make it at the D1 level.

But my underlying question was this: Why would we surrender such a profound home-court advantage? I had never lost in Manley as a head coach. Do you have any idea what the phrase *never lost* sounds like to a coach?

Plus, we were playing in front of 9,000 people—9,500 if the fire marshal's head was turned. Now we were moving to an arena where capacity could be as high as 35,000? What, we were going to start playing the Celtics and the Lakers? I never thought we'd draw 15,000 fans, let alone 35,000. I was wrong about that, and looking back, I realize I made one profoundly stupid business decision. I should've gotten a clause in my contract that read: Boeheim gets $1 for every fan over 15,000.

Cliff heard me out, but, as I indicated earlier, he oversaw what food would be served and who would plow the snow, so he was sure as hell going to decide where the basketball team was going to play.

At some point, he said, "Jim, we're going." Which was like saying, "Jim, shut up." So I shut up. No one at Syracuse foresaw a day when patrons would pay $7,000 for seat licenses and we would have crowds as large as 35,000. Except for Dave. And maybe Cliff.

As far as scheduling went, we pretty much got the Dome whenever we wanted, even in the early years. But there were problems, as there were bound to be in a facility of that size. In the beginning, they kept the Dome at 66 degrees, which is too cold for practice. It has to be at least 70; these days we keep Melo at 72. They tried space heaters, but you can imagine how effective space heaters were in a football stadium. So eventually they just turned up the heat to get it from 66 to 70, which cost between $3,000 and $4,000 per day. Of course, they began selling tens of thousands more tickets to games, so it was a net gain. Sometimes we had to deal with dripping water. There were rips in the roof that had to be fixed, and the roof once collapsed, though not during the season.

All in all, though, the transition wasn't bad. There's a lot of wind in there, but, surprisingly, you don't feel it at court level.

So here was the timetable:

Move to the Big East for the 1979–80 season.
Move to the Dome for the 1980–81 season.

And if there's one juncture when the past came crashing down and a bright future unfolded (though we couldn't see it at the time), it was the evening of February 12, 1980, our last game at Manley in the first season of the Big East, a conference that had not yet made a large footprint in the college basketball sand.

Georgetown was the opponent.

Of course it was.

LET THE RECORD show that the first time I met John Thompson, I tried to calm him down.

The first time I saw John Thompson, however, was not on an opposing bench, staring me down with a towel draped on his shoulder. It was at that playground in Washington, D.C., in the summer of 1965, the one Dave Bing had invited Bradley to the summer before.

I was on Dave's team. (You think I'd be anywhere else?) There were two other really good players in the game: Ollie Johnson, who was an All-American at the University of San Francisco, and a playground legend named Garnett Logan.

Suddenly, this big guy named Thompson, who had gone to high school at Archbishop Carroll, in Washington, and was an All-American at Providence, shows up. John was two years older than Bing and me, kind of an awkward player, but he certainly knew the game. At that time he was preparing to go into the NBA, where he would play three years for the Celtics.

So he gets his shot blocked by this Garnett Logan guy, and John is all upset. "Relax," I tell him. "We'll get 'em back."

John and I didn't connect again until we were coaching against each other. Pre–Big East, Syracuse–Georgetown was just another game on the ECAC schedule. I didn't think much about him, and he didn't think much about me, I'm sure. That would all change on February 12, 1980.

John was an intimidating figure, no doubt about it. He carried an us-against-the-world attitude that he imprinted on his teams. He felt he needed that to be successful. There was always an undercurrent of race with John, but that came mostly from the outside. I never thought that black and white had much to do with the sometimes hostile relationship between our schools. After all, we had mostly African American players, too. It was more that orange just never got along with blue and gray.

We had a great team in that first year of the Big East. We came into the final Manley game ranked number two in the country, a loss at Old Dominion the only blemish. Bouie and Louie were seniors. Danny Schayes was a terrific backup for Rosie. They were both six-eleven, and Louie Carnesecca, in his inimitable fashion, used to croon about "Syracuse's orange trees." We had balanced scoring with Bouie (17.7), Orr (15.4), Marty Headd (11.9) and freshman forward Erich Santifer (9.9). Marty had shaved his head by that time; he wasn't our best player, but he was a singular personality in college basketball. Our defense was great; we could gamble outside, because Rosie was such a great protector of the basket.

The atmosphere in Manley, where we had won 57 straight games, was electric. One of the student signs read KILL THE HOYATOLLAHS, a reference to what was going on in the Middle East. (It must've been drawn up by political science majors.) The seniors got introduced, and the band played "Jesus Christ Superstar" when Bouie was announced.

It would turn out He was exactly Who we needed. If anyone involved in that final Manley game was being honest, he would admit that, yes, there was too much pressure, too much emotion, too many memories, too much desire to win.

Still, on the force of our energy and talent, we're up 38–23 with about 14 minutes left. If we could hold the lead, it would mean my seniors—Rosie, Louis and Hal Cohen—had never lost a home game in their entire careers. At one point the crowd started singing "Auld Lang Syne" in homage to Manley. Some in the crowd were already crying. It's impossible to overestimate how much coaches hate premature celebrations. They almost always come back to bite you . . . as they did on this night.

Later, it would be written that I slowed down the pace after we got the double-digit lead. I don't agree with that. There's a natural tendency to play more cautiously when you're way up, I suppose, but the big problem was that we started to miss free throws—a bunch of them down the stretch as Georgetown edged closer. Finally, they tied it in the final minute and, with five seconds left, we fouled Eric "Sleepy" Floyd with the score tied at 50. Over the years, Georgetown has gotten a lot of attention for its big men, but the Hoyas have had some great guards, too, and Sleepy, with his laid-back style, was one of the best.

I called timeout. The place was going insane. And Floyd goes up there and makes both of those damn things . . . and we lose 52–50.

It's hard to describe my level of despair that night. Seven years later, it would be worse when we lost an NCAA championship final we should've won against Indiana. But not much worse. Fifteen minutes after the game, there were still hundreds of fans sitting there, stunned, immobile. I was distraught and a little hoarse in the postgame press conference.

Conversely, John Thompson was elated and in rare oratorical form. Then he uttered these gleeful words:

"Manley Field House is officially closed!"

On the surface, it doesn't sound like much of an insult. But you had to have been there. John took great joy in twisting the knife, and it wouldn't be the last time he drew blood.

The barb enraged our fan base. It felt as if John were stomping on all that proud history in our little old-school fortress. The words kept getting resurrected. Nobody ever forgot them. And though we didn't realize it at the time, it heralded a new era, both for us and college basketball. *Welcome to the Big East.*

A COACH'S NOTES III

John Calipari is on the phone. The Kentucky coach wants to talk about our zone defense, because he might be interested in using it from time to time, the key phrase being "from time to time."

A lot of coaches are curious about our zone. They contact me as if inquiring about an exotic pet, some kind of lizard or snake that they might want to keep around the house if they're not too scared of it. And in the end, we usually have some version of the conversation I had with Coach Cal, who, I hasten to add, doesn't need my help.

ME: John, you don't really want to play zone, do you?
JOHN: I do. I really do. Just not all the time.
ME: But as soon as your guys give up a couple of three-pointers, you'll get out of it and go back to man-to-man, right?
JOHN: That's probably true.

On my tombstone, I suppose the following will be written: HERE LIES JIM BOEHEIM. HE WORE GLASSES AND PLAYED ZONE. (As the son of a funeral director, I can tell you that inscription wouldn't come cheap.) I get calls about the zone all the time, from junior high coaches, high school coaches, junior college coaches and major college coaches. We are among just a few major programs to commit to it on a full-time basis, a decision I made in 2009 after we managed to get beaten by a Division II team. And if you don't *commit* to the zone, you're not really *playing* zone.

A disciplined zone requires practice and precision. No, it doesn't require high-level, mathematical thinking, but there is some spatial geometry to it. It's the defensive counterpart to the Princeton offense, with all kinds of reads and counters.

It has certainly worked so far this season. We played terrific defense in winning the Maui Invitational title, holding Indiana to 36 percent from the field and 28 percent on three-point shots in a 69–52 win. I think it's helped Tyler Ennis a lot. He's been asked to be the quarterback of our team as a freshman, and he's looked comfortable—partly, I think, because he is concentrating on offense and hasn't gotten burned defensively by strong and quick point guards because of our zone. In fact, he and Trevor Cooney make a good perimeter defensive duo out there.

Like most things in sports, parts of our zone have been stolen from coaches who came before me, so I hope it's clear that I never claimed to have invented successful zone defense. You might never have heard of John Egli's "sliding zone" at Penn State and Charles "Buzz" Ridl's "amoeba defense" at Pitt, but both were revolutionary in their times. Jud Heathcote at Michigan State played a great 3-2 matchup. Rollie Massimino at Villanova played a great matchup zone, as did Boyd Grant at Fresno State and Jerry Tarkanian at UNLV.

But I will say, with some modesty, that the two best zones I've ever seen are the matchup that John Chaney played for years at Temple and ours. The reason for that is simple: John and I played it virtually all the time. We committed to it.

The zone is an evolving organism. I brought back a few wrinkles from my stint with the U.S. national team in the 2008 and 2012 Olympics. We talk among the staff all the time about little tweaks that will make us more effective. Our players from the 1980s and '90s who watch us now have commented on the subtle differences, particularly in the increased role played by the forwards, who come out a lot higher than they used to. There is much more matching up and much more aggressive trapping, which is why we now tend to look for a slightly different kind of recruit: players with long arms and quick feet who can execute our defensive slides, as well as defend perimeter shooters, double in the corners and still get back to defend a post man.

We make subtle alterations from game to game, just as man-to-man defenses do. Most zones conform to a formula, but ours doesn't. We change up on ball screens, sometimes going over them, sometimes under. We can push up on shooters or sag back, depending on the situation.

There are five major advantages, I believe, to playing zone:

- In a tournament, it can be highly effective, because teams haven't faced zones—good zones, anyway—very much during the season.
- You tend to get into less foul trouble with a zone, because you can "hide" a defender better than you can in a man-to-man.
- A zone gets into the opponent's head a little bit more than man-to-man. *The Syracuse zone. The Syracuse zone.* I know that's what happened when we made it to the Final Four in 2013, particularly in our Sweet Sixteen and Elite Eight games against Indiana and Marquette. As the game went on, the zone increasingly befuddled both of those opponents, especially Marquette, a Big East team that should've been familiar with how to attack it. Offenses start thinking instead of reacting, which is what you tend to do against man-to-man.

- When you play both man-to-man and zone, you're constantly trying to decide which is better in which situation. That can waste precious seconds of planning time. That decision isn't a factor for us, because we're always playing zone, even when we're trailing by three points late in the game. Sure, we're trapping, but we're still in our basic 2-3 alignment.
- And the biggest advantage comes in saving preparation time. We put in our basic slides early and, as I said, we're always prepared for subtle alterations. But we don't have to spend a lot of valuable time on defense in practice. We identify tendencies, of course, but we're going to do basically the same things, no matter what the team and what the personnel.

As I said, it wasn't always that way. For years we played very good man-to-man defense at Syracuse, sometimes with full-court pressure. We mixed in the zone, like most teams do. I remember a game in 1985 against Marquette in which we played zone and were getting hammered in the first half. In the locker room, I was so mad I threw a stool and almost hit Wendell Alexis. So we went man-to-man the rest of the way and killed them.

Truth be told, I'd still like to coach man-to-man. I don't love playing zone all the time, because it does have an effect on your offense. Against our zone, even really good offensive teams take longer than usual to get into their patterns, maybe 30 seconds. So we're locked into playing defense for that long, much longer than the average team, whose man-to-man can give up a lot of matador layups. So it's hard to run on offense after you've been hunkering down on D for that long. Plus, you tend to be a little more cautious on offense, because you don't want to throw it away after playing defense for 34 seconds on a 35-second shot clock. I've never been known as a deliberate offensive coach, but to a degree that has happened since we've become zone-centric. If I were 40 years old again, we'd probably be playing man-to-man, but I can't see 40 in my rear-view mirror.

There is a built-in prejudice against zone coaches, as if they're mad scientists running amok in the lab. College basketball commentator Doug Gottlieb uses the success we've had as a zone team in his argument that I'm not a very good game coach, that zone is a great "change-of-pace" defense but not suitable for the long haul. He names a bunch of Syracuse players who he feels have underachieved in the NBA and wonders if their lack of success is due to their having played mostly zone defense.

First of all, some on Doug's list played a lot of man-to-man. Also, the reverse could be true—that zone helped them become valued college players who got drafted a little too high. But in any case, the argument is simple-minded; players succeed or fail in the NBA for a variety of reasons.

Someone asked me once why I don't—just for the pure, unadulterated fun of it—suddenly jump into man-to-man defense out of a timeout. I'm not going to do it. It would just open up a whole can of worms.

Plus, it would confuse the hell out of Doug Gottlieb.

7

A LEAGUE OF EXTRAORDINARY GENTLEMEN

Since I've never been involved in a sitcom, I'm not sure how the shows are cast. I assume they look for different personalities who can connect in some way, play off one another for laughs, like Kramer and George.

While there was no casting director present at the formation of the Big East in 1979, the league somehow came up with an ensemble of coaching characters that I'll wager is the equal of any at any given time in any sport. I'd guess that SEC football coaches—guys like Nick Saban, Les Miles and Steve Spurrier today—might come the closest, but even they are not as across-the-board colorful as we were.

What the coaches did was give the Big East a sharply defined profile, a name, a presence, an "It" factor—whatever indefinable thing you want to call it. Because once the Big East got rolling, we became known throughout the land as a full-throated insane asylum, with inmates running the show from the sidelines.

I've never believed in the idea that coaches sell tickets. I suppose a few people over the years came to see if Bob Knight would throw another chair, and a couple rows in Cameron Indoor Stadium might be filled because Mike Krzyzewski is there, but by and large, fans show up if a team is winning and stay home if they're losing. If Syracuse University had consistent 25-win seasons with a trained giraffe making the play calls, the fans would still fill the Carrier Dome. But coaches do build programs, foster energy and coax the maximum out of their players, and in those formative years of the Big East we had a group of coaches who did that as well as anyone. Did it more loudly, too.

So before I go into the players who made the Big East—and emphasize that they were the key—let me reintroduce the characters who roamed the sidelines. In alphabetical order by program:

BOSTON COLLEGE. Most of the Big East coaches would register high on anyone's Intense-O-Meter, but I would argue that Gary Williams, who replaced Dr. Tom Davis in 1982, could go from ZERO to BOILING in the shortest time. Gary just *smoldered* on that bench. P. J. Carlesimo had an affectionate nickname for him: Wacko. Gary didn't seem to mind. Somebody would be reading off the golf pairings at the meeting like this: "Okay, P.J., you're playing with Boeheim. . . . Paul Evans, you're with Wacko . . ."

Gary was the only head coach to routinely "fire" his assistants *during the game.* Gary went on to great success at Ohio State and Maryland, where he won a national title in 2002, reaching that pinnacle a year before me, damn him. He may currently hold the title of Best Coach Not Coaching. Gary's distaste for recruiting is a big reason he isn't boiling over on someone's bench right now.

CONNECTICUT. Jim Calhoun became such a central figure in the ultimate success of the conference that it's easy to forget that the Huskies' first Big East coach was Dom Perno, who was well known as a player, too. In the 1964 Sweet Sixteen, he stole the ball from Bill Bradley to give UConn a 52–50 upset victory over Princeton. Dom's contributions got lost in the Irish tornado named Calhoun, who followed him. Jim was the classic tough guy, somebody who worked as a gravedigger when he was 15 and never let you forget it. "If you want to pick a fight with me," Jim always said, "you won't have to work hard."

GEORGETOWN.   John Thompson was on the Hoyas' bench from the beginning of the Big East until 1999, after which the reins eventually went to his son, John Thompson III. John the Son is a good coach, but John the Father cast a huge shadow— figuratively and literally—over the Georgetown program, the conference and, to an extent, all of college basketball. In a league known for outsize characters, John stood alone.

PITT.   In much the same way as Calhoun came to dominate UConn basketball, so did Paul Evans dominate the Pitt of the old Big East. Dr. Roy Chipman was the coach for Pitt's first four years in the Big East, which began in 1982. If Dr. Roy had a soothing bedside manner, Paul acted like someone on the other end of the stethoscope, a wild-eyed patient. That's perhaps why he's not coaching right now and living on a houseboat in Annapolis, no doubt engaged in screaming matches with fish. But he could coach the hell out of a basketball game.

Paul was followed by three terrific coaches: Ralph Willard (one of my assistants during our 1987 NCAA tournament run), Ben Howland and Jamie Dixon, who is still there and whose hard-boiled defense will be as annoying as ever in the reconfigured ACC.

PROVIDENCE.   The Friars follow the UConn/Pitt pattern. Rick Pitino looms over the program, but he wasn't there in the beginning and he wasn't there for very long—in fact, for only two seasons before he went to the Knicks. But such was Rick's personality that his short stay was memorable.

Providence has probably had the most turnover in coaches—Mike Tranghese, who followed Dave as commissioner, says that it pained Dave that the Friars could never reach the Big East heights of many others. But Providence had arguably the greatest array of coaching talent: Gary Walters and Joe Mullaney before Rick, and Rick Barnes, Pete Gillen and Tim Welsh after Rick.

ST. JOHN'S.   Somebody once said that if a popularity poll had been taken among the Big East coaches of the 1980s, we would all finish last. In truth, it would be a two-man race between P. J. Carlesimo and Louie Carnesecca. Louie was cagey. Most of us—John, Jim, Paul, me—stood up to rant at the refs, right there where everybody could see us, but Louie used to get down low and snipe away. What, it doesn't count as harassment if you bitch and moan at ground level?

SETON HALL.   It's a testament to how much of a quipmaster P.J. turned out to be that many people forget that Bill Raftery, no slouch in front of a microphone, guided the program for its first two years in the Big East. P.J. had a way about him; he was able to show respect for his elders, who were most of us, while also being a wise guy. He's probably my best friend in coaching, but he's a lot of people's best friend, too.

SYRACUSE.   Yours truly. Still here. Still whining. Can you believe that?

VILLANOVA.   They should've made an opera with Rollie Massimino in the Pavarotti role. He coached as if he were performing an aria. He did a fantastic job in leading the Wildcats to the 1985 championship, a win over Georgetown that John Thompson will never forget, but most of us in the league saw a change in Rollie after he won the title. Not that we were ever exactly an all-for-one, one-for-all alliance, but there was an understanding that we would do what was best for the league, follow the plan that Dave laid out for us. I'm not sure Rollie always did that. But he was certainly instrumental in forging the Big East's identity as *the* conference for coaches.

Jim Calhoun got some advice from Bob Knight when Jim was thinking about taking a job at Northwestern. Stay at UConn, Knight told him, because the Big Ten is a conference of institutions, while the Big East is a conference of coaches. How true.

The headlines didn't say SYRACUSE HOSTING GEORGETOWN. They said BIG JOHN IS COMING TO TOWN. You didn't play Villanova. It was ROLLIE SQUARES OFF AGAINST BOEHEIM. You didn't entertain St. John's. It was LOUIE BRINGS HIS BAD SWEATER ACT TO THE DOME.

It seemed like we all had shown up at the stage door and passed an audition, Big John with his towel, Rollie with his Italian-uncle bit, Calhoun with his booming bluster. But I can assure you of this: There was no acting, none at all. We were all just that nuts.

The best show happened away from prying eyes, at the Big East spring meetings. I'm quite sure there's never been anything like them. We had sessions that lasted from eight in the morning until six at night. Big John would be up there on the high altar, proclaiming, "DON'T YOU TRY TO TELL ME WHAT TO DO!" Paul Evans and Rollie almost came to blows at one meeting. Carnesecca accused Paul's assistant of telling a recruit that he, Lou, was dying. That assistant went on to have a little success: a fellow by the name of John Calipari. (Both Paul and John denied the allegation.) You know how you say about some people, "He doesn't care what you think about him." Well, Paul Evans *really* didn't care what people thought about him.

One time, the minutes showed that we had uttered 36 "MFers" in the first ten minutes. Most of the time, though, there weren't any minutes; Dave wouldn't let them be taken, for fear of what they'd reveal.

Blackballing referees was a major activity. If one guy liked a ref, you could be sure that five other guys didn't. You have to remember that we argued about that even though, according to NCAA rules, the likes and dislikes of coaches have nothing to do with referee selection. One year, the ten best refs in the league all had at least one blackball, even though we all agreed they were the ten best refs in the league. Another year we blackballed three guys who had constituted 75 percent of the Final Four crew the year before. There was so much talk about zebras, you'd think we were starting a zoo. When a new official would come into the league, John Thompson would want to see a photo of the guy. What . . . like he could divine whether he was a good official or not by looking at him?

Jim Calhoun always remembers me standing up one year and saying, "Look, *somebody's* got to ref, right?" And I don't mean to present myself as a conciliator.

One year, the meeting reached a crescendo over . . . basketballs. MacGregor was going to do a ball deal through Rollie, but everybody had to agree on it. We would each get something out of it, but it wasn't that much, a few grand.

"Well, I deserve the most money," said Rollie, who was coming off that unforgettable title win over Georgetown.

"You don't deserve any more than I do," somebody else said. I remember Rick Pitino really spoke out about it. P.J. would pour fuel on the fire, because that's what he did. "You tell him, Rick," P.J. would say. "That's not right."

On and on it went. Then Gary Williams chimed in. "I can get my own balls." One normally argumentative coach didn't say anything and, it's funny, after it was all resolved, he came out the following season with a lucrative ball deal from another company. I think he was from the nation's capital. The argument lasted for hours, and I'm not sure it was ever resolved to anyone's satisfaction.

Basic insecurity is in the DNA of most coaches anyway, but this went well beyond that. We all believed we needed an edge in this new league to survive. It got so contentious in our meetings that Gavitt, realizing that diplomacy had its limits, was smart enough to stay away much of the time. But here's one thing Dave would do: He made the guys who didn't get along play golf together. Or at the annual banquet he would make them sit at the same table, all the while pretending it was just coincidence. Dave knew that this competitiveness was good, but he absolutely did not want it to get out of hand.

Carnesecca had a great line when our meetings were breaking up. "Listen," he would whisper, as if we were Mafia guys who had just pilfered everything in the room, "leave the chandeliers."

What was my role? Well, I was no angel. I was in every battle. I was hard to get along with, fought for what I believed in until the bitter end, and to an extent I'm still like that. But over the years I became an elder statesman, even got elected to be the coach who ran the Big East meeting. I would still battle, and I don't think you could exactly call me a consistent peacemaker, but I did settle some disputes, and the meetings became a lot calmer. It was: Meet for two hours, no yelling and screaming, and let's go play golf. Jim Calhoun once said, "My first ten years in the Big East were magical. Then we got civilized and it ruined everything."

In a league of strong personalities, though, Big John stood out. When John was present, he was *extremely present*, but he also believed that if he associated with other coaches he would lose an edge. It's possible that he saw the rest of us as being in a little fraternity together and himself as an outsider, though in point of fact we didn't necessarily like one another more than we liked John. Anyway, there were times when John did everything possible not to be in attendance. One year we were meeting at Hilton Head. It was 75 degrees all up and down the East Coast. Nevertheless, we got a call from sunny Georgetown: "The weather is bad here. Coach can't get out."

John's paranoia extended to his team, as has been famously documented. Georgetown requested the right to review interview tapes with players before they aired. John instructed his team to sit together in airports and not interact with other terminal passengers, even—and especially—if a rival happened by.

Yet it might be John who speaks most eloquently to the complex camaraderie we enjoyed in this highly competitive league. All of us—even John, sometimes *especially* John—understood that we had to come together, that the most important thing was growing the game, not growing an individual program. When he, Massimino, Carlesimo, Carnesecca and Pitino were in the conference together, John good-naturedly accepted the title of "the Black Italian" and was sometimes known as John "Thompsonsino." Calhoun points to the history of him and Pitino as an example. They were bitter rivals who never spoke when Jim was at Northeastern and Rick was at Boston University. But when they came into the Big East, even though they were still rivals, there was an understanding that they would have to communicate, even if that communication was at a high-decibel level.

P.J. remembers the year that he got Seton Hall to the NCAA final, where they lost to Michigan. Two of the first calls of congratulation came from John Thompson and me. Take my word for it: That doesn't happen in every conference. Some conferences have the veneer of civility, but it's nothing but ice-cold water under the surface. The Big East looked from the outside like a war zone, but inside it had a big heart.

Big John didn't just love the battles—he loved the spoils that came with them, the big contracts, the endorsement deals, the speaking engagements. John was the ultimate capitalist, and he loved the title. We were more than happy to follow his lead. As the Big East rolled, our endorsement deals went up, and so did our salaries. In the early 1980s, I was making about $75,000, up from the $25,000 I made in 1976, when I took over. My negotiations with Jake Crouthamel, our athletic director, were simple. I would go in, say how much money I thought I should make, and Jake would say nothing. I would keep talking and Jake would say nothing. That was how he negotiated: with silence. Eventually I'd just walk out, and sooner or later I'd sign a contract for not quite enough money.

But the Big East turned us into stars. By the end of the 1980s I was making about $300,000, plus about $150,000 from Nike. And I was by no means the highest-paid coach.

Out of that anger and competition and all those amplified voices evolved a mystique, something that transformed the league into the embodiment of eastern basketball. It was as though we had created something new. It wasn't UCLA basketball, it wasn't Kentucky basketball, it wasn't Duke/North Carolina basketball. It was chip-on-your-shoulder, every-night's-a-war, you-wanna-make-something-of-it basketball. *Big East basketball.* Chris Mullin once described a Big East game like this: "There was a menace to it."

Remember that I said how riveting those Syracuse–St. Bonaventure games were in the old ECAC? Well, after only one or two years of Syracuse–Georgetown, everybody forgot that we had ever played the Bonnies. But Syracuse–Georgetown? Nobody will ever forget that.

SO WHAT STARTED out as an unknown enterprise suddenly became the Next Big Thing. In retrospect, it was incredible how clearly Dave Gavitt saw it from the beginning. Jim Satalin, who went from St. Bonnie's to Duquesne in the early 1980s, remembers attending a gathering in Pittsburgh at which Dave was speaking. It was when

Pitt was coming into the Big East, and Dave confidently predicted, "You will not be able to buy a ticket within one year. In fact, you'll eventually have to build a new facility." Everybody thought Dave had lost his mind, but he was spot-on.

It happened all over the place—Georgetown, Seton Hall and St. John's all eventually moved to larger arenas. Dave loved the Carrier Dome from the beginning, because he understood the optics: TV cameras zooming in on a Sunday-afternoon or Monday-night game, 30,000 fans screaming their lungs out in a sea of orange, the Big East in panoramic vision.

To achieve his goals, Dave had to put up with a lot of Neanderthal thinking. In the beginning, for example, there were complaints from athletic directors about the cost of keeping the lights on for extended practices and dire predictions about what would happen when we moved to larger venues. Dave always kept his patience, held everybody's hand and led them through the forest.

Around the time that the Big East was formed, Joe Paterno, who was then the athletic director at Penn State as well as the football coach, was trying to put together a league that would've been called the Eastern Conference, with schools like Syracuse, Pitt, Maryland and Boston College, oriented, obviously, more toward football than basketball. Paterno wanted Gavitt to run it. Some of the schools might have leaped at the opportunity, had there been a more equitable distribution of the football revenues than what Penn State wanted. But it didn't happen, thank God.

Stories differ at this point. Paterno said that Penn State was invited as a basketball-only member but declined. Then they were invited again but wanted to keep too much of the football revenue. Finally, they applied and were considered for across-the-board membership but lost on a 5–3 vote. That was when the conference decided to take Pitt.

Later, Mike Tranghese would say that not taking Penn State was a huge mistake because, in the long run, any major conference needs to pay attention to football. Ultimately, Mike was proven correct when the Big East broke up because of football, but, speaking as a basketball man, we clearly had the right teams in the mix.

As a side note, when Penn State applied to become a member of the Big Ten in the late 1980s, I got myself into trouble with JoePa by making an offhand comment. Had I been smarter back then, maybe I wouldn't have said it. Live and learn. Anyway, I was doing a local interview and was asked about Penn State moving to the Big Ten. I said that, just as it would be tough for us to compete in the Big Ten, I felt it would be the same for Penn State. I was talking strictly about basketball. Recruits are by and large city kids who would have a hard time relating to Penn State. There is no convenient airport and not much basketball tradition. And traveling to many of those Big Ten sites can be very, very difficult when you play games during the week, as you do in basketball. I didn't mean it as a personal slight against Penn State.

But a headline goes out, something to the effect of BOEHEIM SAYS PENN STATE CAN'T COMPETE, and Joe really takes offense. He goes on *Nightline* and says, "I don't know what that coach up there is talking about. I don't even know him. My people tell me he can't win anything, never won anything, never will win anything."

I tried to straighten it out. I told everyone who would listen that Joe Paterno was a great coach who ran a great program, but that I still thought they would struggle in basketball. Which has turned out to be the case over the past 25 years. Anyway, I never met Paterno before he died and always felt bad about the whole exchange.

WE GREW UP fast in the new conference. All of us. Sure, Dave Bing had played at Syracuse, and we had been to a Final Four, but we were basically nobody until we got to the Big East. I distinctly remember playing Maryland in the NIT in 1972 when I was an assistant, and it was like playing the Knicks, like we were playing a program two steps up from us. That feeling prevailed even though we lost by only six, 71–65. I had tried to recruit their star big man, Tom McMillen, a couple of years earlier, but he wouldn't even talk to us. Around that same time we supposedly had an "in" with Mitch Kupchak, a highly regarded big man in Long Island. Mitch barely gave us a sniff on his way to North Carolina. That was just the way it went back then. ACC trumped ECAC almost every time. But that changed after the Big East got rolling.

Fortunately—and this was a big factor—we had momentum going into the league. To an extent, Dave's commissionership can be compared to David Stern's in the NBA. Stern possessed both vision and exquisite timing. He took over as commissioner in 1984, the year Michael Jordan came into the league and right at the height of the Magic Johnson–Larry Bird rivalry. Similarly, Dave began the Big East at a time when there were a lot of strong teams and a lot of really good players coming in.

But it's still the job of a commissioner to leverage and maximize what you have. Both Daves did that.

All you need to know about the first year of the Big East is what happened after the "Manley Is Closed" game. John Thompson has commented that the last Manley game grew more important as time went on, and he's absolutely correct. It wasn't as if we shriveled up and stopped playing basketball. Exactly four days after that devastating loss to Georgetown, we beat St. John's 72–71 in an incredible game on the road. We're down by one point and they have Curtis Redding, a good shooter, on the line for a one-and-one. Looks like a loss. But Curtis misses, Danny Schayes grabs the rebound and outlets to Hal Cohen as Louis Orr just flies downcourt. Hal finds him, and Louis lays it in at the buzzer as Reggie Carter slides over to draw a block. Block or charge? We wait . . . and we get a block. We run out of there with a win.

In the Big East tournament, we trampled UConn but got beaten by Georgetown 87–81. This rivalry was not starting out well. We beat Villanova in the East Regional 97–83 (even though both Bouie and Schayes fouled out), but Iowa ended our season 88–77 in the next game.

We had gone 26–4 in our first Big East season, but it felt a little empty. Two of those losses had come to Georgetown. Manley was gone and, worse than that, Bouie and Louie were gone. I'll never forget those guys for the kick start they gave me as a head coach.

WE STRUGGLED A bit the next year but saved the best for last in the second Big East tournament, this one held at the Carrier Dome. Gavitt, bless his heart, had the vision to move the tournament there, even as some opposing fans were already wondering if the Dome was a white elephant.

We beat Georgetown 67–53 in the semifinals and Villanova 83–80 in triple overtime to win the championship. John and I got into a tiff in that semifinal and went at each other at midcourt. We were comfortably ahead, and I think John just wanted to energize his team by getting a technical foul. He had wandered so far onto the court I thought he was going to take a charge, so I came over to see if I could, you know, help him find his way back to the bench.

The sight of two head coaches apparently ready to go ten rounds horrified Mike Tranghese, who was then a young man in his role as Big East public relations director. Dave wasn't there, because Selection Sunday was the following day and he was chairing the committee. Mike called Dave after the game and said, "Listen, Jim and John really went at each other. It was bad." And Dave says, "Don't worry, it'll all be fine." And it was. Perhaps because he had been a coach himself, Dave never seemed to worry that we would get completely out of control—emphasis on "completely."

The Villanova game remains one of the most memorable in Syracuse history. Leo Rautins came in from the baseline to tip in a missed shot and give us a two-point lead in the final overtime. Rollie then called a timeout that he didn't have, and Danny Schayes made the subsequent technical. I alerted the refs to the timeout infraction, but they had already seen it. Maybe Rollie blamed that on me, and maybe that's why he later made some negative comments about our fans and the Dome, which almost no visiting teams cared for in the beginning.

That year, 1981, was the last time the Big East tournament winner did not get an automatic bid, and, sure enough, we got snubbed. The NCAA, which back then took 48 teams instead of 64, selected Boston College, Villanova and Georgetown but not Syracuse. We should've been invited. We were good enough. Ironically, Gavitt, the ultimate salesman, couldn't convince the committee to take us. We went all the way to the NIT final before losing to a terrific Tulsa team 86–84 in overtime.

One historical note about that Big East final: We drew about 15,000 fans. That's the number the administration was hoping for when it started drawing up plans for the Dome. That was a big deal. And now? Fifteen thousand is about half the total we draw for even a relatively meaningless game.

The Big East had arrived, but it was still not ready for prime time. That would happen the following year, when two extraordinary players came into our league. Welcome, Patrick Ewing, and welcome, Chris Mullin.

And they would soon be joined by a Pearl.

8

THE PEARL AT THE CENTER OF THE ORANGE

Patrick Ewing was a phenomenon, the consensus high school player of the year, a seven-footer who ran the floor like a guard and played every possession like his life depended on it. He was made for Georgetown, and it became evident early that John was going to get him. Maybe 15 schools came in to visit with Patrick at Cambridge Rindge and Latin, but he was pretty much heading to Washington from the get-go, something that the Boston fans took a long time to get over, if they ever did. Plus, Patrick had the gall to make the announcement at a restaurant owned by a Celtics legend, Satch Sanders. Patrick has said in recent years that he was scared away from North Carolina by reports of a Ku Klux Klan rally nearby. I hadn't heard that before and never thought that Patrick was going anywhere except to play for John.

Patrick was every bit as good as advertised, the real deal, the warrior John needed to install his vision of a tough, determined, intimidating, almost-cross-the-line, defensive-oriented team. Coaches love it when they get players who reflect a vision of what they want to do, and there has rarely been a better match than Ewing and Thompson.

And remember this: John didn't give Patrick much freedom offensively. In considering Patrick's greatness as a college player, we don't even think about offense. It was all about how he could intimidate on the defensive end, set the tone, block shots, change shots, discourage shots, clog lanes, compensate for overaggressiveness on the defensive perimeter, get rebounds and start the break. Over the years, we had some success against Ewing, but here's how good he was: Any day of the week, I would have rather faced the 1-2 punch of Alonzo Mourning and Dikembe Mutombo, who were pretty damn good themselves, than one Patrick Ewing.

And here's how important he was to the league: As soon as Patrick committed, Gavitt told Mike Tranghese, "We'll be taking the Big East tournament to the Garden very soon." We were there by 1983.

Chris Mullin came along to St. John's the same year that Patrick went to Georgetown. Chris had been recruited by Mike Krzyzewski and for about five minutes considered heading south. But he was a city kid, and Louie was a city coach, and St. John's just seemed like the right place. What can you say about Mullin? He stayed for four years, like Patrick did. He played the game the right way. He shot 55 percent from the floor and 85 percent from the line and seemed to be what Naismith had in mind when he invented the game.

Patrick got Georgetown to the NCAA final in his freshman year, where he lost to North Carolina and its freshman star, Michael Jordan. Patrick wasn't a one-man team, but he was *that* kind of difference maker. We in the Big East owe Georgetown a debt for making that big an impression in only our third season. And you don't know how hard it is for me to say that.

We didn't get there that fast. The year after our NCAA snub, we had another NIT season, with a 16–13 record that stands as my worst as a coach. We had good players, just not the kind to take you all the way to the top.

But it's not like you don't remember those guys with fondness. Like Leo Rautins. And Red Bruin, one of those six-foot-four guys who jumped over everybody and didn't bother to do much more than that. We had Andre Hawkins, who could stand up to anybody at center, including Ewing, despite being only about six-six. We had Erich Santifer, a terrific all-around player who led us in scoring and rebounding in 1982 but was only about six-three. Even Leo, who was six-six, played more like he was six-three, since he was a finesse guy. All in all, we were just not *equipped* to take on the likes of Ewing, although we did beat them 75–70 in Patrick's first season, when they made it to the NCAA final.

Leo and I see each other from time to time, since our sons play on the same junior high basketball team. We had our moments, as a coach and player will. There are always little dramas that take place behind the scenes, just like in any business or relationship.

Midway through the 1980–81 season, for example, we played at St. Bonnie's, a holdover game from the ECAC. We lost 74–71, and Leo—with whom I was always disagreeing about how much he should handle the ball on the outside (he thought he should be handling it there more than I thought he should be handling it there)—had as many turnovers as points, about ten. So we played Old Dominion four nights later, I didn't put Leo in at all and we won 71–58. Leo had been a major addition to our team, a transfer from Minnesota, so the benching was a big story in our small world.

We got into it the next day, and I told Leo, "Well, it just went that way." Leo felt that I was showing him up by not playing him, and he really came after me. I thought about it for a minute, then I told him, "Okay, maybe I could've handled it better."

These things pass. Leo went on to have a good season—climaxed by the tip-in—and two more after that. The same knee injury that followed him around at Syracuse robbed him of an NBA career after two seasons.

There's not an exact science to this who-plays-how-many-minutes issue. Fans and media think there is, but there isn't. And contrary to what people might think about the drama that comes with the job, the hardest emotional facet is not dealing with the press, the refs, or the personal agony of the close losses—it's keeping a kid you like on the bench. You know his parents. You understand that they sent him to you partly because they trusted you. You see how hard he works and how much he *wants* to play. Yet for the good of the team, sometimes you *can't* play him.

The sad truth is that at the highest level of college basketball, you have to be heartless. I know people think you should play a kid just because he works hard, but that's not how programs like ours work. Dozens of players, I would guess, think that they got shafted here. Danny Schayes played behind Roosevelt Bouie for three years, and I'm sure he thought he didn't get enough minutes. Danny went on to play in the NBA for 18 years, longer than any other Syracuse player, but that's not proof he should've played more than Rosie. In fact, Danny might've gotten better *because* he played behind Rosie. But I understand why Danny looks at it differently.

I have some regrets about the way I doled out playing time. Herman Harried, a six-seven forward, was a really great kid who came here as a big-time recruit out of Dunbar High School, in Baltimore. They called him "the Helicopter" because of his leaping ability. When he got here, we had players like Raf Addison and Wendell Alexis, so that reduced his playing time. Then he got hurt, and when he recovered we had players like Derrick Coleman and Billy Owens. One year, Herman went on an off-season trip for Big East all-stars and was the leading scorer, but when he got back to Syracuse he was again a role player. I feel bad about that, even though I stand by my decision to use him as a role player. Herman has done quite well as a coach and athletic director and remains one of our biggest supporters.

The important thing is not to have any preconceptions about a player—either that he's really good or really bad. Okay, it's impossible not to have some of those notions—after all, you base your recruiting on them—but you have to be able to *change* those preconceptions. Don't keep playing somebody because he was *supposed* to be good.

But it works both ways. I thought Mike Hopkins, my top assistant, would never play here. He redshirted his first year. The next year, he played against Stevie Thompson and Sherman Douglas, and every day he got crushed. I remember one practice when Sherman stole the ball from him every time. But Mike kept busting his ass. We had a wager among the coaches about how many times he would end up on the floor during games, the over-under usually around 10. And Hop kept getting better, turning into a reliable shooter and a terrific defender. By his junior year he was a starter, and by his senior year a co-captain. Our brains told us he wouldn't be a good player, but, eventually, our eyes saw something else.

SO THE BIG East had ferocity with Ewing and finesse with Mullin. What it needed now was flash.

In his senior year at Boys and Girls High School, in Brooklyn, Dwayne "Pearl" Washington was the most exciting player in the country. There wasn't a close second. He had gotten his nickname back in junior high, after Earl "the Pearl" Monroe, the Knicks player who spun and danced and seemed to be in his own world out there.

Pearl announced his college choice on CBS to Al McGuire, which was rare back in those days, and getting him was a big deal for us. We didn't usually attract the McDonald's All-Americans.

Remember that the Dome ticket-sale issue was big back then. The administration had been happy with the attendance after our move out of Manley—we averaged 16,440 in our first year in the

Carrier Dome—but there was still much trepidation about ticket revenue. For a few years our games were blacked out locally, because we were afraid that TV would hurt attendance. (If you want to know the truth, I wouldn't mind if they were still blacked out; despite our attendance numbers, I'm convinced that they keep people away.)

But by the time Pearl left, in 1986, we were leading the nation with over 26,000 fans per game. So I'm not sure any player ever was more important to our program than Pearl. He lifted us to the same level as Georgetown, which, after its runner-up season in 1982, won the NCAA championship in 1984, Pearl's first season.

Plus, Pearl might have been the first true manifestation of Dave Gavitt's Big East vision. Ewing was going to John Thompson, and Mullin was going to stay in New York City to play for Lou Carnesecca—the conference didn't matter all that much to either of them. But Pearl wanted to play in the Big East, and, beyond the fact that he felt comfortable on our campus, that's the main reason we outrecruited North Carolina State to land him, which was not an easy battle. First of all, the Wolfpack had Jim Valvano, among the greatest salesmen in college basketball history. During Pearl's visit, Jim's recruiting ace, Tom Abatemarco, did a kind of striptease, tearing off his sport coat and shirt to reveal a T-shirt that read WEL-COME PEARL. They turned off the lights in the arena and, when Pearl walked in, turned them on to display a Wolfpack jersey with his name and number draped over a chair at midcourt.

I stay away from that Hollywood stuff here. Particularly the stripteases. And I guess Pearl noticed, and preferred it that way. Ewing, Mullin . . . Washington. I'm sure any of us coaches would've loved any of those players. I could've coached Patrick and Chris, and Louie could've coached Pearl and Patrick. John could've coached Chris and . . . well, I'm not so sure about Pearl. He liked his quarterbacks a little more in control.

Pearl's high school coach, Paul Brown, used to install a seven-man zone to practice against Pearl. He had a rare gift for a point guard, even at 18. He was strong and quick with the ball. I had never had a player like him here, and it was a seismic change for a team and a system.

Pearl was the epitome of the "city point guard," the New York or Philly kid who grew up on the playgrounds, cocky, wily, creative, fearless, showmanship in his blood and bones. You don't think of that type as much anymore, since the most talented kids now go to prep schools. It's hard to imagine Pearl at a prep school, but that's probably where a modern-day Pearl would end up.

I don't want to go overboard, though, in making distinctions between "city" players and "prep" players. To an extent, yes, four years of prep school might wean some of the flash and dash out of a player, some of the "street." But you're not going to change an athlete's basic nature. For example, Shabazz Napier, who led UConn to the 2014 NCAA championship, would've been the same style of player—flashy, cocky, a million moves—even if he had gone to a prep school instead of Charlestown High School, in Boston. And you could've stuck John Stockton in the middle of Philadelphia and he still would've been solid, efficient, unspectacular John Stockton. You know who I consider the ultimate "city point guard" right now? Chris Paul. And he grew up in the bright-lights metropolis of Clemmons, North Carolina.

At any rate, when you have a player like Pearl, the casual fan wants you to wind him up and let him go, while the traditionalist wants you to rein him in.

But here was the best thing about Pearl: As unpredictable as he was, he rarely threw the ball away. Sure, he made bad decisions; so did Magic Johnson. But Pearl led the Big East in assists, not turnovers, for three straight years. You have to give a player like Pearl the room to play his game, let him dribble into trouble once in a while, because chances are he'll dribble out of it. Pearl couldn't have fit into a standard offense, and it would've been a big mistake if I'd tried to make him.

What you have to do, though, is get him the ball on the move once in a while. When you have players who can get to the hole, the tendency is for them to dribble, dribble, dribble, which can kill an offense. Back then, we didn't have many plays that were designed for Pearl to come off picks and get the ball from someone else. We do that more now with our point guards, although our guy this season, Tyler Ennis, had the ball in his hands probably as much as Pearl did.

Pearl didn't want a ball screen. He wanted everyone flat, almost on the baseline. When someone's defender left to double Pearl, which happened most of the time, that unguarded player moved to where Pearl could find him spotting up. However, there was a flip side. Pearl could go either way, so you couldn't plan it in advance. He was a little better with his left hand, even though he was right-handed.

And it was uncanny how he could almost always get to the basket and finish, a God-given talent to some extent, like broken-field running for a tailback. And it's one thing to get to the basket, but it's another to convert. Pearl converted and did it, for the most part, without dunking. He was only six-two and not a leaper.

As a coach, you try to think the game more than watch it. What I mean by that is that you don't get caught up in what individual players are doing beyond how they are impacting the game as a whole. But Pearl was the first player since Bing who made me just stop and watch him do his own thing from time to time. What I remember most is the way he just *froze* his man, stood him up, blew by him and laid it in over, around or through a help defender. Flashes of Pearl live on in my memory to a degree greater than thoughts of any player I've ever had, my ultimate mind's-eye treat.

. . . .

IT TOOK PEARL exactly 14 games to become a certified Syracuse legend. When Boston College came to the Dome on January 21, 1984, a B.C. player named Martin Clark tied the game 73–73 on a follow shot against our best defender, Raf Addison, with four seconds left. Clark also got fouled but missed the free throw, and up the court comes Pearl.

He releases the shot at about midcourt, and the ball is not even halfway to the basket when he starts running toward the locker room, like he knew it was going in. Which it did. Clean. Like it was nothing. It is not an exaggeration that Pearl was halfway to the locker room when the ball finally swished through.

Just about everyone else, however, rushed onto the floor. Students were trying to tear down the basket, as if we had won the national championship halfway through the season.

The B.C. coach, Gary Williams, stood transfixed, staring at the basket as if he expected that another would appear in its place, Pearl's shot would bounce harmlessly off the backboard, and B.C. would take it into overtime.

"Gary," I said.

He didn't even look at me.

"GARY!" I repeated. "The game's over. Your team played well. You could've beaten us."

I'm not sure he heard a word I said.

There's no explanation for a shot like that, really. Of course, there's an element of luck, but it is one of those moments that you get only from great players.

The big hole in Pearl's game was outside shooting, long-range miracles like that notwithstanding. Sure, it frustrated us from time to time and really exasperated the fans who reasoned, "Well, he's such a great player . . . he should be able to shoot." But if you've been around the game as long as I have, it's not a mystery.

It might begin with the fact that, from the day Pearl picked up a basketball, he could get to where he wanted to go without shooting from a distance beyond three feet. And to an extent, shooting, like driving, has a God-given element to it. It's just that we never look at a shooter like, say, Reggie Miller or Gerry McNamara and wonder, "Gee, why can't he drive better?" It's always the drivers we want to be better shooters, not vice versa.

You can work on mechanics all you want, but sometimes you just can't turn a player into a good outside shooter. We tried like crazy with Stevie Thompson, but he never could get it quite right. Pearl did improve, and one of the things he was able to do was hit clutch outside shots to win games. But he never could be consistent from the perimeter.

Also, it's no secret that Pearl did not love the game, was not driven to succeed in the way that guys like Sherman Douglas and Gerry were. He never got himself into prime shape. When Pearl retired from the NBA, after only three injury-scarred seasons, he said, "I lost my love for the game." That had probably happened years earlier.

I remember in the summer of 1984 we scrimmaged against the Yugoslav national team before they went to the Olympics, where they would get a bronze medal with players like Dražen Petrović. The first night, Pearl doesn't bother showing up and we lose by 30. I tell their coach, "We have another kid coming tomorrow. He's pretty good." So Pearl plays and gets, like, 40.

"Yes, this Pearl is pretty good player," the coach told me.

Pearl was one of those guys who would've been a beneficiary of the individual in-season workouts that take place now. But back then, you weren't on top of a kid all summer, and Pearl was as liable to be in upstate New York riding horses as in a gym working on his jumper. Pearl's older brother, Beaver, pushed him hard, and if it weren't for his prodding, I don't know that Pearl would've played the game at all.

As a coach, it's frustrating when you see a great player who doesn't love the game, but you can't *will* someone to have that passion. You'll drive yourself crazy trying to do that. And let me be clear about this: Pearl worked hard during the season. He never gave me one minute of trouble. He was not intransigent or rebellious. (Sometimes I wish he had been, since it would've better prepared me for Derrick Coleman.)

To the outside world, Pearl was thought to have a personality that matched his nickname. But he really didn't. Raf Addison used to say that fans thought of Pearl as Superman, but around the locker room he was more like Clark Kent. Pearl was not a big personality.

To the average fan, though, he was larger than life on the court. In his last Big East game, against St. John's in the 1986 championship final in the Garden, Pearl steamed downcourt for a potential game-winning shot, but Walter "the Truth" Berry blocked it from behind and we lost 70–69. Everybody in that building, except maybe Berry, figured that Pearl would make that shot.

Their coming together at that climactic moment spoke to the essential character of the Big East. In their schoolboy days, Pearl and Berry had captivated summer crowds during pickup games in Harlem. One time Pearl arrived on a motorcycle, wearing a dark helmet. That is inner-city style all the way.

All in all, I think there is a feeling in some quarters that I was somehow disappointed with Pearl, disappointed that we never won a Big East tournament championship with him, disappointed that we never won an NCAA championship with him, disappointed that he didn't become an all-star in the pros. Before Pearl left after his junior year, Mike Lupica, a well-known columnist in New York, wrote something like, "Jim Boeheim will be happier when Pearl is gone." The next day I got a call from Pearl's mom, who was crying on the phone.

Nothing—and I mean nothing—could have been further from the truth, which is what I told her. I loved coaching him. Pre-Pearl, I remember recruiting on the West Coast and having to explain where Syracuse was. Well, Pearl comes, and the next year I'm out there again. "Hey," somebody says, "you're Pearl's coach." I hate to think what this program would be like and how many more years it would've taken us to build it if Pearl Washington hadn't come here. We had a 71–25 record in the three years he was here, and he was first-team All–Big East every season, in a conference that had point guards like Mark Jackson at St. John's, Charles Smith at George-town and Michael Adams and Dana Barros at Boston College.

Pearl had some tough times after he left Syracuse. He carried the weight of expectation into the NBA, his nickname alone a burden. He got injured and fell out of shape. At the age of 32, he was watch-ing a football game one Sunday afternoon when he suffered a sei-zure. A six-hour operation was required to remove a tumor from the front of his brain.

But in May of 1998, he was back on campus fulfilling a promise he had made to his mother by getting his degree. I was as proud of him that day as at any of those game-winning moments he had for us on the court. And when I see him courtside now, it makes me smile. And I don't smile all that often.

A COACH'S NOTES IV

There are certain games that you mark on your mental calendar from the beginning of the season. North Carolina is one of them. But as I sit in my office, making out that day's practice schedule, it would be impossible to forget it anyway. There, flashing across the TV screen in my office, is an old clip of Michael Jordan.

Michael's been gone for years, but to a large extent Carolina is still the School That Michael Played For.

He's not on my mind right now, though. It's their coach, Roy Williams. I've been reading about the spells of exhaustion suffered by Roy, who has had a difficult season. The NCAA suspended his top player, guard P. J. Hairston, who allegedly got impermissible benefits, involving a luxury car, from a third party. That was a big loss. I don't know how many teams could lose their "glue guy" and go on without a hitch.

Roy's exhaustion led to headlines and stories about the "burnout factor" among college coaches. When you get to the top in most professions, you can relax a little. It's understood that business goes up and down all the time—great years, good years, bad years, great years again. But because of the constant media scrutiny, sports are always about *this* year. A coach is too often evaluated by what he does in the short term, not the long haul.

On the other hand, the idea that many coaches have these kinds of burnout issues is a myth. There are 380 Division I head coaches, and maybe two or three per year will have some kind of health-related problem. And you're talking about a population mostly between the ages of 40 and 60 and in some cases, like mine, nearly 70. If you look at a few hundred CEOs from the world of business, I guarantee that you will see just as many medical scares. So I don't think that coaches get sick at any higher a percentage than anybody else.

Yes, there is stress and pressure, but a coach has had that for his entire professional life. If people like us hadn't learned to adapt, all of those 30-year-old coaches would never have made it to 50. You'd be doing radio or TV, which, as a matter of fact, is where you find the smarter guys who finally *did* something about the pressure.

Trust me on this: Roy Williams is a great coach. He's won two national championships, and almost half of his games against Mike Krzyzewski. A couple of years ago, a website polled about a hundred college coaches—anonymously, of course—and Roy emerged as the "most overrated," with 23 percent of the vote. How is that possible? (By the way, I got 4 percent of the vote and finished ninth.) "Overrated" is one of those words tossed around far too indiscriminately in the sports world.

No matter what its record, North Carolina is one of those special teams in college basketball. Duke, Kentucky, Kansas and North Carolina—that probably represents the magic quartet, now that UCLA has slipped. I'd like to think that we're lurking on that next tier, along with teams like Louisville, Michigan State and Michigan. And if you consider just the ACC, it's pretty much become *only* Duke and North Carolina, something we hope to change.

Going back to the early 1990s, when Duke started drawing even with Carolina, these two schools have won 19 of 23 conference championships and seven of the eight NCAA titles won by the ACC—Duke has four, Carolina three and Maryland one. Carolina has had more ebb and flow than Duke, but that's mostly because Krzyzewski has kept his team on such an even keel, not because Carolina has slipped a lot.

I have history with Roy, since it was his Kansas team we beat to win the NCAA championship in 2003. I've played golf with him several times on Nike trips—first I was better, then he was better, now we're both probably mediocre—and always enjoyed his company.

But it was Dean Smith who got the Carolina program rolling. He coached UNC from 1961 to 1997 and was on top of his game for most of those years. Dean was maybe the best "system coach" ever, and it was a system of multiple attacks. With most teams, you know what you're getting. Bob Knight, for example, would come after you with a motion offense and man-to-man defense. John Chaney, at Temple, would get after you with his matchup zone, and Rick Pitino is going to full-court-press you. It was less predictable with Dean. His offense was built around the fast break and the high-low-inside game; no team did a better job than North Carolina of entering the ball into the post. But though they ran, Dean was also the master of the delay game with the four-corners offense, back before there was a shot clock.

Dean had multiple looks on defense, too. His teams trapped and played both man-to-man and zone. It can be argued, though, that Dean did so many things that it hurt him in the postseason, where having multiple looks is not necessarily an advantage. Sometimes the best style in the tournament is to do one thing really well, to keep wearing down a team and coming at them with what you do best. Dean was in the Final Four eleven times and won only twice; Krzyzewski has won four in ten trips.

We played North Carolina twice when Jordan was there and, as if some cosmic force were at work, they beat us by identical 87–64 scores, one home, one away—a 23-point margin that corresponds to Jordan's jersey number. But it wasn't just Michael who killed us; the one who really hurt was Sam Perkins. Sam remains, to this day, my saddest recruiting story.

Perkins played at Shaker High School, in Albany, and I saw every game he played as a senior, all 30 of them. I'd finish practice at six, drive to Albany, which is over 140 miles away, always staying under the speed limit (well, maybe not), get there at 8:00, 8:15, bump into Sam and say, "How you doing?" and drive back. We had started out way behind, because everyone wanted Sam, but I believed that we had worked our way up to his second choice, right behind North Carolina, which is where his coach wanted him to go. After the season was over, I went to Albany every day in the spring, when recruiting rules were looser, and it was terrible. You practically *lived* in the city of a kid you really wanted. One coach took an apartment in Albany. It was stalking as much as recruiting.

Anyway, we were told not to have any contact with Sam for a week, after which he would make his decision. I really thought we had a chance, since I had done so much more work than Carolina's guys.

But then I got a call on a Saturday morning.

"Sam's going to Carolina."

I didn't get out of bed until four in the afternoon.

My second biggest disappointment would probably be losing Kenny Anderson to Georgia Tech, but it's really not that close. Still, I did learn a valuable lesson. We almost never recruit against Duke or Carolina anymore. If they really, really want a player, they will get him. End of story. Billy Owens was maybe the first and only kid we got that Carolina really wanted, and that was because his big brother, Michael, was a star football player at Syracuse. He would've gone to Carolina, too, if not for blood.

As for the game?

In front of 32,121 at the Dome, we beat North Carolina 56–44. It's the lowest point total the Tar Heels have had in an ACC game since 1979. We don't shoot that well, but our defense collapses and locks down on their interior star, James Michael McAdoo, an example of how we can change up with the zone, depending on what the offense wants to do. The win raises our record to 16–0.

9

GENERAL SHERMAN

arch 12, 1987. New Orleans. The night of the biggest professional heartache of my life, courtesy of Bob Knight and the Indiana Hoosiers. A national championship game we had won slipped through our fingers. Had we not been able to redeem ourselves 16 years later—in the same building in the same city—I'd probably be dead from lack of sleep, or at least retired. But it still hurts. I wish I could concentrate on the journey, remember what it took to build the team that got all the way to the final against a legendary coach. I wish I could focus on the memories of a team maturing and coming together.

Instead I can only imagine an alternate history. Or think about the one we finally won.

WE HAD SAID good-bye to Pearl, his decision to leave after the 1985–86 season being pretty much a sure thing. He went 13th to the New Jersey Nets, the ideal team for him. Pearl had had a great career here and was ready to move on. We were eliminated in the second round of the East Regional in his final season—played, incredibly enough, at the Carrier Dome—and I lay the blame for that defeat on a piece of bad scheduling.

Early in the year, we had invited Navy and its star, David Robinson, to the Carrier Classic. We just mauled them, 89–67. What a mistake that turned out to be. David must have been nursing some real bad feelings all season long, because he came up and just destroyed us 97–85 in that East Regional game, Pearl's last appearance in orange.

I'm not sure I've ever seen a more athletic center than David. We had gone up against Ewing for four straight years, but David, while not as ferocious a competitor as Patrick, was as skilled offensively as any center I ever coached against.

Pearl left behind an indelible legacy, but one of his major achievements goes unremembered. In the residue of a hundred scrimmages, battles witnessed by no one except our team, he helped create the unlikely quarterback that became Sherman Douglas. Had Pearl returned for his senior year, I'm quite sure Sherman would've transferred and we would've lost another guard who became All–Big East for three straight seasons.

Sherman had not been our main recruiting target by a long shot. First we were after Boo Harvey, who ended up going to St. John's. Then we thought we had our point-guard answer in "the next Pearl," a California kid named Earl Duncan who had been recruited by Kansas, North Carolina State, Georgia Tech and a bunch of other major programs. The basketball magazines raved about him and rarely included a word about Sherman. Duncan even had a basketball name, right? Earl "the Next Pearl" Duncan. But he signed with us. And even though he was a Prop 48, meaning that he had not qualified scholastically and had to sit out a season, he could practice with the team for a year and slide right into the starting role the following season.

But Sherman was ready for "the Next Pearl," largely because he had spent the 1985–86 season getting torched every day in every way by the real Pearl. No disgrace in that. Sherman was about 150 pounds back then, and Pearl could dominate anybody. I'm sure there were times when Sherman got discouraged—he averaged only 11 minutes a game in his freshman year—but he never quit.

It's impossible to impress upon a recruit that getting schooled in practice might help you in the long run. Adrian Autry emphasizes that you have to choose more diplomatic words and tell a kid that he can *compete* against so-and-so every day rather than telling him that he can *learn* by performing as a backup.

Sherman wasn't exactly unknown. He had been a high school teammate of Michael Graham, an extremely physical player at Georgetown. And his high school wasn't exactly unknown to Syracuse people: Springarn High, where Dave Bing had played. The Hoyas didn't recruit Sherman, but Connecticut and Maryland had shown interest. Sherman picked Syracuse, he always said, because he had only one player to get by, and he figured—accurately, it turned out—that he would be under Pearl for only one season.

Sherman didn't know much about Earl Duncan, but it didn't matter. Throughout the 1986–87 season, Sherman basically treated Duncan the same way Pearl had treated *him*: with competitive contempt. Sherman didn't dominate Earl in the same way that Pearl had dominated him, in that physical, bouncing-off-guys style, but he ran the team with utter confidence, spreading the ball around, getting in the lane and releasing what Stevie Thompson (showing surprising historical acumen) called "that little Bob Cousy floater" and perfecting what became perhaps the best lob-off-the-drive ever. At the same time, Sherman demonstrated that he could get his own shot when the offense broke down.

To be blunt, Sherman ran Duncan out of town. Earl played in a reserve role for us as a sophomore but transferred to Rutgers, where he went on to have a respectable two-year career. Earl was, for a while, a sheriff down south, but he was never a general. That designation belongs to Sherman.

One other thing about Sherman: He developed as an individual to a greater degree than any player I ever had. He came from extremely tough circumstances in Washington, D.C. He didn't have a home life, he lived in an apartment that didn't have a front door, and he didn't express himself well at first. I'm sure some people thought he was dumb. But he overcame all of that and became one of the greatest players in Syracuse history and a guy who played in the NBA for 12 years. His daughter is a student here now.

Ironically, the Miami Heat drafted him, in the second round, because they weren't entirely satisfied with another point they already had there: Pearl Washington. I remember that one general manager had a negative comment about Sherman, even as he was praising his competitiveness. "He's a little wild and a little out of control," the guy said. To which I added, "Yes, he was a wild and out-of-control All-American."

Kids like Sherman Douglas are why you stay in the game.

STEVIE THOMPSON WAS another player you could chalk up to Dave Gavitt's genius. There he was out in L.A., a kid who grew up within a bus ride of two major Pac-10 schools and a short plane ride from several others, a kid who as a young player wanted to go to UCLA, a kid with a mother who wanted him to stay on the West Coast . . . and we get him in snowy Syracuse.

Like so many kids, Stevie would come home from practice and there on his TV screen would be not UCLA or USC, but a typical Big East throwdown. Stevie fell in love with it, when UCLA was in a down cycle, and we got him early in his senior year, when he was just 16 years old.

The book on Thompson was clear, and it wasn't all good—he was a six-two shooting guard who couldn't shoot. But he knew how to get shots, jumped like a forward, rebounded and competed every single play. He never complained about not getting the ball, figuring that he would collect enough leftovers to be effective, which turned out to be the case. He came here expecting to play with fellow Californian Earl Duncan and ended up having incomparable chemistry with Sherman. And Stevie Thompson was—still is—a terrific person who is now a coach himself.

YOU'D LIKE TO think that recruiting is a science, a careful analytic study of pluses and minuses that lead you to go after certain kids and leave others alone. But sometimes a recruit comes up and just taps you on the shoulder.

"Coach, I'm thinking about coming to Syracuse," this big guy with the beginnings of a heavy beard said to me one summer.

"How old are you?" I asked, turning around. "Twenty-five?"

"I'm seventeen," he said.

That was the first time I met Rony Seikaly.

Rony's aunt lived in town, and that's how he had settled on Syracuse. He had been to one of the top summer camps, and his physical attributes (a well-sculpted six-ten, 235 pounds) were obvious, but he was raw and unschooled. He was born in Beirut and lived there until he was nine. Then his family left and settled in Massachusetts before moving to Athens when he was ready to start high school. He never even picked up a basketball until he was fourteen. Then he came back to the United States for his senior year of high school. All that moving around kept him from playing much organized basketball. He couldn't play for the Greek junior national teams, for example, because he was Lebanese by birth.

Now, why did I settle on Rony? Simple. His athletic potential was off the charts. He was big, strong, mobile and quick. Those guys don't come around that often. But he still had to be coached—and coached hard—though Rony didn't always see it that way.

One day he said to me, "Why are you always yelling at me? Why aren't you yelling at Stevie?"

So I stopped practice and yelled: "Stevie! Stop working hard! Stop pushing! Stop running! Stop going after every ball! Stop being a good teammate!" I turned to Rony and said, "There . . . I just yelled at Stevie Thompson."

Understanding what working hard and playing hard entails is not always easy. Some players do not understand what it means to go all out. They think they are when they're not. Basketball-wise, Rony's big problem—besides fouling too much, the plague of many big men—was that he overdribbled in the lane. He always thought he could get free in there when he couldn't. Before one game I said, "Rony, you bounce it in the post, I'm taking you out." Ball goes in, he bounces it, turns, makes a shot. I had a sub at the scorer's table almost before the ball dropped through.

"Coach, I made it," he said to me when he sat down.

"Did you hear what I said?"

I put him back in. He catches, bounces, turns, misses. I take him out. Happens again. Finally he gets it. He was a difficult guy, a stubborn guy, and he was trying to win a debate with a guy who is pretty stubborn himself.

It's my opinion that Rony never fully realized his potential. He disagrees. He had a quite respectable 11-year pro career with four teams. But Rony was looking for more of a warm-fuzzy coach, and I've never been a big hugger. There was one point, though, when he thought that I wasn't such an ogre.

In the summer of 1986, he played for our national team in the World Championships under Arizona's Lute Olson. Rony came back that fall and said to me, "Coach, you're not so bad. Lute Olson didn't like me *at all*."

But I know to this day that Rony is not a Boeheim fan. He

always thought that I demonstrated what the psychologists called "displacement," that I hollered at him because I couldn't holler at Derrick Coleman. Not true. I hollered at Rony because I *wanted* to holler at Rony.

As for the one and only Derrick Coleman?

That's another story altogether.

10

THE ENIGMA

The locker room is going crazy. Bedlam. Jubilation. Utter joy. It is March 21, 1987, after the final whistle at the Meadowlands for the East Regional final, and we have just beaten North Carolina—hallowed North Carolina—79–75. It will be my first Final Four as a head coach and the first for the program since the "Roy's Runts" team of 1975. For our players, this is the reason you come to a big-time program.

But amid the screaming and backslapping, I notice one strange sight: Derrick Coleman, our star forward, possibly the best rebounder in the country as a freshman, a kid who just outplayed J. R. Reid, the highly touted Carolina freshman, is sitting at his locker and staring at the floor as he shakes his head.

Derrick Coleman is *pissed*?

"Derrick, what's the matter?" I ask him.

"Man, this ain't no damn good," he says. "It's spring break. I was going to visit my grandmother. I don't want to miss that."

"Derrick, you can go later," I said. "This is the Final—"

"I want to go *now*," he says.

That was the enigma named Derrick Coleman. Nobody in the Big East—and I mean *nobody*—wanted to mess with Derrick during the four years he terrorized everyone. Jayson Williams of St. John's?

Tough guy? He started looking for the nearest exit when Derrick walked into Madison Square Garden.

But with the 1987 Final Four looming, Derrick wanted to see his grandmother.

That wasn't the end of it. On our way to New Orleans, we had to connect through Detroit, Derrick's hometown, and when the layover was just about over, I noticed Derrick's mom by the boarding gate. (Security was a little looser back then.)

"Coach," she says, "I have to talk to you."

"Okay, Mrs. Coleman. What's up?"

"I think Derrick should stay home tonight and come down to New Orleans tomorrow," she says.

I am almost speechless.

"Mrs. Coleman, we can't do that," I say. "There's a lot of reasons, but mainly we just have to stay together as a team."

It takes some convincing, but Derrick finally gets on the plane. He wasn't nervous or apprehensive about the competition. He just wanted to spend the night at home.

DERRICK'S HOMESICKNESS NOTWITHSTANDING, we were rolling by the time we got to New Orleans. We had lost in the finals of the Big East tournament to Georgetown, but in the NCAAs we played some of our best basketball. We beat Georgia Southern 79–73 and Western Kentucky 104–86 and really hit our stride the following week. Seikaly was a major reason. He kept mispronouncing the name of the Florida center, a peculiar character named Dwayne Schintzius, but he dominated "*Shin*-zis" with 33 points. Then Rony had 26 and 11 as we beat Carolina to reach the Final Four and disturb Mr. Coleman's vacation plans. Derrick got over it; he and Rony were running up and down the hallway the night before the game in their boxer shorts, shouting, "I'm going to get J. R. Reid!"

Once in New Orleans, our semifinal win against Providence was perhaps our best performance of the year, a 77–63 victory, the third time that season we had beaten the Friars. It's hard to beat even a mediocre team three times, let alone a team coached by Rick Pitino with a point guard like Billy Donovan running the show. To this day, when I see Billy, who has become one of the best coaches in the country at Florida, he says to me, "Jim, I just couldn't handle that damn Sherman Douglas."

So there we are: the biggest spotlight in college basketball, and Indiana's Bob Knight, the biggest name in coaching at that time, on the other sideline.

I didn't really know Bob. And anyway, you try not to coach against coaches (though my rivalry with John Thompson had become a little personal). But it would be silly to pretend that seeing Knight on the other sideline didn't add to the intensity. It hadn't been that long ago that his 1976 championship team had accomplished the near-impossible feat of going undefeated.

I remember that '76 team well. It was my last year as an assistant under Roy, and I had to scout Virginia Tech for our final regular-season game. I watched Tech's game against Indiana, and I don't think Tech got off a good shot in the first eight minutes. Yet Virginia Tech later murdered us 92–81, and it wasn't even that close. That's how good Indiana was. The Hoosiers were tough, talented and disciplined. All five of their starters—Quinn Buckner, Scott May, Bobby Wilkerson, Kent Benson and Tom Abernethy—made the pros, in an NBA that had only 22 teams. That kind of utter domination will not happen again.

The 1987 version of the Hoosiers was good but not great, and I believe to this day that we had the better team, if a less battle-hardened one. We had a freshman, Derrick, and a sophomore, Sherman, who hadn't played much the previous season, in key roles. Also, Derrick was moody, and not just because he was a freshman.

He would be moody when he was a senior. You never could predict what frame of mind he'd be in.

And Sherman had gone south on me once, during a game at Michigan. It had an intense atmosphere from the start. Derrick had a few dozen family members there from Detroit; he eventually fouled out going against their big man, Loy Vaught. The Wolverines also had Glen Rice, a fantastic shooter, and a tough guard named Gary Grant, who was giving Sherman problems. I was yelling at Sherman—I do that from time to time—and suddenly he walks off the court and sits down on the bench. I watched in amazement and did the only thing I could do: I called timeout to pretend that he was heading to the bench as a matter of course.

"Sherman, you can get mad," I said, "but you can't do *that*."

Lack of maturity was not something that Knight had to worry about. Indiana had returned almost everyone from a strong team the year before, including their top three scorers—Ricky Calloway, Daryl Thomas and Steve Alford, one of the best shooters in NCAA history. And they had added two junior college transfers (not usually Knight's M.O.) in Keith Smart and Dean Garrett.

It was Alford who killed us early. He drained three-ball after three-ball, forcing us into a triangle-and-two defense that we hadn't practiced that much. These days it would be different; we would make all sorts of adjustments to our zone.

Still, we had control of the game, up by eight with about six minutes left, when our 2 guard, Greg Monroe, pulled up on a fast break and clanged a three. Then they came back and scored. Had we pulled it back in that situation, killed more clock and maybe gotten a two-pointer . . . who knows? But one vision I still have in my mind's eye. The scoreboard reads Syracuse 73, Indiana 72. There are 27 seconds left. Derrick is at the line with a one-and-one.

He misses the front end and they get the rebound.

Every Syracuse fan knows the rest. Indiana works the clock until

Smart gets a decent look in the left corner. It's not a difficult shot, but it's not a particularly easy one, either, since he's drifting to the left, toward the baseline. It goes in with four seconds left to put Indiana ahead 74–73. Ironically, up to that point, Knight had been furious at times with Smart's play. He had taken him out because Smart had been ineffective and was taking bad shots. And as the years roll on, I wish more and more that he would've kept Smart on that damn bench.

We had one timeout left, and no matter how much you talk about those situations in practice, panic can set in during a game. Rony, Derrick and Howard Triche were closest to the officials, and none signaled for a timeout. But Greg Monroe did, probably with three seconds left, and it was not granted until only one second remained.

We had only one play at that point: Derrick, our best bomb-throwing quarterback, trying to get it into the frontcourt for a desperation shot. Coleman was incredibly good with that long pass. He could throw a bullet from the baseline and hit somebody square in the hands at the other foul line. (Strangely, he threw with his right hand, even though he was left-handed.) But this Hail Mary was intercepted by Smart, and that was that.

I'm not sure that getting a timeout with four seconds left would've made much difference. My philosophy is that you can't go full-court with a short inbounds pass in that amount of time, so even with three more seconds, we probably would've called the same play.

One other comparison resonates. In our 2003 title game, Hakim Warrick came bounding out of our zone to block a shot—more on that later—and we had asked Derrick to watch out for that same corner, because in a triangle-and-two, the corner is a vulnerable area. But he stayed behind his man, Daryl Thomas, and maybe he could've gotten out on Smart.

Still, there was one move I made—or, rather, didn't make—that haunts me. On the play that led to Derrick's missed free throw, we were inbounding against full-court pressure. We have an automatic play in that situation in which Sherman and Greg Monroe cross, then Sherman heads upcourt for a possible long pass. I noticed that they had pushed up, and I thought about calling timeout to tell Derrick that a long pass to Sherman would probably be there. But I didn't want to surrender my last timeout and also figured that Knight, if he knew what we were talking about, would put a man back in the free-safety position.

So I let it go and, sure enough, Sherman started to break free. But Derrick didn't see him and made the short inbounds pass, which happened to be to Rony, who wanted no part of accepting the foul. He threw it quickly back to Derrick, and he was the one Indiana fouled.

Look, there is an element of good luck in most close games you win and an element of bad luck in most close games you lose. You would like to think that the breaks even out, though if you poll most coaches—as well as most golfers, stockbrokers and blackjack players—they would all say that they get screwed more often than they get saved.

This game was definitely in the bad-luck column, I'm sure of that. A lot of unfortunate things had to happen for us to lose to Indiana: Our reputation as poor foul shooters was born that night, since we missed a few key free throws down the stretch. Some writers even suggested that I didn't have my teams practice them enough. Let me tell you, there's no more helpless feeling a coach can have than when one of his players is on the free-throw line with the game in the balance. There is literally nothing you can do besides clap your hands and utter a silent prayer.

But the margin between Indiana and us was not that great. Rarely does a team get upset in an NCAA championship game when it's *far better* than its opponent. Oddly, two of the bigger upsets had already happened right around that time. In 1983, Jimmy Valvano's North Carolina State team beat a powerful Houston team (with Hakeem Olajuwon and Clyde Drexler) 54–52. State had a lot of luck in that game, including the final shot, which was a put-back after a bad miss.

Two years later, Rollie Massimino's Villanova team beat John Thompson's Georgetown team 66–64 on April Fools' Day 1985. Many still call it the biggest upset in NCAA history, but I don't buy that. Yes, Villanova had ten losses coming into the final game, but they had played Georgetown tough in both of their regular-season matchups. Villanova had beaten us by 12 in one of our games that year, and we had a really good team. Villanova was an underdog, but that's about as far as I'll go.

There wasn't much to do after the Indiana loss but return to the hotel and replay the game in your head, over and over and over. I think I've still never watched the whole thing. I remember my father was there—my mother was gone by that time—and though he wasn't the warmest guy, it made me feel better to talk to him.

What made it somewhat easier was the thought that we could get another crack at it very soon. We were losing Howard Triche and Greg Monroe, two reliable seniors, but we still had Rony, Sherman and, of course, Derrick.

What could possibly go wrong?

THE CHINESE HAVE a saying: "May you live in interesting times." As I understand it, it's as much a curse as a wish, since "interesting" implies anxiety, insecurity and unpredictability.

In other words, life with Derrick Coleman.

To really arrive at the essence of the guy who was the third-best (behind Bing and Carmelo) player Syracuse ever had, you have to go back to those moments before the Final Four. Home, mother, grandmother—all of those things meant a lot to Derrick. After that game in Michigan, I can still see the Coleman family waiting to say good-bye to Derrick, Dessie Coleman in her DERRICK COLEMAN'S MOTHER shirt. She absolutely wanted to get on the plane back to Syracuse with Derrick, and he absolutely wanted her to come. That kind of love is understandable and admirable, but within the context of a team, you sometimes have to make sacrifices that conflict with your personal wishes. It was hard for Derrick to understand that when it came to his family.

Predictably, I always had trouble getting him to return from Christmas vacation. In his sophomore year, early in the 1987–88 season, he told me that he simply was not going to come back for a team meeting on Christmas Day.

"Derrick, every player wants to be with his mom over Christmas, but you have to come back," I told him. "Stevie Thompson's flying to California, and he's coming back. If you're not here, I have to bench you."

People outside of sports must understand this truism: A coach has only one true weapon to use with a player—minutes. Running at 6:00 A.M., hollering at him and all that other stuff? It pales in relation to playing time.

Derrick had started 47 straight games to that point, but, as promised, he missed the meeting, and I kept him on the bench for the first 13 minutes against Morehead State on December 28. We still won easily, and everyone wondered if I would've done the same thing had Georgetown been the opponent. The answer is yes. Then again, I'm not sure that Derrick would've missed the meeting had the punishment been sitting against Georgetown.

Derrick was not a troublemaker, a bad kid or anything remotely like that. His teammates loved him. I've never had a better kid in the program than Stevie Thompson, and to this day he likes and respects Derrick like no other teammate he ever had.

But Derrick walked a tightrope—that I will concede. For one

thing, he loved practice only when there was competition. If we were running a drill, he didn't care all that much, but if we were running a drill in which he could beat someone's brains in, he cared a lot. Sometimes I put him against other first-team players, like Seikaly or Billy Owens, just so he would stay engaged. So to say that Derrick didn't practice hard is not accurate; he just didn't practice hard if there weren't sufficient reason as he saw it.

From that perspective, he had a little Pearl Washington in him. In the summer of 1988, after his sophomore year, Derrick was invited to the Olympic Trials. I was there to help John Thompson, our coach in Seoul, assess the talent.

My phone rings at 6:00 A.M.

"Coach, I'm going home," Derrick tells me.

"I know, Derrick," I answer. "We're all going home. We have this exhibition game tonight, and then we break camp and—"

"No, I'm going home *now*," he says.

"You're crazy," I tell him. "You have a really good chance of making this team."

"That's just it," he answers. "I don't want to make this team. I want to go home."

He was at the airport before I could get to his room to change his mind.

If you pushed Derrick too hard on a bad-mood day, someone on that court was probably going to end up with a bloody nose. The rumor among the team was that he wasn't happy with the play of our point guard, Mike Edwards, who had taken over after Sherman Douglas left, so Derrick hung Mike up in a locker. I never wanted to confirm that one.

Derrick came in a couple of years before the "Fab Five," the group of Michigan freshmen who changed the culture of the game, and let's just say that Derrick would've blended right in with them. If fans insulted him, he would insult them back, sometimes with words, sometimes with a gesture. Athletes are supposed to suck it up and tune out all distractions, but that wasn't Derrick. He liked to get fans riled up, sometimes waving good-bye to an opponent who had fouled out or pointing to the scoreboard when we were ahead. He got in the habit of pumping his fist after dunks, an image that ended up on T-shirts sold around campus. To any Syracuse basketball fan in the late 1980s, D.C. did not stand for District of Columbia.

AFTER WE HAD beaten Providence in our first meeting during Derrick's freshman year, Rick Pitino, who was coaching the Friars, said, "Derrick Coleman is one of the top young players in the country, but he's got a little bit of the mustard in him." To which I would add: So do some coaches.

Stevie Thompson used to say that when Seikaly thought he wasn't getting the ball enough, he would complain to my assistant, Bernie Fine; when Derrick wasn't getting the ball enough, he would complain to *everyone*. But that attitude was part of what made him great. With those kinds of players, you have to take the good with the bad, because sometimes it's hard to discern where the line is.

Billy Owens says that Derrick and I were like an old married couple. I think I understood Derrick because we're somewhat alike, even though we're from different worlds. Even before his freshman season ended, Derrick had grown tired of repetitive postgame questions, for example, and did not do a good job of pretending otherwise. That did not endear him to the press. I know how he feels.

Off the court, Derrick liked to hang out, people liked to hang out with him, and therefore trouble sometimes found him. In his sophomore year, he got involved in a melee with a bunch of football players and got arrested. There were 30 guys at this party, and he was the only one who got charged with harassment and disorderly conduct. I asked the policeman why it was just Derrick who got nabbed and the guy told me, "Because he's who we recognized."

In the 38 years that I've been in charge of the program, we've had some off-court incidents. Sometimes my players were in the wrong, other times they were innocent but got burned anyway. Anything a Syracuse basketball player does in Syracuse will be magnified. We get that. It's the way it goes.

But also keep in mind that well over 200 players have come through our program since 1976. If you took a random sample of any campus group, you would find a similar percentage of kids who got into some kind of trouble without it becoming public knowledge. I understand the trade-off. Our games get covered, so our screwups get covered. But my interest is in emphasizing that athletes, as a group, are not troublemakers.

How far can you go in trying to keep your players out of trouble? And what exactly constitutes trouble? Do you ask athletes to refrain from doing things that you wouldn't ask or even reasonably expect normal college kids to refrain from doing? These are questions that coaches have to deal with every day of every season, and over the years my general philosophy has evolved this way:

You can't have rules that you can't enforce. For as long as I've coached, I've had players who drank alcohol, but why should I put in place a no-drinking rule that I can't monitor? What if I set a no-drinking rule and someone comes to me and says, "I saw your player having a beer." Do I get backup verification? If I find out it's true, do I suspend a 21-year-old for having one legal beer? One year, the Syracuse football players made a pledge not to drink. So what happens? They win a big game and three dozen of them are out drinking on Marshall Street on Saturday night. And anyone who finds that surprising is crazy.

If you're under 21, you shouldn't drink because you're breaking the law. My players know that. But I don't tell the ones who are over 21 that they can't drink. They go to bars for the same reason that kids have been going to bars since bars were invented—to meet girls. You want the truth? I'd rather they didn't go to bars. I'd rather not hear from someone, "Hey, I saw one of your players out last night." But I just will not put in a rule I can't enforce.

Now, if drinking becomes a problem—and you will usually find that out—I will step in. I will say that over the years drinking has not been much of an issue, at least in comparison with pot smoking. Pot is a problem because—quite simply—there are laws against it and there is testing. I've had a few kids test positive for marijuana who have paid the price. But again, I would look to comparative metrics: If you consider the number of kids who have come through the program, the percentage of pot smokers is less than in most campus groups.

I don't have a curfew, either. When I was in college I played cards until two in the morning, sometimes three. Why? Because I liked to. I didn't drink, but I did stay up. I can't remember whether we had a curfew, but, if we did, I broke it three dozen times during the season. Plus, stuff happens. Let's say you put in a curfew of midnight and one of your players leaves his girlfriend's apartment at 11:30, has a flat tire and gets in at 12:30. Is that a suspendable offense? You would end up spending half your time adjudicating curfew offenses instead of coaching basketball.

For the most part players live together, but they're spread out all over the place, some in dorms, some in apartments. I have no desire to be a policeman. The last time I was in a player's room was 40 years ago, when I was an assistant. Roy had a curfew, and I was assigned to enforce it. So what happened? I walked in on a player and his girlfriend. It was embarrassing for all three of us and clearly under the category of Too Much Information.

Truthfully, I wish my players didn't stay out late, because I don't like to hear about it. I used to kid them: If you have to stay out until 2:00 A.M. to convince a girl to like you, then you need to work on your game.

So here are my rules: Be on time. Go to class. Do the things you're supposed to do as students and basketball players. Mostly my players toe the line. If that's not good enough for critics who want you to be on your players all the time ? Tough.

Some coaches make a great show of having a lot of rules and do it this way. They'll suspend a player who's misbehaved for a game against a lousy team. Or they'll announce a suspension over the summer, so the kid misses the first easy game and he's back for the second. Is that honest? Does that show your program has integrity? It's hypocritical.

Finally, I don't believe in suspending kids from games unless it's really egregious. I have done it very, very infrequently, most recently with Dion Waiters. I've gotten criticism for that, because people think it's all about protecting me. It's not. Suspensions punish not just the player but also the team, the program and the fans.

I'M SORRY THAT a discussion about Derrick ended up being about rules. Because when I think about Derrick Coleman, I absolutely do not think about the few times he went off the side of the road. I see a player of immense talent who came to me as maybe the best young rebounder I had ever seen, stayed four years and left as one of the greatest college rebounders ever.

And I see a player who had an immensely competitive personality and a fierce pride. Which brings me to a final Derrick story.

March 5, 1989, Derrick's junior year, Sunday afternoon, 30,000 in the Dome, national television, Georgetown the opponent. An assistant comes to me about seven minutes before the game and says, "Derrick's not coming out."

I run into the locker room, where I find our All-American sitting in the altogether.

"Derrick, what's going on?" I ask.

"I'm not wearing that uniform," he said. "It's bullshit."

That day was one of those "special uniform" days that still happen from time to time (we wore a particularly egregious one against Boston College this season), and this one was hideous, a skintight unitard that was more appropriate for the ballet. It showed *everything*. And Derrick Coleman was not putting the damn thing on.

"I'm sorry," I told him. "We should've tried it on first, and I admit it's not that great. But it's not that bad, either."

"Well, I'm not coming out in it," he said.

"Derrick, it's not the best situation," I said. "But you need to put on that uniform and you need to be out there in a few minutes. Or you're done at Syracuse." And I left.

The buzzer sounds. They announce the Georgetown starters. No Derrick. The lights go down. They start announcing our starters.

"And at forward . . ."

And out he comes.

Until that moment, I had it at 50-50 that he would show.

And then Derrick Coleman kicked Georgetown's butt.

A COACH'S NOTES V

I can't remember when there was this much hype for a regular-season game. Maybe never in our history.

It's February 1, and Duke is coming to town.

We've just concluded our team meeting/film session in a hotel close to campus, like always. I've been taking my team to a hotel near campus the night before home games since the late 1980s. Derrick Coleman was here then. Actually, Derrick wasn't the only reason. Michael Edwards had something to do with it, too. Derrick and Michael enjoyed the nightlife, and they weren't the only ones. The night before a game with a noon tip-off, I'd always hear that a couple of my players were out on Marshall Street. They weren't doing anything that a normal college kid wouldn't be doing, but it looked bad, a case of perception over reality. I got tired of hearing about it, so we started bringing them to a hotel and haven't stopped.

Can I swear that no player has ever left the hotel or imported companionship? I'm sure it's happened. But by and large going to a hotel the night before a game—a noon game, a four o'clock game, a nine o'clock game—has resulted in fewer problems . . . even though the players hate it.

Our meeting was nothing out of the ordinary. We went over what we have to do in the game, not what the game *means*. But all the time you're talking, you know that your players know it's not just another game, and they know that you know it's not another game.

There are several reasons for all the excitement. Duke is probably the most polarizing program in the country. Millions love them; millions love to hate them. We're really good, up to number two in the rankings, and they're really good, like always. They have one of the most watched freshmen in recent years, Jabari Parker, a six-eight superstar-to-be out of Chicago. Jabari has a little Carmelo Anthony in him—live body, strong, can step out and shoot threes but does a lot of inside post-ups, too. Predictably, we were not able to get in on the Parker recruiting. We don't recruit much in the Midwest, and it would've been tough to beat Duke in any case.

Also, this is one of the first showdown games of the "new ACC," kind of like a marriage being consummated. Duke has won the most games in the ACC, and we won the most in the old Big East, so it's a natural. Duke just finished playing (and routing) Pitt, another new ACC team, but our program has a higher national profile than Pitt's. Pitt has been in the conversation for the past 10 years; we've been good for the past 40.

ESPN will hold its *GameDay* broadcast from the Dome. Nobody does hype like ESPN. I still marvel when I think back on where it all started in 1979, this little joke of a station broadcasting box lacrosse and slow-pitch softball. I played basketball for four years here and was interviewed exactly once, by a local writer when I was a senior. I never did a TV interview, and I'm not sure Dave Bing ever did one, either. Now my phone is ringing every ten minutes. One time it's Dick Vitale and he sounds like he's yammering into the end of a tin can. "Dick," I tell him, "you gotta pay your phone bill."

My relationship with Mike Krzyzewski only adds to the intrigue. We've been through two Olympics together, and he's become one of my closest friends in coaching. Although it might not look like it from the outside, Mike and I have a lot in common. The Syracuse *Post-Standard* even ran a story with the headline EIGHT SIMILARITIES BETWEEN MIKE KRZYZEWSKI AND JIM BOEHEIM.

The information came from Tim O'Toole, an assistant at Stanford who worked under both Mike and me. He said we both like to keep things simple; we both recruit well; we have been extremely loyal to our respective institutions and understand how basketball fits into the university structure as a whole. There are a few other similarities, but I'm too humble to list them. Okay, what the hell. According to Tim, we're both also humble.

YOU HAVE TO prepare your team in multiple ways for Duke. Their system is based on pressure defense, which means that it's not easy to run your set plays. They disrupt you, and they have great athletes. They keep coming at you and deny, deny, deny. They jump into the passing lanes better than anyone. It's difficult sometimes to use a ball screen, because they double-team the screens and pressure you hard.

And it's not like they just send five guys after the ball in a mad rush. Mike is organized and disciplined, and that's how his team plays. I tell my guys that the only way to beat an aggressive defense is with aggressive offense; they have to take the ball to the basket. We would've been better equipped for it last year with Michael Carter-Williams and Brandon Triche, both of whom could drive. Right now the only guy we have who seems comfortable slashing to the hoop is Tyler Ennis (and C. J. Fair, once in a while). The one positive is that there *will* be driving lanes. And Duke probably takes fewer charges than it used to when the annoying (but effective) Shane Battier would always be standing in someone's way.

On the other side of the ball, Duke has four guys who can shoot, never mind what Parker can do, which is everything. So our zone has to identify the shooters: Andre Dawkins, Rasheed Sulaimon and Rodney Hood. Parker is getting the most publicity, but Hood is a very, very good player. He can shoot, put it on the floor, pass, rebound and defend.

True, Duke has had a couple of bad losses this year, to Clemson and Notre Dame, teams that shouldn't beat them. But you don't even bother looking at those games on film. They're anomalies. They just pounded Pitt 80–65 on the road, and *that's* what you look at.

We'll have 35,000 in the Dome, but with teams like Duke, that's not much of a factor. In fact, they'll enjoy that. Some teams come in here and see all that orange and it's over. But those aren't the kind of players Krzyzewski recruits.

We're still undefeated, but it's a minor miracle. We could've lost at Miami; they got off to a big lead and missed several chances to bury us. Boston College had us down by eight points in the second half. Pitt had us down three with two minutes left and the Panthers almost always win those games. Our margin is an inch wide, the lowest of any good team I've had here. We lost DaJuan Coleman for the season after knee surgery, and our depth has become a real problem.

MONTHS AGO, MY wife had a great idea: Invite Syracuse grad Vanessa Williams to sing the national anthem for the home Duke game. Even ESPN has noticed—they almost never broadcast the anthem, but they're doing it tonight.

Yesterday, my assistant coaches and I visited "Boeheimburg," the enclave at the Dome where students camp out to get prime seats inside, a show of solidarity for freezing their asses off. There are not as many kids at Boeheimburg as there are at Krzyzewskiville, the long-running campout near Cameron Indoor Stadium, but then again, it's a helluva lot colder in Syracuse than it is in Durham.

Then last night, Mike and I sat down for a long joint interview with Rece Davis of ESPN. We talked a lot about the relationship between us, the Olympic team and how much we're looking forward to our friendship continuing into the ACC, even though we'll both be trying to beat each other's brains in. Mike doesn't usually do that kind of pregame interview, another indication of how special this game is.

EVEN AS LONG as I've been around, I can't say that I feel a Classic Game coming. But a lot of times you're almost certain that a game will be very, very close, and very, very intense, and that's my assessment of this one. Our teams are evenly matched. We have ways to score and stop them, they have ways to score and stop us. But if either team is going to blow the other one out, it will almost certainly be Duke blowing us out. Whereas Duke has terrific athletes who can pressure you and create easy baskets, we don't have much blowout capability. We're a very good team with a very small margin of error.

At game time, courtside seats are going for $3,400, and the first ten rows are at $1,500. Longtime fans will tell me later that they didn't recognize half of the people around them because so many folks had sold their tickets for profit. As I said, no regular-season game in my memory, which goes back a long way, approaches the hype of playing the Blue Devils, at home, when you've got a pretty good team.

Vanessa's anthem is perfect; then she comes over and hugs me.

It's Duke.

It's on.

C.J. IS MAGNIFICENT. Guarded mostly by Hood, Duke's best defender, he looks confident, both shooting it outside and taking it to the rim. C.J. is an example of someone who made the right decision about returning for his senior year. He contemplated coming out and ultimately decided against it, and for those of you who think that's an easy decision for a young man, I assure you it isn't. There is the lure of money, friends telling you that you can make it and the tantalizing sight of other players leaving. But C.J. weighed it all and decided that he should stay. He's more of a complementary player, and that's not a criticism. That's exactly why he *could* be a really good NBA player. He's efficient, he doesn't need a lot of shots to get his points, he sneaks up on you with his production, he can rebound and he's a good teammate.

We play hard and get out on their perimeter shooters, but Duke makes tough shot after tough shot—15 three-pointers altogether, the last of which really hurts. We're ahead by three with four seconds left, and they have the ball without a timeout. We have one left. The advantage of taking a timeout, of course, is that you can figure out whether or not to deliberately foul and thus take away a potential game-tying three. But my philosophy is: I'm not going to take a timeout to let you set up your offense.

As a general rule, with ten or more seconds, you want to foul, because the offense has way too much time to get a good look. Even with six or seven seconds left, we would've fouled. There's one other factor: We're a bad rebounding team on free throws, prone to letting the outside guy come in for a follow shot.

So let's see if they can go full-court in four seconds and . . .

That's exactly what Sulaimon does. Not only that, but he goes right to the three-point line whereas most players will pull up 10 feet behind it and turn a 20-footer into a 30-footer. It goes in. Tie game, 78–78. End of regulation.

It looks bad when they make a three early in OT, but Tyler Ennis makes a great recognition play, spotting Jerami Grant on the low block against a smaller defender, and Jerami gets a dunk. During a timeout, we tell Tyler to go there again. It works twice. There are several reasons Tyler will be a good pro, and his court sense is foremost among them.

We dominate the final two minutes of overtime, hitting seven of eight free throws and allowing them only two points. One of the great things about sports is how you can overanalyze games, but things happen all the time that you can't explain, like Jerami and Tyler making all of their free throws in pressure situations and, moreover, converting 18 of 18 for the game. Jerami is an average foul shooter, but in the last five minutes of games so far this season, he is 17 for 17. It makes no sense, but there it is in black and white.

We win 91–89. C.J. has 28 points and Jerami has 24. Yes, we gave up those 15 threes, but nobody really killed us. We limited Parker to 15 points.

One of the first things I see right after the game is Derrick Coleman rushing the court. He's just as excited as our players. Sometimes we have to stop Derrick from coming out and yelling at them, but this time it's just pure joy.

Mike Krzyzewski and I talk briefly.

"Unbelievable game," I say. "Sorry someone had to lose."

"We made the first one a great one," Mike says.

Later, people will comment that it's among the ten best

they've ever seen. I'll have to think about that, but I won't rule it out.

Finishing up the postgame interview on the court, that's when I notice that the fans are staying, an image I'll never forget.

Yes, this is one of those days. And on Monday morning we'll be voted the number-one team in the country.

11

BLUE CHIPS

In the fall of 1987, a few months after our championship-game heartbreak, I went to recruit the most complete high school player I had ever seen. Maybe not the best, but the most complete. If he were in baseball, he would've been labeled a five-tool player.

Billy Owens was ambidextrous, he rebounded, he was an excellent passer, he defended and he had court sense. He probably never became a great shooter, but that gets back to that foolish criticism—if he did *everything* he'd be somebody else, in Billy's case a six-foot-eight version of Michael Jordan. As it was, I like Stevie Douglas's description of Billy: the small-forward version of Derrick Coleman.

Owens appeared for a while to be Perkins 2.0—in other words, a player destined for another team. Dean Smith wanted Billy badly, and, as I said, whomever Dean and Coach K want, they usually get. Plus, Billy was coached at Carlisle High School, in Pennsylvania, by Dave Lebo, and played alongside Lebo's son Jeff, who would go on to UNC. They won four straight state championships at Carlisle, with Billy playing every position.

We had one thing going for us—Billy's older brother, Michael, was a running back at Syracuse—but it still didn't look promising.

I'd see Billy on campus once in a while, visiting his brother and hanging around with Derrick, and I'd give him the subtle pitch. But he never paid me much mind.

My recruiting visit to Carlisle started out very badly. I was in a four-seat plane on the windiest day of the year, bouncing around like a jelly bean in a shaken jar, and it was one of those times when my mind flashed to that embalming room at the Boeheim Funeral Home.

Plus, Billy had forgotten that I was coming. He was in and out of the house like a flash—hi-how-are-ya!—before heading for the playground to play pickup. (At least he blew me off to play basketball.) Billy's father did all the talking, and his mother never came downstairs. Bad sign. The key to recruiting more often than not is Mom, and not just in African American families. So I get up to leave and I'm thinking, *Sam Perkins all over again.*

But as I'm leaving, Mrs. Owens comes running out the door.

"Coach, I just wanted to say hello," she said. Then she added, in a conspiratorial voice, "You don't have to worry about this much. I think it would be good for Billy to be up there with his brother."

"Mrs. Owens," I said, suddenly relieved, "I couldn't agree with you more."

Still, Billy didn't commit until late. Alonzo Mourning and Chris Mills were the other two top recruits that year, and one weekend Alonzo was visiting. I already knew that he was going to John Thompson at Georgetown, so I said to him, "Have a nice visit, but please convince Billy to come here and play against you."

Finally, Billy said yes, marking the first time I had beaten North Carolina on a recruit.

Billy is a good example of the mental transition a high school player has to make in college. He started for me as a freshman in the 1988–89 season, and we won 13 in a row before Pitt beat us. Then we won another before Villanova beat us. Billy was disconsolate in the locker room. He had come off a 33–0 senior season.

There they are, the best bridge players in central New York—my parents, Janet and Jim Boeheim. The biggest reason I rarely forget anything is that I inherited my parents' gift of memory.

(Courtesy of Juli and Jim Boeheim)

Here I am in my playing days, taking off just inside the free-throw line.

My first year of coaching (1976) was all about hard work, dedication and stimulating talks at the chalkboard.

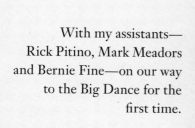

With my assistants— Rick Pitino, Mark Meadors and Bernie Fine—on our way to the Big Dance for the first time.

That '77 team was led by Louis Orr (55) and Roosevelt Bouie (50); the Louie and Bouie Show.

Pearl Washington helped turn us into a nationally recognized phenomenon. Here he is dribbling away from Navy's David Robinson, who would get his revenge later that season.

I had to be careful about overcoaching creative players like Pearl; they have to have the freedom to make their own mistakes.

Rony Seikaly was looking for a warm and fuzzy coach, but I was never a big hugger.

There was never a dull moment when you coached Derrick Coleman (44); frankly, I could've used a few.

Mike Hopkins, now my top assistant, was always a good listener.

Sherman Douglas lived up to his nickname, "The General," with his court sense and leadership.

Even as a teenager, Carmelo Anthony was a pleasure to coach.

Gerry McNamara did most of his damage from long range, but he could take it to the hoop, too.

This block by Hakim Warrick to clinch the 2003 championship is the most famous play in Syracuse history.
(Courtesy of the Syracuse Post-Standard)

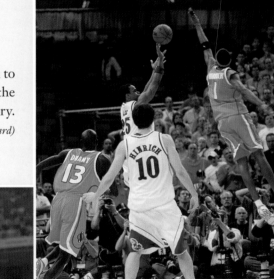

Maybe my greatest postgame moment: cutting down the nets after the '03 championship.

Notice who's playing above the rim (Bing) and who's earthbound (Boeheim, 35).

People used to say, "Who's the white guy with Dave Bing?" After almost fifty years, I hope they know now.

One of the keys to my success is my upbeat, fun-loving team of assistants—three former players: Gerry McNamara, Mike Hopkins and Adrian Autry.

Our two games with Duke and Mike Krzyzewski in 2013–14 set the standard for the first year of the "new" ACC.

You try not to personalize rivalries, but the one between John Thompson and me got a little personal at times.

UConn's Jim Calhoun was the classic tough guy, a former gravedigger. I can relate.

Dave Gavitt, who started the Big East, was one of the great college basketball visionaries.

(Courtesy of Juli and Jim Boeheim)

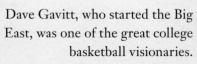

I still think Tyler Ennis should have stayed for his sophomore season, but no matter what, Tyler's maturity will serve him well in the NBA.

Coach K and I split two memorable games last season, but at the end of the second one I had a polite disagreement with an official that went viral.
(AP Photo/Gerry Browne)

Sharing the Beijing bench with Coach K, Mike D'Antoni and Nate McMillan.
(NBAE/Getty Images)

Lebron told me, "Coach, tell me whatever you see that might help. You've been doing this a long time."
(NBAE/Getty Images)

I started to become more of a human being when my oldest daughter, Elizabeth (Lizzy), came into my life.
(Courtesy of Juli and Jim Boeheim)

The love and support of my wife, Juli, my children (from left: twins, Jack and Jamie, and Jimmy III) and our dog, Lulu (in my arms) are the reason I'm still in game as I hit 70.
(Courtesy of Juli and Jim Boeheim)

Even going into the 2014–15 season with 948 wins, coaching is humbling enough that you shouldn't get a big head.

"What's the matter, young brother?" Derrick Coleman asked him.

"Man, I can't take all this losing," Billy said, head buried in his hands.

"Well, get used to it," said Derrick, slapping him on the back, "and welcome to the Big East."

SOMETHING HAPPENS TO you as a coach when you get great players. You are no longer this teacher of basketball, this old sage who rounds up a group of dedicated kids and gets them to play together. Rather, you are the CEO of a *Fortune* 500 company that is supposed to perform at the highest level, obligated to return premiums to your stockholders. After Jim Calhoun started getting blue-chip recruits at Connecticut, I told him, "Jim, get ready. Now you'll be an idiot if you don't win it all."

So over that period from the late '80s to the early '90s, we started to have those studs at Syracuse, the kind we hadn't gotten before— Derrick, Sherman, Rony, Billy and Stevie Thompson. We won 139 games and lost only 37 in the five seasons between 1986–87, Derrick's freshman year, and 1990–91, Billy's junior year, after which he went to the NBA. We got within one game of the Final Four and two games of the Final Four. But we didn't win it all, and that made it disappointing for us and our fans.

We were loaded, yes, but you have to remember that this was a different era of college basketball. In 1988–89—Sherman and Stevie were seniors, Derrick was a junior and Billy was a freshman—we faced Illinois in the final of the Midwest Region, with the winner going to the Final Four. And here's who Illinois had: Kendall Gill, Kenny Battle, Nick Anderson, Marcus Liberty and Steve Bardo, all of whom would play in the NBA. That Illinois team had put up 127 points against LSU and scored 100 seven other times.

A couple of the players describe that Illinois game as the best they ever played in. I would never say that, since we lost. If the NCAA final against Indiana in New Orleans two years earlier had been a tactical battle, this was a high-flying trapeze act. I thought we had it. We had a 12-point lead at one point and were still up by seven at the half. I remember Derrick and Stevie walking back to the locker room together, talking about how they would be going to see the president soon.

Man, do I hate premature celebrations.

It was give-and-take in the second half, and in the end they just played a more athletic game than we did. Kendall Gill, maybe the most gifted kid out there, jumped in and got a rebound off a missed shot to preserve their 89–86 win.

The White House would have to wait.

EVERYBODY FELT CERTAIN that Derrick was going to leave after the 1988–89 season. In today's game, he wouldn't have played for me more than one year. He would've rocketed to the top of the draft boards after collecting 19 rebounds in the championship game against Indiana. But Derrick, as you've seen, was cut from different cloth. He wanted to be the number-one pick in the draft, and, had he left after his junior year, he would not have been. Pervis Ellison, Danny Ferry and Sean Elliott would've almost certainly maintained their spots, and Derrick would've slotted in fourth, right ahead of Glen Rice. Fourth might've been good enough for some, but not for D.C.

The way he informed me that he was coming back was pure Derrick. I'm in my office after the season and he strolls by, stops, hollers in, "I'm staying," and keeps on walking. Sure enough, he was the first pick in the 1990 draft, right ahead of Gary Payton.

Over the years, people have tried to goad me into saying that

Derrick had a "disappointing" NBA career. Nonsense. He played for 15 years and averaged 16 points and more than 9 rebounds. No, he didn't become Karl Malone or Tim Duncan. He was D.C.

Anyway, I'm the coach at Syracuse University, so when I consider a player's career, I think first about what he did for me. Derrick had incredible hands—I literally never saw him juggle a ball—and incredible court sense. He could've scored 20 a game easily, but he was more interested in facilitating the offense. You told Derrick something once and that was it.

In short, Derrick had a better understanding of the game than any big man I ever coached. And it's not even close. I also see someone who loved this program, who still comes back and worms his way into the team huddles. Sometimes when we're in the middle of a tough battle, I wish Derrick were sitting on that bench, even if he were pouting, so I could tell him to get back in there and take no prisoners.

RICHMOND. IF YOU coach long enough, you're bound to have a Richmond.

Krzyzewski has a couple of Richmonds. As a number 3 seed, he lost to Mercer, a number 14, in this past year's NCAA tournament. As a number 2 seed in 2012, he lost to number 15 Lehigh.

Jim Calhoun has a Richmond. As a number 1 seed in 2006, UConn lost to number 11 George Mason.

Lute Olson has a Richmond. As a number 2 seed in 1993, he lost to number 15 Santa Clara, which had a point guard named Steve Nash.

Jim Harrick has a Richmond. In 1996, the year after he won the NCAA championship, 4th-seeded UCLA lost to 13th-seeded Princeton.

That's not the end of the list by any means, but you get the picture. We just happened to be one of the pioneers. In the 1991 NCAAs, we became the first 2 seed to lose to a 15 when Richmond beat us 73–69 in the first round of the East Regional at the University of Maryland. You mention the name Richmond to our fans and they're likely to reach for the nearest weapon.

I understand why such defeats seem inexplicable to the outsider, but if you're in the eye of the storm, they make perfect sense. Look, let's be clear: It was an upset. We had a very good team. A few weeks before dreaded Richmond, we had handled Florida State 88–79, and we had beaten Pitt, Villanova and Georgetown in our final three Big East games.

But the tournament is a crapshoot. Neutral sites, strange tip-off times, unfamiliar opponents, different ways that refs call the game, added pressure and teams that are better than their seeds, which was the case with Richmond, a veteran squad that had beaten a good Bob Knight Indiana team in the previous season's NCAA tournament. We could've been on top of our game and still lost to Richmond . . . and we were definitely not on top of our game.

I do have one out, though. Two of my assistants, Adrian Autry and Mike Hopkins, were on that team, so I can blame the defeat on them.

Actually, there is a backstory to the loss.

Around tournament time in 1991, the NCAA was nearing the end of a two-year investigation of our program that led to our being barred from the 1992–93 postseason. Investigators were around for the entire week of preparation. One of our starters, Conrad McRae, was involved, and we were working day-to-day to get him cleared.

Anyone who knows me will tell you that one of my strengths is eliminating distractions. The investigation had gone on for too long, it wore on everybody, and I didn't do a good job of keeping it from interfering with our preparation. At that time, our players were much more involved with our booster organization, the

Hardwood Club, and, yes, sometimes those guys took their enthusiasm over the line. Back then, college basketball was more Wild West than it is today.

The violations centered around a number of little things: free meals at restaurants around town, discounts for records, rides that shouldn't have been given, laundry that shouldn't have been done. The official statement from the NCAA read, "There were problems in the basketball program. I would *not* describe it as a program out of control." But little things add up. I was singled out for criticism by the NCAA—that's okay; the buck stops here and all that—but the investigators also said that "there was no evidence that the coach was aware of the violations," which is true.

A so-called street agent named Rob Johnson illegally left tickets for and gave gifts to recruits. We found out about what he was doing and cut ties, but the violations were retroactive; since he was considered a "university representative" when they occurred, we got tagged.

Was Rob Johnson a close confidant of mine? Absolutely not. But I did talk to him to gather information about players, just like a lot of coaches did. Would I do things differently now? Yes. I'm older and more careful. The term "street agent" makes it seem like seedy characters are running amok within the program, and that's just never been the case.

Now there's the "AAU coach," which in some quarters has assumed a completely negative connotation. Let's get this straight: There are bad AAU coaches. But there are bad high school coaches, too, despite the perception that the high school coach is always the old, fundamentally sound guy looking out for the player, and the AAU coach is the flashy opportunist who's invested in the kid only out of self-interest. It simply isn't true. I've had high school coaches tell me, "Jim, my kid just isn't interested in Syracuse," and meanwhile the kid is on the other line calling me.

Of course I deal with AAU coaches. All the time. I go to AAU tournaments every summer, including some in which my own kids play. Everybody does, because they've become so important, much more influential than "street agents" ever were. So who do you talk to—the high school coach or the AAU coach? Well, you run into all kinds of combinations in recruiting. Kids who want you to talk only to their high school coach. Kids who want you to talk only to the AAU coach. One parent who tells you to talk to the high school coach and another who tells you to talk to the AAU coach. Those are the parents who need Dr. Phil.

It can be a minefield. My philosophy is to tell the parents, "I'm going to talk to you first, and anybody else you want me to talk to." The ideal situation is that you talk only to the parents, but that's not reality. In many cases today, the AAU coach has the kid from sixth grade. He's working with him, transporting him, taking him around the country, guiding him and sometimes becoming a de facto parent.

Having said that, I end up dealing with parents the majority of the time. Virtually all of my current players were in AAU programs—in fact, any player, if he's any good, will be in an AAU program—yet the parents were the ones most involved in recruiting. To recruit C. J. Fair, I talked to his parents mostly and his high school coach a little bit. Same with Trevor Cooney. I dealt with Tyler Ennis's father, period, but his father was also his AAU coach.

Anyway, how can I say that AAU ball is a bad system? One of my sons has played on an AAU team since sixth grade, in some cases flying to tournaments. My daughter also plays on an AAU team. Adrian Autry began his coaching career in AAU programs, which, on balance, have helped college basketball, not hindered it. Most AAU coaches know what they're doing, and the programs provide a structure after the high school season ends.

Even if the AAU coach is ineffective, kids are playing and learning about competing at the highest level. It helps players. And if a college coach can't wean out some of the fundamental flaws that a player might've developed in AAU ball, he shouldn't be coaching.

Plus, there's a stark reality about recruiting: An AAU coach might have five or six players a year who are good enough to be in your program, whereas the high school coach has one.

When we went on probation for the 1992–93 season, we had plenty of company—23 other schools were in that situation for various violations, including Missouri, Michigan, Maryland, Illinois, Texas A&M and Auburn, all for basketball. Looking back, two decades later, do I think the penalty was fair? I suppose. We broke some rules, and there are always consequences for breaking rules. But the whole thing was very hard on Conrad McCrae, and when I reflect back on that year, it's even sadder because of what happened later. Conrad signed a ten-day contract with the Denver Nuggets in 1999 but blacked out twice on the court, and the contract was voided. The next year, while playing for the Orlando Magic's summer league team, he collapsed on the court and died of a heart attack. He was 29.

It's very difficult to tune out the criticism that swirls around when you're on probation. It didn't help in this situation when one of my buddies, Dick Vitale, said my job was in jeopardy, which was never the case. But we got past our little contretemps and, for some odd reason, he felt compelled to challenge me to a one-on-one game for charity. It was to be held on a street court in downtown Rochester in the summer of 1991.

I was 48 at the time, hadn't even shot around, much less played, in years, was in terrible shape and, moreover, had gotten in 18 holes on the morning of our epic battle. It had to be 90 degrees when I showed up. There was a large crowd, an announcer, and 54-year-old

4

4

4

Dick in all his glory: wrists taped up, kneepads, the whole nine yards. Of course, that was in direct opposition to our agreement that we shouldn't try to kill each other.

The game starts, I get the ball, and Dick—whose playing career consisted of . . . tell you the truth, I don't even know—jumps in my face and starts pushing me. What? This is how we're going to play? So I made a halfhearted up-fake, drive, laid it in. Blocked his shot. Did it again. Did it again. A few minutes into the game, I'm dying, but it doesn't matter much, since Dick is already dead.

To summarize, I crushed him, 15–3. Over the years Dick always accused me of playing easy games, but *that* was the easiest game I ever played.

BEING OUT OF the tournament for a year is harsh punishment. You never know how many recruits make their decisions based on what happens in March and April. And if you're not there, you're nothing but a missing person. Plus, as the investigation goes on, there are reports that vastly exaggerate the violations, and you know of course that your opponents are using the sanctions against you in recruiting. I can't tell you if there was any player we failed to get because of the looming penalty, but I can tell you a player who never backed off his commitment.

Which is why a kid named John Wallace might have been the most *important recruit* in the history of Syracuse University.

12

THE KENTUCKY CONNECTION

t's not much of an exaggeration to say that John Wallace saved our program. He was the only big-time recruit we could get with the specter of probation hanging over us. John was from Rochester and loved Syracuse from the moment he started playing ball. It's as simple as that. He told me that he would've come here even if there had been a two- or three-year ban on tournament play. I'm not sure that's true, but he insists that it is. One of his future teammates, Otis Hill, remembers that he and John met at a Nike camp when they were in high school and John told him, "Everything will be good if we go there. One-year probation, then the Final Four."

Which turned out to be the case.

We mostly filled in around John, with guys like Otis (an undersize center with a big heart), and specialists like Lazarus Sims (great passer), Jason Cipolla (great shooter) and Todd Burgan (great versatility). That team would get us to the NCAA championship game against Kentucky in 1996.

But all of them had considerable assistance from another player who had graduated the season before that Kentucky game. In some ways, that player is the most surprising I've ever had at Syracuse.

Lawrence Moten was relatively unheralded when he arrived in

1991, the year before Wallace got here. Lawrence had been a stand-out high school football player, a wide receiver/safety, tough and smart. Still, he wasn't a high Division I football prospect (not big enough), and for whatever reason, he wasn't highly sought after for basketball either. As the recruiting expression goes, we liked him, but we didn't love him. Our athletic director said, "Do you really need this guy? Should we give him a scholarship?" And I said, "Yes, we need him. I think he's pretty good." But I didn't pound my fist on the table and might've backed off had opposition to giving Lawrence a scholarship been stronger.

Maybe it was his seeming lack of athleticism. Nothing Lawrence did left you bug-eyed. He was one of those players who make you remember that the game is basketball, not track and field. Lawrence got everything within the flow of the game. You'd peruse the box score at the end of the game and say, "Wait . . . Lawrence had 25?"

Adrian Autry says that he never paid much attention to Moten during pickup games before Lawrence's freshman season began. Everyone was more interested in what we could get from Luke Jackson, the son of an NBA star and a much better-known recruit from Texas. I told Lawrence that he probably wouldn't play much with guys like Adrian, Dave Johnson and Mike Hopkins in front of him.

Even before our first tough game, in the ACC–Big East Challenge, in Atlanta, against a loaded Florida State team (which included future NBAers Sam Cassell, Doug Edwards and Bobby Sura, a kid I should've recruited, by the way), I was wavering on our final starter between Lawrence and Scott McCorkle, a shooter from California. At the last minute, I thought, "Well, Lawrence is probably a better all-around player. Let's go with him." It was almost a coin flip. So Lawrence scores the first eight points of the game and 13 of our first 18, we win 89–71 and Lawrence continues doing that for the next four years. There was always the supposition that Lawrence might not make it in the NBA, which turned out to be the case. But he was great for us, and you can probably win some cash by asking this question of any non–Syracuse fan:

Who is the all-time leading scorer in the Big East? It's not Chris Mullin, Michael Adams, Otis Thorpe, Ray Allen, Pearl Washington, Derrick Coleman or anyone from Georgetown.

It's Lawrence Moten.

WE WERE BARRED from the tournament and played like it—we lost eight games in the Big East in 1992–93. But in some ways, the season was sweet. Lawrence had a great sophomore year. Freshman John Wallace began to show the kind of ferocious competitiveness that would lead us to that 1996 championship game. John likes to boast that he drove every teammate vying for his spot out of town. While I'm not sure that's precisely true, Glenn Sekunda did transfer to Penn State after John's freshman year, and, later, Chuck Gelatt left for a junior college and eventually DePaul. Let's put it this way: John didn't make either of those guys feel much at home.

I didn't know then that Adrian and Mike would end up as assistants on my bench, but they competed every single day on every single play. It's amusing to see them as close friends and colleagues now, because much of their intensity was directed toward each other. Both remain among the all-time favorites of Syracuse fans.

Hop has a starring role in one of Syracuse's most famous plays. In a late-season game at Villanova, we're up by one point with time running out. It's our possession under our basket. I tell Mike that we have one timeout left, but Villanova pressures us, the five-second count is running down and Mike throws a poor pass that gets deflected. Kerry Kittles picks it up, he hits a shot and the buzzer goes off. But they put 1.3 seconds back on the clock and we're down one with a slim chance of pulling it out.

In the timeout huddle, I have Mike in a "loving" headlock, trying to find out exactly why in the hell he didn't call for the timeout instead of throwing it away. As I'll find out later, Mike's mom is back in California saying, "Isn't that nice? Look how Coach Boeheim is consoling Mike."

Anyway, we draw up the "Laettner play." This was a year after Christian Laettner caught the three-quarter-length pass from Grant Hill, turned and nailed the jumper that beat Kentucky in possibly the most famous finish in NCAA tournament history. Hop gets it to Conrad McRae, who is no Christian Laettner when it comes to making jump shots. But it doesn't matter. Conrad turns and hits it, and I run up the court to hug Hop. "You are the luckiest SOB ever," I tell him. I'm sure Mrs. Hopkins was even happier with me at that moment.

We made a brief run in the Big East tournament, beating Pitt and St. John's to reach the final. With no postseason in front of us, we flamed out in spectacular fashion. I should say *snowed out*. Our final at the Garden against Seton Hall and its great shooting guard, Terry Dehere, was on the same day as the Blizzard of '93, and we lost 103–70, in many ways the worst defeat of my career yet in some ways the most predictable. We weren't going anywhere but home anyway.

Hollywood came calling in the summer of 1993 when I filmed *Blue Chips*. Through a mutual friend I had met the director William Friedkin, a Hollywood power broker who had directed *The French Connection*, one of my favorite movies ever. I was such a natural that they flew me to locations in Los Angeles, Chicago and French Lick, Indiana, home of Larry Bird. Or maybe that's just what the script called for.

A working actor prays for a speaking role, because that's where the money is, and for whatever odd reason, I was given two lines, neither of which will go down in movie history.

"I don't think he can play for you," I told Coach Bell, the character played by Nike Nolte. "He takes too many bad shots."

"Can he play for you?" Nolte answered.

"Well, maybe," I said in return. Friedkin wanted that phrase to be uttered "slyly," and I have to say, I think I nailed it. (He probably gave Gene Hackman the same direction in *The French Connection*.) One thing I didn't nail was my clothing choice in the scene at French Lick, where I wore a pink polo shirt. I can't remember whether it was my choice or someone else's, but I'll say someone else's.

Each of us basketball types—Knight, Pitino, Vitale, George Raveling, Marty Blake, Jerry Tarkanian, Lou Campanelli, and, of course, myself—made about four or five thousand bucks, but we still get residuals. Recently I received a check for—I'm not making this up—$8.67. Hey, it's found money, right?

We were good in the 1993–94 season but not great (23–7, lost to Missouri 98–88 in overtime in the Sweet Sixteen). That was Adrian Autry's last Syracuse game, and he made it memorable. He went scoreless in the first half against Missouri, and I told him he wasn't being aggressive enough. He got the message. So he went out and scored 31 points in the final 20 minutes, still a Syracuse record for points in one half.

LIFE BEING A series of what-ifs, I can't help wondering from time to time: What if I had skipped that Derby Day party in Lexington, Kentucky, in May of 1994? Or what if I had gone, but left before two striking women made a late entrance together? By then I might have had a couple of mint juleps (one is already out of my comfort zone) to loosen my tongue.

"I'll take either one," I said to the room in general.

But let me back up for a minute and explain my status. At the time, I had been divorced from my first wife, Elaine, for a year, although our marriage had died long before. I assumed I would find someone else down the road, but it's not like I was looking just yet. Sometimes it just happens that way.

Elaine and I had married in June of 1976, two months after I got the head job, and I will concede right now that it wasn't easy being my wife. Our life in Syracuse was a fishbowl, and my entire focus was on basketball, except for those few summer weeks when golf drifted occasionally into my thoughts. And you really didn't want to be around me in those days. I was insecure and had convinced myself that I would be fired at any minute. After a loss, I would take out that anxiety on Elaine. Our emotional bond began to fray early in the marriage, and while I know this happens to a lot of couples, it doesn't make me feel any better about it.

I was 41 when Elaine and I adopted a beautiful daughter, Elizabeth, the progeny of two college kids in no position to raise a child themselves. The arrival of Elizabeth was the biggest change in my life up to this point, and as a middle-aged man, it was about time I explored a relationship with someone or something other than basketball.

I know that Elaine had moments when she resented me during this period, but, to her credit, she never made her feelings public or turned our divorce into a bitter war of words in the press—and I couldn't be happier that she, too, found someone new to share her life with. She once kept a newspaper clipping on our refrigerator door about the memorial service for a young boy who had been accidentally shot and killed by his friend. The article said that at the service, the dead child's parents each sat with an arm around the boy responsible for their son's death, and Elaine had underlined the minister's quote. It read, "Forgiveness frees you."

Lord knows I've made my share of wise-guy comments over the years, too many of them in a public forum. But one thing you'll never hear from me is an ex-wife joke—because mine happens to be among the best. My own kids feel close to her, too. They call her Aunt Elaine.

. . . .

ANYWAY, BACK TO Kentucky and the belated but welcome entrance of those two stunning women. They were, as it turned out, sisters— the Greene sisters—one of whom was engaged. Juli, the other, was a free woman, and I was a free man. And even though getting re-attached wasn't my goal just then, I couldn't help gravitating into her orbit.

At first, Juli kind of kept her distance. She knew who I was, but that didn't mean much—until we started playing backgammon. Then we seemed to hit it off. She had a bit of Kentucky pedigree, since her brother had been a Wildcats cheerleader in the 1970s and she attended some of their games. But Juli wasn't zealous in the manner of many Kentucky fans who can't get back to their lives after the game is over. Put it this way: It did not take long at all to wean her off Kentucky.

Juli had many things in her favor, homecoming-queen looks being near the top. The youngest of six children from a musical family, she had worked in Chicago as a model, but after a year, the ugliness of the business had driven her back to Kentucky. Her new goal was to become a special education teacher.

For me, the attraction was instant and strong enough that I im-mediately rebooked my flight back to Syracuse, delaying the return for two days so we could spend time together. On our first date to-gether in Lexington, we saw *Tombstone*—appropriate, I suppose, for the son of an undertaker.

When an attractive younger woman decides to share her life with an older man—Juli was 27 and I was 49 at the time we met— it plays into the standard narrative of the young gold digger and the old lecher. In our case, there was another challenge: The older man is a big fish in the relatively small pond of Syracuse, while the younger woman already faces the geographical upheaval of being a native Kentuckian transplanted to central New York. Syracuse can be a tough place: tough weather, tough people. That toughness was in my DNA, but it was not in Juli's.

Before we were married, I took her on a Nike trip, and she could feel the tension. At the very least, people were curious about us. I could sense them thinking: How the hell are they going to make this work in a small town like Syracuse? And is something wrong with that beautiful young lady's vision?

There was Juli, tiptoeing around and trying to be unobtrusive, which is difficult when you're five-eleven and happen to look like a model. By dinnertime, we were literally trying to sneak into the room—and what's the worst thing that could happen in that situation? I'll tell you: You run into Charles Barkley. Charles spotted us coming down this wide stairway that led to the dining room—like a scene from *Titanic*—and bellowed:

"JIM BOEHEIM? HOW DID YOU MANAGE THAT? NORMALLY YOU CAN'T RECRUIT AT ALL!"

One of the people to whom Juli confided her fears about our relationship was Micki Krzyzewski, Mike's wife.

"I feel like everybody's talking about me," said Juli. To which Micki replied with typical candor, "Well, you are every wife's worst nightmare."

Then again, we were able to have fun with our relationship before it became widely known. P. J. Carlesimo was along on the trip, so I goaded Juli into knocking on his hotel door and saying, "Oh, I'm your biggest fan, and I was hoping to get an autograph." I should have let the scene play out, but I couldn't contain myself for too long before I jumped out and yelled, "Gotcha!"

Juli didn't want to get married right away. She wanted to see, understandably, if this was going to work and how much she liked Syracuse, particularly in the winter. So she came to town and enrolled in Syracuse Graduate School, where she eventually earned a master's in early childhood education. Sometimes she felt anonymous, and other times she felt like she was on stage with a spotlight shining on her. And that's with the relationship staying out of the newspaper. We couldn't have pulled this off in today's world. On our first public appearance together, there would've been hundreds of tweets. Eventually she told one writer, "I know some people are just waiting for me to show I'm just a dumb bimbo, but I gave up a lot to come here. I miss the South. I miss my family."

Finally, her hesitation about getting married appeared to be waning, so I decided on my best romantic move. I wrapped an engagement ring in a pile of dirty laundry. She said no and yes.

No, she wouldn't do the laundry.

Yes, she would marry me.

Her maid of honor was my daughter Elizabeth, which required Elaine's blessing. From the beginning, Elaine had gone out of her way not only to be nice to Juli but also to share Elizabeth with her. "You're one more person to love Elizabeth," she told Juli. One writer was amazed that Elaine had been so magnanimous. "Juli is a wonderful person," Elaine told him, "and I can't think of anyone I'd rather have Elizabeth be with."

Juli had an impact, beyond the personal one. She brought the idea of Midnight Madness from—this hurts me to admit it—Kentucky. She was a natural with people, so my charitable work, which now involved her, started to grow. If people at first were hesitant to welcome her, it has become clear that Juli is now more popular than I am. I see it all the time. *Oh, there's Jim Boeheim. Wait—here comes Juli. Thank goodness. We'd rather talk to her.*

There were a few comments from time to time—Jim Rome, the broadcaster, referred to her once as a "trophy wife"—but gradually they stopped, partly because people began to realize that this relationship was for real.

The differences between us are obvious. I'm grumpy, she's sunny. I'm closed, she's open. She was born with a sense of style; I was born with a sense of how to look, as one writer described it, "like a harried headmaster." We've been together for almost two decades now, so it's clear that some of each of us has rubbed off on the other. Okay, mainly she's rubbed off on me, particularly that style part. Almost immediately she got me to retire what used to be known as my game "uniform"—blue blazer, gray slacks. Truth is, I might have been ready for a makeover myself, but Juli certainly helped.

The biggest mistake someone could make, though, would be to consider Juli soft. She's nice, not soft. When you've been doing this as long as I have at one place, you reach the position where nobody tells you you're wrong. I could walk out of my office with my shirt buttoned the wrong way and nobody would say anything to me. Well, Juli tells me I'm wrong. Every day. Maybe it's just me getting my comeuppance after all these years.

When I think back on that time we met, I breathe a sigh of relief that Juli and I were at that same party and that, for whatever reason, she saw something in me. I have to think it was meant to be. Because two years later, that Kentucky girl found herself behind the Syracuse bench, cheering like hell *against* Kentucky, on college basketball's largest stage.

A COACH'S NOTES VI

John Clougherty, the supervisor of officials for the ACC, calls me in my office in the late morning a couple of days after our win over Duke. It's not unusual. There should be some contact between coaches and referees during the season, friendly feedback.

So as long as I have John's ear, I might as well present my number-one complaint so far this season. Which is:

Against our zone, opposing centers tend to camp out in the lane for as long as seven seconds. It's a huge advantage for the offensive team, and it hurt us against Duke. In a typical situation, the center gets it, and, if we don't collapse on him, which we tend not to do if he's not a scoring threat, the center just waits and looks, looks and waits, while his shooters get set all around.

Plus, the forward on the weak side sneaks into the lane to get rebound position or ducks in to catch a pass. That means sometimes there are two guys in the lane for more than three seconds. Even when a center makes his move, you usually don't get a good count. A guy is in there for maybe *one thousand one, one thousand two*. So our defense is reacting to it. Then he gets the ball . . . *one thousand three.* He turns, still in the lane . . . *one thousand four* . . . and starts to make his move . . . *one thousand five* . . . and finally shoots the damn thing . . . *one thousand six.*

So I'll ask the ref about it and he'll say, "Well, he's going to the basket." And I say, "Yeah, and he watched an episode of *60 Minutes* in there before he finally shot it." It should be called. To this point, through 21 regular-season games, three seconds has been called for us once and against us once. That's it.

I'm particularly attuned to the three-second call because (a) teams like to place centers in the lane against our zone to find shooters, and (b) we don't tend to post up our centers much, because they're not major offensive threats. John hears me out, which is all he can do. Every coach has his own little soliloquy, and a supervisor must hear them all.

What makes a good referee? On the one hand, that question carries the easiest answer in the world. A good referee is one who makes the correct call most of the time. But I'd estimate that 25 percent of calls are impossible to make. Ten refs could look at them on film, take all the time in the world, and five would call it one way and five the other way. What you're looking for is someone who is consistent and who keeps the game under control.

In truth, officiating has gotten better over the years. The new rules clamping down on physical play have helped. Some teams still get away with holding an opponent—I'd like to point out that zone defenses don't hold nearly as much as man-to-man defenses—but on the whole, referees make the right call. They're also more liable to whistle for the block than the charge, which is a good thing. You don't want to see defenders constantly stepping in front of drivers who have already committed to a move.

Also, the three-referee system has been a huge plus, because it keeps the veteran officials around. You can't have three old guys out there who are constantly trailing the play, but in big games I would rather have at least two graybeards who might move a little slow but who have better control of the game. You tend not to get those results where the home team shoots 32 free throws and the visitors take five.

In a game at Providence in the late 1990s, Etan Thomas, our center and the key to our defense, got two ticky-tack foul calls in the first four minutes. I'm going crazy, and Clougherty, who was then a regular referee, runs over and says to me, "I'll take care of it. I got it." And there weren't any more silly calls on Etan.

The best officials, see, are fans of the game—not in the sense of favoring one team over another, but in the sense that they want to see the best basketball played by the best players. They *manage* the game, which is different from calling every single violation. That's *micromanaging* the game.

Still, here is another stark reality: Across the college basketball season, the better players and the more respected coaches probably get a slightly higher percentage of calls, even from veteran refs. It's not like 80–20; more like 55–45. But—and this is a good thing—there is also the control factor of "visitors' refs," that is, refs who are really homers for the visitors.

I said that once to Jim Burr, a Big East ref who called more than his share of memorable Syracuse games.

"Jim, if there's a close call, can you deny that you go most of the time with the visiting team?" I asked him once.

And he said, "I can't deny that."

"Well," I said, "isn't that as bad as being a homer?"

Appearances to the contrary, I've actually had decent relationships with most referees over the years. I never got technicals as a player and, as a coach, I've gotten fewer and fewer as the years have gone on. A small minority of my players ever got technicals, and I've never had a player tossed, even Derrick Coleman, whom I cautioned all the time about flapping his gums. It's my job to jabber at the refs, not theirs. If a ref gets down on a player, he will make calls that go against that guy and, just as important, he will tell his fellow whistle-blowers. Then it will spread like a virus.

One final referee story: We're playing Boston College in the early 1990s and their center, Bill Curley, sticks his hand up through the basket on a Lawrence Moten layup. They don't call goaltending, I go ballistic and Tim Higgins comes over to calm me down.

A minute later, there's another questionable call and I give it the arms-spread look I'm famous for. Tim, who's on the far side of the court, charges over and T's me.

"I didn't even get up, Tim," I say. "I'm capable of much worse than that."

"What it was, Jim, was cumulative," he tells me.

"Tim," I say, "you don't even know what that word means."

13

THE LAST LOSS OF THE OLD BOEHEIM

don't know whether heartache is the best teacher, but it is a tough SOB. And few games in Syracuse history withered my pulse as did our loss to Arkansas in the Midwest Region, in 1995, which will forever be known as the Lawrence Moten Timeout Game.

Is that fair? No. Lots of things lose a game.

Is it reality? Alas, it is.

We had had a terrific 1994–95 season, a string of 14 straight wins that got us as high as sixth in the rankings, although we stumbled a bit at the end of the year. Still, with Lawrence in his senior year and junior John Wallace having firmly established himself as a scoring machine and team leader, I thought we had a chance to make a run in the tournament. I thought that even though we had drawn a powerhouse Arkansas team, the defending national champions and a second seed, in the Midwest Regional at the University of Texas.

The Razorbacks had three star players: shooter Scotty Thurman, point guard Corey Beck and interior scorer Corliss Williamson. But John Wallace had a simple solution. "All you have to do is be better than Thurman," he told Lawrence. "And all you have to do is be better than Corey Beck," he told Michael Lloyd. "Because I will *own* Corliss Williamson." I'd like to have a dime for every player John said he owned over the years, though most of the time he was correct.

Down 62–50 with about 14 minutes left, we made a great comeback. John and Lawrence were spectacular. We go up 82–81 with 6.5 seconds left. I call a timeout. We want to set up our defense. We talk about that and remind them that we have the possession arrow.

The huddle breaks, and I do something I almost never do: call another timeout to go over things again. Why not? I figured. If we get a steal or a held ball, we're not going to need a timeout anyway. The game will be over.

"We have no timeouts left," we remind everyone when the huddle breaks. Then we remind them again: *"We have NO timeouts left."*

Cue the heartache track. Lukey Jackson steals the inbounds pass—that's good. He sprawls on the floor—that's not good. Gets tied up—that's okay, because it's our possession arrow.

Except that back at midcourt, Lawrence has motioned for a timeout. It's what players instinctively do when there's a scramble for the ball. There's no rule on whether it's a smart play or not. Sometimes it is, sometimes it's not, but Lawrence, an intelligent player, had done it throughout his career.

However, it's definitely a disastrous decision when you have no timeouts left, which is what Michigan's Chris Webber had discovered two years earlier in the NCAA championship game against North Carolina, a much more enduring gaffe than Lawrence's.

Thurman makes one of the two technicals, we go into overtime and we lose 96–94. We had two looks to win or tie the game, but shots by Michael Lloyd and Jackson missed.

I felt terrible for Lawrence, who had had such a stellar career and who owned up to the mistake after the game, his last in Syracuse orange. "I just had a mental lapse," he said. The thing is, there's a little gamesmanship involved in that kind of play. The refs can ignore the timeout call. In fact, the official closest to Lawrence did let it go, while the guy who called it came flying out from under the basket, either because (a) he thought he was doing us a favor or (b) he knew we were out of timeouts and should be penalized for it.

Either way, it was an agonizing way to lose a basketball game.

WITHOUT LAWRENCE, WE were picked as low as 42nd for the 1995–96 season, which is one step up from invisibility. Even pundits who kind of liked us didn't rank us in the top 20. But I knew we had a chance to be good, particularly since John Wallace had decided to come back, although not before making us sweat. With two hours left to announce his decision, he still hadn't made the call. John had thought about coming out after his junior year when the Denver Nuggets told him they would take him at 15. But John had worked himself from a second-rounder to a first-rounder and thought that with another year he could become a top-five pick. That didn't happen. In retrospect, though, John looks at his senior year in another way: Our team in 1996, which was largely *his* team, was what cemented his legacy as a certified Syracuse legend. That was important to him.

I'm not sure what I expected, but we got a great win early at Arizona, 79–70. At one time we were up by 20 points, and I started thinking, *This could be a special season, especially if we can sneak up on people.* We did from time to time, but in other games we struggled. We had one reliable scorer—John—and sometimes that's just not enough.

But we had tough, resilient kids like Otis Hill, who had been brought up by a tough-minded father who ran a group home for disadvantaged boys. Otis always said, "I thought I had 14 brothers growing up." Otis's father had died right after his freshman season, and he struggled throughout his sophomore year. But we stuck with him, and he proved to be one of those gritty overachievers who couldn't be intimidated in the pivot.

Lazarus Sims was a terrific guard for us, not because he was explosive like Pearl and Sherman but for almost the opposite reason: He was reliable and almost always made the correct decision. One could argue that he was the best passer we ever had here, because such a high percentage of his passes found the intended target.

We had one other leader on that team whom people might forget about: Donovan McNabb, Syracuse's All-American quarterback. He had been a good high school player who could've possibly been a recruit for us—emphasis on "possibly." Donovan wanted to come out as a walk-on after his freshman football season, and, somewhat reluctantly, I agreed. It is very, very hard to play two sports at this level, even for an exceptional athlete like Donovan. Certainly the football staff didn't want him to play. But he insisted and I agreed, figuring that his athleticism could possibly help us at some point.

The experiment didn't start out well. One day in January I got a call from Donovan's father, who very politely said that he wanted to talk to me "about Donovan's playing time," which had been scarce.

I explained my philosophical position, which was, and remains today, the following: I do not talk about playing time with parents. Every parent—and that includes me—believes that his/her son/daughter should be playing more. It's the nature of parenthood, like assuming that the story behind the dented fender goes deeper than "I backed into a tree." This means that I would be terribly unsuccessful as a high school coach, whose job description, far too often, is explaining to parents why Johnny or Joanie is sitting on the bench.

"But, Mr. McNabb, your son is a great kid, and I respect you as a father, so I'll tell you this," I told his father. "Donovan came in a month or so later than he could've because he wanted to rest after football season. I understand that. But he's out of basketball shape, we have a terrific team and I'd be a pretty bad coach if I put him in ahead of the players who are better and more fit."

Over the years, I've had very few problems with parents. We even used to allow family members in the locker room after games, which sometimes made it look like a Thanksgiving Day gathering in there. Against all odds, we never had a single incident—no uncle from one family jawing at a cousin from another family—but we finally realized it was just too many people and asked everyone to wait outside. To be honest, sometimes I miss it. I don't see parents all that much, and sometimes they like me more than their sons do.

At any rate, I never heard from Mr. McNabb again. And you know what? Donovan was unbelievable on that bench. Cheering, slapping people on the back and just being a positive presence made him an important player on that team.

STILL, AFTER LOSING to UConn 85–67 in the Big East championship game, there was zero chance, as I saw it, that we could claw our way to the national championship game. Talk about bad harbingers: John missed the flight to Albuquerque, the site of our first- and second-round games. There was a power outage and his alarm clock didn't go off, which sounds like a dog-ate-my-homework moment but happened to be true. (I will say, though, that while John never had much trouble getting up for games, clocks gave him problems.) He still made it to Albuquerque that evening, but it was potentially a big story, and a lot of coaches would've made it bigger.

There were calls for me to bench John, make a public example out of him. I spoke to John, and it was over. I've told you before about my philosophy of discipline: If an offense is so beyond the pale, okay, it must be punished. But stuff happens. There are power surges. Clocks malfunction. Kids oversleep. If I had penalized John by not starting him in the first NCAA game, I would be punishing his teammates, the fans and, yes, if you want to look at it that way, myself.

Plus, sitting him only calls more attention to the incident. His missing the flight just did not rise to the level of a capital offense, never mind the fact that John played his ass off from the opening tip to the final buzzer and had a kind of contagious optimism about him. All season long, he had gathered his teammates at his house for dinners on Sunday night. They believed they were better than they were, and sometimes that's as important as anything.

So I called the team together and said, "Look, John is starting. There's nothing to talk about. No one answers any questions except me. It's done." And you know what John told me later? "An ease came over me when I heard that."

Unfortunately, no ease came over me in the first round of the West Region when we were up on Montana State by only one point early. Then we went zone the rest of the way and crushed them 88–55. Then we zoned up on a tough Drexel team and beat them 69–58.

Then came two of the most wonderful back-to-back tourney games in Syracuse history.

In the third round in Denver, we drew a talent-rich Georgia team. We went up early, then surrendered a 20–3 run in the second half to go down by 10. Worse, John was on the bench with four fouls. But I never believe in sitting a good player and watching the game slip away. So John comes back. Lazarus Sims, who wasn't much of a three-point shooter—hell, wasn't much of a shooter at all—hits two treys. We press all over the court and force turnovers. Still, we're down two with 2.4 seconds left, our ball on the sideline around midcourt. The odds are not promising.

John is our go-to option, obviously, but he's also our best passer in that situation, the one most likely to make a smart decision. But our options—Sims on a drive and Todd Burgan for a jumper—are all covered, and John lets loose with a long crosscourt pass to the opposite corner, the kind of pass that has every coach in America screaming, "Noooooo!" Somehow it just eludes a Georgia defender—it might've brushed his fingertips on the way over—and gets to Jason Cipolla, who takes an awkward, falling-toward-the-corner jump shot that goes in to send a 70–70 game into overtime.

(I would never call Jason graceful, but he did have enough post-basketball moves to have a long relationship with Lorraine Bracco, the actress from *The Sopranos*.)

Overtime is back and forth. John scores inside to put us up 80–78 with 15 seconds left, but Pertha Robinson hits a three-pointer from the corner, and now we're down one with seven seconds left. We do have a timeout, but things move quickly in that situation, so I made a quick decision not to call one. The court was open. And we had Wallace, the ultimate confident scorer. For some reason, they let John receive the inbounds pass just before midcourt. He takes a couple of dribbles, crosses over and lets fly with a kind of leaning jumper as a defender rushes up. It goes in for his 28th, 29th and 30th points of the game. We win 83–81.

John's foot was actually on the line, so it should've been a two-pointer, but that was enough for the win anyway. At our next practice, I say to John, "I bet you could never make that shot again." We stop practice and he tries—a couple of dribbles, crossover, shoot. He misses it five times.

But he made the one that counted.

NO ONE COULD believe we were a win away from the Final Four. It was widely predicted that we were ready to go home, because we faced number-two Kansas, which had a starting lineup loaded with future NBA players (Raef LaFrentz, Jacque Vaughn, Scot Pollard), a great shooter named Jerod Haase, who was their leading scorer, and, for good measure, a future certain Hall of Famer named Paul Pierce.

You want the truth? I didn't think we could beat them, or, at the very least, that we would need a near-perfect game, the kind that Villanova had in the '85 final against Georgetown. And that doesn't happen very often. But Wallace thought differently. "We don't lose to West Coast teams," he said. When I reminded him that Kansas was actually in the middle of the country, John, no geography major, said, "Doesn't make any difference."

Later on in LaFrentz's career, you would hear that he was "soft," and I'm not sure that rep didn't originate with this game. John and Otis owned him. And our defense shut down Haase, who missed all nine of his shots; it might've been the first time I've seen a player tell his team, "Don't throw me the ball." We win 60–57 and it's on to Mississippi State in the Final Four. If we beat them, I've got my eye on powerful Kentucky.

I had a different feeling about the Mississippi State game than I did about Kansas. I was almost sure we would beat them, even though they were coming off a victory over Kentucky in the SEC tournament championship. I knew we couldn't do much on the glass against their giant, Erick Dampier, and I was right. We got outrebounded 41–21. But I was pretty sure we could disrupt them defensively—we forced 21 turnovers—and hold on to win a close game by virtue of our composure, which is exactly what happened. We won 77–69.

So now it was Kentucky. And Rick Pitino.

THE ONLY WAY I can describe this game is "surreal."

Surreal that we had gotten this far with a team that was supposed to be worse than 41 other teams.

Surreal that we were going against a team coached by a guy I had hired 20 years earlier.

Surreal that we were playing it in the Meadowlands, almost a home court for Syracuse, despite the fact that at least half the arena would be filled with the most obnoxious fans in college basketball.

Wait . . . did I say obnoxious? I meant *enthusiastic*.

And surreal that the girl I had met two years ago—in Kentucky— would be sitting behind our bench, rooting for *us*. For me.

Juli says to this day that, had she been a debutante, the 1996 NCAA final would be the moment when she entered high society. She was behind our bench, seated near Kevin Costner, who by then was a Syracuse fan—one of his closet friends in acting, George Wyner, was a Syracuse grad—and was wearing a shirt with my likeness on it, something that only a Hollywood leading man could pull off. (Take *that*, Ashley Judd.) The cameras zoomed in on Juli, like astronomers examining a new and particularly interesting planet, while the commentators struggled to explain how in the world she had anything to do with me. What made it easier was that Lizzie, my daughter with Elaine, was sitting directly beside her, with the blessing of my ex-wife, who was sitting two rows behind them.

We did what we had to against Kentucky, a team with eight future NBA players: We dictated tempo. Yes, we turned the ball over too many times (24), but we never rushed, we took good shots (we were 50 percent from the floor) and often frustrated them on defense (they shot 38 percent). What we didn't do was pay sufficient attention to a freshman, Ron Mercer, who came off the bench to score 20 points.

As the years go by, the story line from that game seems to have become: Kentucky was in control almost the whole way, but Syracuse kept hanging close. Which was not the case at all.

We were down by just two with four minutes left and by only five with a minute left and our possession. Lazarus Sims drove into the lane and tried to get it to Wallace. John was calling for it high, but Lazarus made a chest pass, and Mark Pope stole it. John went after it too aggressively and was called for a foul, which was his fifth.

That was it. Our leader was gone, as was pretty much our last chance. We lost 76–67, but it was by no means a nine-point game.

When John and I talked about it later, we agreed on one thing: That was probably the only bad passing decision Lazarus Sims made all season. He and John had been friends and teammates since their early teens, and they had almost always connected. Except this time they didn't. That's basketball.

TO THOSE WHO cared to psychoanalyze me in public, 1996 was the year that the New Jim Boeheim appeared, although glimpses of the Old Jim Boeheim continued to surface with enough frequency that it was impossible to predict what you were going to get on any given day. I've never spent a day in therapy, so I'm not sure what to think about the theory that I morphed into some kind of new, kinder-gentler version of the old me around 1996. I suppose I accept it, but only to an extent.

First of all, yes, I felt "at home" for that Final Four in New Jersey, which was kind of like a Big East tournament on a bigger stage. That loosened me up around the media. It was reported that I even smiled once at a press conference.

More important, getting to the Final Four changes everything both about you as a coach and your program as a force in college basketball. We had been there in 1987, but that was with "overdogs" like Derrick Coleman, Sherman Douglas, Rony Seikaly and Stevie Thompson. As the theory went, I had done everything humanly possible to coach that team *out* of a national championship, whereas in 1996 I had performed like David Copperfield to get an under-achieving bunch to the title game.

If that were true, then I guess if Keith Smart had missed that shot in the corner in the 1987 final, I would have become the Genius Who Beat Bob Knight?

Yeah, right. All of a sudden people were saying, *Hey, maybe this guy isn't that stupid after all.* My throwaway line was always this: "It's funny that I was always considered one of the smartest players but one of the dumbest coaches. I guess I found smart again." Then again, I was in my 20th season as a head coach; if you're not better by that point, you should get out.

And, yes, Juli made a difference. I tapped into a softer side of myself, and that made me a more well-rounded person. Those early years of dating Juli and getting to really know her began an evolution that continues today. We had a son and were surprised when Juli became pregnant with twins. My life became about something other than Syracuse basketball. It became about *everyone else's basketball.* Elizabeth, the wonderful girl Elaine and I adopted, is bright and independent, but she didn't care all that much about sports or the fact that her father coached Syracuse basketball. Basketball is at the very center of our life now. I swear I did not calculate Juli's height when we first met and go, *Hmm, we could have some tall kids.* But it worked out that way. My kids play, watch and talk about basketball, meaning there is a lot less time for me to spend brooding about Syracuse losses.

You begin to catalog your milestones by your family, not yourself. The November 1999 day when we brought the twins home from the hospital? That was the day we ran off a 19-win streak to begin the season. The day in February 2002 when they christened Boeheim Court in the Carrier Dome? That was the day that one of the twins, Jack, wouldn't stop crying.

I started to plan practices around the kids' games and off-season recruiting trips around their AAU tournaments. It is a rare grace to have been given another shot at being a better husband and a better father, and I thank Juli for giving me that chance. And when someone asks just exactly how old I will be when my kids are ready for college, I say, "I was never any good at math."

14

ETERNAL RIVALS

John Thompson retired from coaching Georgetown in 1999. Rollie Massimino had left Villanova for UNLV seven years earlier, the same year that Louie Carnesecca retired at St. John's. P. J. Carlesimo had been in the NBA since the mid-'90s. Rick Pitino and Gary Williams were long gone from the Big East by the late '80s.

And though his legacy loomed above the conference until his death, in 2011, Dave Gavitt hadn't been active in its daily affairs since 1990, the year he left to run the Boston Celtics.

All of that is to say that by the turn of the millennium, the Big East wasn't what it once had been. Don't get me wrong: It was still a force to be reckoned with. Wesley Johnson transferred to us from Iowa State in 2008 and says that the first thing he noticed was how much tougher the Big East was than the Big 12. Nine years into this century, we would engage Connecticut in one of the most memorable games of all time, which took place in the Big East tournament final.

But the conference that we had formed, some of us kicking and screaming, in 1979 was not the same beast 20 years later. Many of the dynamic coaches who had formed the conference's personality had moved on, and a different geometry defined the Big East of

2000, which now included, for football reasons, Miami, Rutgers, Temple, Virginia Tech and West Virginia.

It wasn't as though this was a shock for any of us. When Gavitt left to run the Celtics way back in 1990, he and his successor, Mike Tranghese, talked about the large shadow of football. All of us basketball coaches were sports fans, so we knew about the large shadow cast by college football. We read both the papers and the tea leaves. We talked about it at meetings. But all we could do was keep playing at the highest level possible.

Between the Kentucky game of 1996 and the coming of Melo and G-Mac in 2003 is the right time to look back at what we *really* remember when we conjure up the Big East—the Big East of Pearl, Patrick and Mullie, the Big East of John's towels and Louie's sweaters, the Big East that spilled a bucket of blood, sweat and tears on a nightly basis.

IN ANYONE'S RECOUNTING of the history of the Big East, Jim Calhoun and UConn fans believe that they routinely get screwed.

They are correct.

Calhoun won three NCAA titles (1999, 2004 and 2011). He had a .665 winning percentage in 332 Big East games. In a general sense, he accomplished something that very few coaches have ever done: He adopted a program that was Nowhere and moved it to Somewhere.

But for whatever reason—perhaps because Jim's championships occurred around that time when the Big East wasn't quite as Big anymore—the Huskies get slighted. As Calhoun acknowledges himself, the character of the Big East was forged chiefly in the fire and brimstone of the Syracuse–Georgetown rivalry. But keep in mind that there were other battles that defined the conference.

Those two nice Catholic schools, Georgetown and St. John's,

were bitter rivals. In 1983, Carnesecca assigned one of his guards, Kevin Williams, to harass Ewing at every opportunity, a strategy that led to an exchange of punches between the two. After the game, Big John, never one to spurn the opportunity for a mountaintop sermon, proclaimed that he was considering advising Patrick to leave early because of the double standard of officiating that hurt his star player. I have no doubt that Patrick had to endure more than a few extracurricular blows over his four years, nor do I have a doubt that he delivered more than his share. Nor do I believe that John ever wanted Patrick to leave; if I had a player as dominant as Patrick Ewing who seemed inclined to listen to my advice, I would do everything short of tying him up and stashing him in a garage to get him to stay for four years. Which is what Patrick ultimately did.

Ewing was also subject to racial slurs at certain arenas. There was at least one incident at Providence and another at the Palestra, in Philadelphia, and John threatened to take his team off the court until some repugnant banners were taken down. I backed him on that. To my knowledge, there were no such racial epithets aimed at Patrick at the Carrier Dome. In fact, most of the verbal abuse was heaped upon Big John, just as it rained down on me at Georgetown.

There were always *some* fireworks going off in the Big East. Like Pitino and Thompson going chin to chin at midcourt, in a scene that resembled a jockey arguing with Gulliver. Like Pitt's Jerome Lane ripping down a glass backboard on a layup in 1988. (After receiving the assist, incidentally, from a point guard named Sean Miller, who now coaches Arizona.) Like the Battle of the Allens, Ray versus Iverson, when UConn's Ray hit a jump shot to beat Iverson's Georgetown in the 1996 Big East championship.

And like the home-and-home donnybrooks between Pitt and Georgetown in 1988, the last one, at the Civic Center in Pittsburgh, resulting in the game being stopped four seconds before it was over.

Say what you will about the enmity between Syracuse and Georgetown—at least we finished all of the damn games.

Then there was the time when Big John, in what was maybe his most comic, and canny, moment, wore a replica of the godawful sweater that Louie had taken to sporting on the St. John's sideline. It happened in a 1985 game between the number-one (St. John's) and number-two (Georgetown) teams in the nation. John unveiled it at the Garden and it seemed to take the steam out of St. John's, which got routed 85–69. Two weeks later, at the Big East tournament, Louie came parading down the sideline with a giant white towel on his shoulder, just like the one that had become part of John's sideline wardrobe. It didn't help; Georgetown won the championship final 92–80.

But for sheer tribal warfare, there was nothing like Syracuse–Georgetown. So many games, so many highs, so many lows, and so many controversies. They start with the "Manley Is Closed" game but don't end there. The rivalry between Big John and me could hardly have finished tighter—in 46 head-to-head meetings, the Hoyas won 24 and we won 22, including 13 of the last 18.

The memories come flooding back, and the only way I can make sense of them is to think about the players—and the coach—who made them so indelible.

PEARL
MARCH 10, 1984

As you know by now, Pearl was not a normal freshman. And I'm going to wager that few freshmen—in any sport, at any time—could've come into Madison Square Garden and put on a better show than Pearl did in the 1984 Big East final against the Hoyas.

We were ahead almost the entire game, and Pearl had done everything—spinning, crossing over, driving. He had only 20 points, but he kept us in the game virtually by himself with his scoring and ballhandling.

We're ahead by three late in the game when, during a scramble for a rebound, Georgetown's Michael Graham hauls off and punches Andre Hawkins, our center. I say this without fear of contradiction: Graham was one of those Georgetown players who crossed the line. What Graham didn't like was that Andre, despite not being the most talented of players, never backed down from anyone.

Andre crashes to the floor and referee Dick Paparo instantly thumbs Graham out of the game, which was the correct call. That would give us a two-shot technical and possession. But suddenly the three refs get together and start talking . . . and I know it's always trouble when officials start talking. Sure enough, the horn to resume play sounds and there is Michael Graham—like a condemned man with a reprieve from the governor—still in the game. He was called only for a personal foul.

When I demand a conference at midcourt, Big John looms over my shoulder. Another official, Jody Sylvester, intervenes and says, "No, that wasn't an ejection." What, was Paparo calling someone out at second base? So Graham stays in the game, which goes into overtime, and Georgetown wins 82–71.

Sure, John tried to intimidate officials. No question about it. But how often did it work? I really don't think all that often, not with the top officials, who were usually assigned to Georgetown–Syracuse games. Did his intimidation work in that case? I can't say for sure. Maybe the officials were just concerned that one of those protracted sessions in which a player shoots free throw after free throw would spoil the game. (That would happen in a later Syracuse–Georgetown game, as you'll see.)

At any rate, the non-technical led to a Vesuvian eruption on my part.

"Michael Graham, in front of 19,000 people, punched my player, and the ref had the nerve to call it a two-shot foul," I said at the press conference. "The refs took the game away from us. They didn't have the guts to call it. Today, the best team didn't win."

On my way out, I saw a chair. I had nothing against the chair other than that it was there, doing what chairs do. So I picked it up and threw it against the wall. I'd like to point out that this was a year before Knight, with much more subsequent attention, had his moment with a chair. Then again, Bob hurled it across the court during a game, a move I couldn't have pulled off with his aplomb.

There was no fine, not even a warning from the league office. In the Big East of Dave Gavitt, coaches got a lot of leeway. Dave understood our personalities and our competitiveness and knew that we would never let situations get out of hand. Well, not often anyway.

JANUARY 28, 1985

Georgetown was the defending national champion and the top-ranked team in the nation when they came to the Dome. Ranked 11th, we were good but not great. With Ewing on the foul line, an orange suddenly comes flying out of the upper deck toward the court and goes *splat* against the backboard. It's never been determined where exactly the thrower was aiming, but if it was the backboard, he should've been in the major leagues instead of sitting in our bleachers.

John pulled his team off the court. I decided that something had to be done, so I took the microphone and announced, "If anything else is thrown on the court, I will ask that a technical foul be called against Syracuse."

John and I met at midcourt, two masters of détente, and exchanged back pats to calm the masses. (We're like that.) Raf Addison had a big game, which was why, with 16 seconds left and us trailing by one point, I suggested that he take the final shot.

Pearl suggested otherwise. Like Jimmy Chitwood in *Hoosiers*, he said, "I'll make it." Or words to that effect.

So I call the play for Pearl, who had played a subpar game to that point—4 of 10, with only nine points. But if there's one thing Pearl Washington recognized, it was a crowd-pleasing moment. He let fly with a rainbow jumper that went in and won the game 65–63, our first victory ever over a top-ranked team. Thousands of Syracuse fans spontaneously stormed the court, spilling press tables and knocking around Tom Mees, from ESPN, who, while live on the air, had no recourse but to throw a retaliatory elbow.

Later that year in the Big East tournament, Pearl took a shot at Patrick, nailing him below the ribs. Patrick was momentarily stunned, then swung at Pearl. Tempers flared and benches emptied, but no oranges were thrown. Pearl later said that hitting Patrick was the "best feeling" he'd ever had. He's entitled to that opinion, but he should be glad that Patrick never got a clear shot back at him.

DERRICK COLEMAN
MARCH 5, 1989

We were terrible. We were getting embarrassed against the Hoyas before a home crowd of 32,683—then a record—in our final home game of the season. Maybe it was the unitards that I told you about before. We were losing 57–43 and I told my team, "Well, we have a choice. Lose by 30 or start pressing all over the court and maybe have a chance to win the game."

They chose the latter.

Many people forget that this was actually Citrus Bowl II. Less famously than the one that hit the backboard when Ewing was shooting, an orange was thrown onto the court, which resulted in a technical foul against us near the end of the first half. Things looked bad.

But we went to the press, turned that deficit into a 62–59 lead and finally won in overtime 82–76—not just because of the press but also because Derrick woke up. After having six points, four rebounds and three fouls in the first half, he dominated in the second and finished with 21 and 13. It was classic Derrick. He looked like he was out of it, physically and mentally, but then a switch got flipped and he was unstoppable. Even in a uniform he hated.

DAVE JOHNSON
MARCH 15, 1992

People sometimes forget about Dave, who got overlooked amid the Derrick Coleman–Billy Owens duo but who led us in both scoring and rebounding before John Wallace got here.

It was somewhat of a surprise when we got to the Big East tournament, because we had lost eight conference games during the season. We were unranked coming into Madison Square Garden but beat Villanova and Seton Hall and then took care of the Hoyas 56–54 on Dave's floater over Alonzo Mourning in the final seconds.

DONOVAN McNABB
FEBRUARY 8, 1997

To reiterate, Donovan was a good teammate in his freshman year. Surprisingly, he came back out as a sophomore, even though he didn't get much more playing time. But on this night, Otis Hill and Etan Thomas both got into foul trouble, which necessitated using Todd Burgan at center and putting Donovan into a swingman role.

The Syracuse quarterback made four of five shots and met Georgetown center Jahidi White at the rim for a blocked shot, helping us win 77–74.

I'm glad that Donovan got that chance, because he decided to concentrate on football in his final two years. And, no, his father did not call requesting more playing time for him.

DERRICK COLEMAN, BILLY OWENS AND JOHN THOMPSON

MARCH 4, 1990

It's a truly memorable game when you have to define it through three guys.

First, Derrick. He had been left out of a *Sports Illustrated* story about player-of-the-year candidates. I showed him the cover, and he took it out on Georgetown with 27 points, 13 rebounds and 6 assists as we won in overtime 89–87. The Georgetown center had two more points and just as many rebounds, except that the Georgetown center was two guys: Mourning and Mutombo.

Derrick never wanted to be identified as a center. He felt that centers were clumsy and one-dimensional and, dammit, he was a power forward. But whenever we needed D.C. to outplay centers, he went in and did it. One of my enduring regrets is that Derrick never went against Ewing in the heat of the Big East. Those would've been epic battles.

Next, Billy. We were losing 81–79 with four seconds left when Billy was fouled by Sam Jefferson, who bumped him as they neared midcourt. I concede that it was a foul only in the strictest sense of the word. About as cool as any player I've ever seen, Billy made both ends of a one-and-one to keep us alive.

(Why, oh why couldn't Billy have been on the court three years earlier in that final against Indiana?)

But the real star of the game was Big John, who was not around at the finish. He missed a great one.

With just over two minutes left before halftime and Georgetown ahead 36–33, the Hoyas' Dwayne Bryant was called for a reach-in foul. Derrick made the first of a one-and-one, but over on the Georgetown bench John made such a fuss about Pete Pavia's call that Jim Burr hit him with a T. Then John left the coach's box and started wandering, which he did from time to time. So the third ref, Larry Lembo, came over and gave him a second T. That call propelled John onto the court, where he promptly earned the zebra trifecta—a third technical from Pavia, the perfect geometric ending, since it was Pavia's whistle that had started the whole chain of events—and an early exit. Derrick made the second on the one-and-one call and made five of the ensuing six technicals in what looked like the end of a Syracuse practice session.

If you want me to explain John's action, I can't. He never could, either. It was a seemingly insignificant call at an insignificant point in the game. We had three Final Four refs working the game. Somewhere inside of him he knew he was hurting his team, but he just couldn't stop.

It happens. I know from personal experience.

At any rate, John pulled a brilliant move, as he had with the Louie-sweater maneuver, by raising his hands like a champion boxer when he walked off.

JOHN THOMPSON
JANUARY 31, 1987

We were at Georgetown a few nights after John had his shouting match with Rick Pitino. We met near center court before the game and I make a crack to John, something like, "You gonna fight me, too?" John then goes into a pantomime of a shadow boxer. We laugh. We embrace. Then we go out and try to destroy each other. (He won that one 83–81 in overtime.)

Why do I mention that story? Well, three years later we're playing Notre Dame at home. The Irish, coached by Digger Phelps, are not yet in the Big East. They beat us 66–65 on a last-second shot, and Digger sashays by me, slaps me on the back and keeps on going.

He literally *danced*.

In the old Big East, we fumed and feuded and fought for every inch. We cursed like sailors, battled like marines and schemed like politicians. There was no quarter asked, no quarter given.

But we never danced by each other after a win.

Man, do I miss the old Big East.

15

MELO, G-MAC AND THE BIG ONE

Coach, there's a kid in Baltimore you have to see."

You hear words like that a lot when you're a coach, and more often than not you ignore them. You ignore them when you hear them from your grocer, the guy pumping your gas, or a caller to a radio show. Unless he's a really *smart* caller, and there's not many of them.

But you don't ignore those words when they come from an assistant coach, in this case Troy Weaver.

It was the fall of 2000. We had finished four pretty good seasons since our loss to Kentucky in the 1996 championship game, including a terrific 52–50 win over the Wildcats in the second round of the 2000 Midwest Regional. But we lost to Michigan State in the next round, and we needed players.

Troy, who was from the Washington area and knew the scene, seemed unusually excited about this kid, a tall, skinny, all-over-the-court junior named Carmelo Anthony, from Towson Catholic High. We rearranged our practice schedule so I could see him in a Tuesday-night game in Baltimore.

Right away, Carmelo hits a three. Then he makes a steal. Then he dunks over two guys, makes another steal, hits another three, and I turn to Troy and say, "We can win the national championship with him. He's that good. Why did you wait this long to get me down here?"

"Coach," he said, "I *told* you."

So we got in early on Carmelo. He came up for a visit in the spring and verbally committed. And, fortunately, even when he began to destroy everybody at summer camps and during his senior year at Oak Hill Academy, he never wavered.

When Carmelo came to campus in the summer of 2002, he wasn't the physical specimen he turned out to be in the NBA. But since I had seen him in Baltimore, he had gained 30 pounds and weighed about 225. I was pleasantly shocked. He had turned into a six-foot-seven-inch monster.

Originally I thought of Carmelo as a two-year player, but when he showed up with his new physique, I figured he was one-and-done. I had never had a one-year player—Pearl had stayed for three years, and Derrick and John Wallace for all four—but that was getting to be the way of the college world by then. You don't coach a one-year player any differently, and you sure don't constantly talk about the specter of his leaving, not within the structure of the team anyway. You set your goal—*Win a national championship*—and see what happens after that.

Maybe if we hadn't won the title, he would've come back. I honestly don't know, and I don't think Carmelo knows. Carmelo did his work, went to class and never gave us any trouble. He made four C's and a D in his first semester, and if anyone wants to roll his eyes at that, plenty of freshmen who *aren't* carrying a basketball team on their back do a lot worse. But we couldn't put him in for the Wooden Award because his grades weren't good enough. Nevertheless, this much is certain: No college basketball player in America was better than freshman Carmelo Anthony over the course of the 2002–03 season.

. . . .

JULI AND I had gotten married in 1997—she figured she could live with me since I had demonstrated I could get past losing to Kentucky and Pitino—and was doing a lot behind the scenes to make my life easier. Since 1994 I had been active in Coaches vs. Cancer, an organization started by Missouri's Norm Stewart, and the Syracuse area had really taken to supporting it. In April of 2000, Juli and I held our first "Basket Ball" gala to raise money for the charity, and I was more nervous than I had been before our two national championship games. I was not—am not—a party planner. Juli had instincts for it, but she was a novice, too.

Anyway, we drew a crowd of 650. It seemed that everyone we had asked said yes. The whole evening was so overwhelming that I found myself with tears in my eyes. Everyone thought I had an allergy, but Juli knew. I was carrying around the memory of Jack Bruen, the former Colgate coach and a great friend, who had died of pancreatic cancer in 1997, at age 48. And there was, of course, Jimmy V. Our April gala continues today—soon we'll be at a thousand attendees.

The crusade became a little more personal the following year when I received a diagnosis of prostate cancer, which was what killed my father. I had been having difficulties with an enlarged prostate for a while, and a biopsy found traces of cancer. I could've chosen "active surveillance," which involves monitoring the cancer to make sure that it doesn't get worse, or I could've had surgery to cut back the prostate. But I wanted the cancerous and enlarged gland out of my body. I didn't want to be thinking about repeated PSA tests and biopsies, and anyway I needed relief from the enlarged prostate.

So in November of 2001, I had surgery with one of the experts in the field, Dr. William Catalona. I was out of the hospital in three days, by which time we were into our early-season schedule. I will admit that on a couple of occasions I made phone calls, from my bed and during a game, to Todd Blumen, our video coordinator, asking him to relay messages to Bernie Fine, who was coaching in my absence. We had beaten Hofstra, but then we lost badly to N.C. State and Georgia Tech, and I was on the verge of being rehospitalized, though this time in the psych ward. I'm sure my calls didn't accomplish much, but I couldn't just lie there and do nothing.

After I came back, I coached for a while with my catheter still in place. There is nothing remotely ennobling about it. Other coaches have done it. In fact, there was really nothing heroic about the whole episode. I don't want to be called a "cancer survivor." I don't want to dwell on my "battle with cancer." I had a medical condition and I took care of it.

There's a ten-year-old Syracuse boy named Nicholas Trivelpiece who has been part of our team for a few years now. Nicholas has battled brain cancer for a large percentage of his young life. He's become friends with players, attends our practices, sometimes leads us onto the floor and is one of the main speakers at the annual April gala. He's endured chemotherapy treatments and all the concomitant miseries. He fights every day of his life.

Nick Trivelpiece, not Jim Boeheim, fights a battle against cancer.

SYRACUSE NAMED THE court after me in February of 2002. I felt proud and honored, though my youngest, Jack, wasn't overly impressed—he wailed through the whole thing, believing, perhaps, that it should be named for Dave Bing. Then Georgetown went out and beat us 75–69. Had Big John been coaching instead of his son, I'm sure he would've been able to offer some acerbic comment:

"Jim Boeheim Court is now open . . . and we closed it."

I never thought when I walked onto campus in 1962 that I would have a court named after me. It was truly mind-boggling and remains so today.

But if I were being honest about that time, I would concede that something was missing. I would get asked about how it felt not to have won a national championship, and I would say all the right things. *Sure, it would be nice, but lots of good coaches don't win one. We haven't got the big one, but we're consistent winners.*

Truthfully, though, not winning it all was leaving a hole in my soul.

THE 2001–02 SEASON had ended on a down note, with a 23–13 record and a trip to the NIT. Any coach who says that he's "just as honored" to be in the NIT is full of crap. Major college basketball is about March Madness, and the reality is that it doesn't include the NIT, as hallowed a tournament as that used to be.

So mark this down as an understatement: We were waiting with open arms for Carmelo Anthony.

Frankly, though, we didn't know what else we had. Our other big recruit was Gerry McNamara, a shooting/playmaking guard out of Scranton, Pennsylvania, where I had played many an Eastern League game. Gerry was a winner who had played in three state championship games, but he was also a normal-size kid who lacked outstanding quickness.

Gerry had one of the most unique college basketball experiences of anyone who ever played, like one of those feel-good stories you read about small-town Indiana basketball. A friend of Gerry's father ran a travel agency, and he began taking Scrantonians up to our home games, about a two-hour ride. It kept growing until the Carrier Dome became a kind of northern extension of Scranton, almost a suburb. The total for Gerry's Senior Night game was 52 buses.

Of course, none of that fan support would determine whether he could actually play or not. Turned out he could.

Hakim Warrick was another important player, a six-eight forward with the spidery reach of a seven-footer. I knew Hakim would be devastatingly effective in our zone defense—we were still playing some man-to-man back then, and he could guard people, too—but he developed into a much more solid offensive player than I expected. The first time I saw him at a summer camp, he was long and agile, but he tended to get outmuscled during the scrimmages. We stayed on him, figuring that he would get stronger, and all he did was help us win a national championship.

Our center was Craig Forth, a big body who shot and rebounded just well enough to be effective. It can be a bad thing when you don't have a so-called dominating center, but it can be a good thing when your center doesn't need touches, which was the case with Craig. More to the point, Craig continued a Syracuse tradition of intelligent pivotman. Danny Schayes is a really bright guy. So is Etan Thomas. Craig was an Academic All-American in both his junior and senior years and the Big East Scholar-Athlete Award winner in 2005. That is not to say that smart people are necessarily the smartest players; sometimes the best players don't think at all. But our smart centers used their brains. In the case of Craig, I wish he had used his brawn a little more.

Our fifth starter was a senior, Kueth Duany, a solid defensive player, gifted athlete, good person, natural leader. I moved him to shooting guard to accommodate Carmelo, which was somewhat of a joke, since Kueth couldn't shoot. But he found ways to become a double-figure scorer and was also an effective rebounder.

We played 35 games in the 2002–03 season, and that was our starting lineup for all 35.

Plus, we had three terrific bench players in Jeremy McNeil, Billy Edelin and Josh Pace. Each of them had a role, and each of them knew it. Jeremy could come in and block shots . . . when he wasn't fouling. Billy, whose career at Syracuse would be hurt by personal issues, was immensely talented, a guard who could handle, penetrate, score and play tough defense. That meant that our level of play almost never went down when he came in for Gerry or Kueth. And Josh was the classic all-arounder, a swingman who played hard and smart.

In a way, we had a "perfect" team—not because it was so overpowering, but because we had all bases covered. Gerry could handle and shoot. Kueth picked up the garbage and could guard people. Craig plugged up the middle. Hakim gave us low-post scoring and a shot blocker.

And Carmelo was the Difference Maker, the Man, the best player on the court every time he was out there. In basketball, you don't have to have that, but when you do, you have an awfully good chance of winning. Just ask anyone who played against Michael Jordan's Bulls during the 1990s.

We just fit well together, and any coach will tell you that balance—on offense and defense—is a blessing. From time to time I'm tempted to hold up this team as a paradigm, not just because we won it all but because it was so perfectly constructed. But that doesn't help. You don't always have a player like Carmelo; in fact, you almost never do.

THE REST OF the nation was so impressed with our "perfect" 2002–03 team that we went unranked until mid-January, when we slid into 25th. We never did get higher than 13th, which says all you need to know about rankings.

We knew how good Carmelo was going to be, even if the rest of the nation didn't. Before the season, Gerry had had a come-to-Jesus moment similar to mine the first time I went against Bing. They were scrimmaging in Archbold, and Carmelo was just eating up Duany, who knew all the defensive tricks. Gerry called his father back in Scranton. "Dad, I just went against the best player I ever saw. It's not even close."

How do you describe greatness? It's a combination of so many things—talent, confidence, toughness, physical ability—that it's almost impossible to quantify it. But you saw it in Carmelo right away. I've had four players here who were ready to play at a high level right away: Pearl, Derrick, Billy Owens and Carmelo. And Carmelo is at the top of the list.

What you have to understand about Carmelo, too, is that he worked hard. He *wanted* to be a great player in a way that, say, Pearl did not. He also wanted a great team, and to that end he elevated the play of those around him. Carmelo knew that we would achieve greatness only if Hakim Warrick could be a beast inside, so he made sure to get him touches and work with him.

Don't forget that we were young—two freshmen, Carmelo and Gerry, and one sophomore, Hakim, were our core—and things didn't always run smoothly. Gerry was playing that peculiar position known as "combo guard," trying to both quarterback the team and find shots for himself. He had to figure that out. Carmelo needed to learn that he couldn't win every game by himself. He had to know that Gerry was sometimes not just hunting shots but trying to make plays for him and Hakim.

I had to figure out a few things, too. Yes, you have a great player, but you can't completely scrap your offense. You have to get a player like Carmelo the ball, and maybe you do that with calls from the bench, but it can't be just Carmelo *stuff*. We ran stuff for Gerry, we ran stuff for Hakim and we ran stuff for Billy Edelin and Josh Pace when they were in the game.

We won 15 games that year with second-half comebacks, and, while it might be fun for the fans to follow a team nicknamed "Cardiac 'Cuse," it is hard to play that way. Plus, the comebacks happened not so much because of our flair for the dramatic, but because it often took us 30 minutes to figure out what the hell was going on.

Chemistry takes time, and in a late-January game at Rutgers, it seemed like we had lost most of ours. We got beaten 68–65 and we were all out of whack. Carmelo got 17 shots and Gerry got nine. Great players invariably have people around them, a Greek chorus talking into their ear, and Carmelo probably had a few of them who were telling him that he had to do it on his own. But it wasn't just a Carmelo-Gerry problem. Kueth Duany took one more shot than Gerry in that Rutgers game, for example, and made only one, and Kueth was no gunner.

This balanced team was unbalanced on that night, and we talked about it. I stressed the usual message: We have to work together, because we're not good enough on our own. But if we do play together, we can beat anybody. With the exuberance of youth, the team had taken to shouting "Final Four!" when they broke from a huddle. After the Rutgers game, I suggested that we can that for a while until we regained our bearings.

Those kinds of moments are normal in college basketball. A team gets out of kilter and you have to regroup. What made this unusual was that this team, not highly regarded (we went into the Rutgers game ranked 19th), went on to win a national championship.

WE JELLED FROM that point on, losing only two games before the NCAA tournament, both of them to Connecticut. Truth be told, I thought that Jim Calhoun had the best team in the country, with players like Ben Gordon, Emeka Okafor and Rashad Anderson. After they beat us 75–61 at UConn and 80–67 in the Big East tournament, I wanted no part of the Huskies in the Big Dance. As it turned out, providence—good fortune, not the college—kept them away from us.

We didn't exactly get off to an auspicious start in the tournament. We barely beat Manhattan and might not have beaten them at all without Edelin's 15 points off the bench. Against Oklahoma State we were down 23–8 when I went with a defensive pressing team, using Edelin, Pace and McNeil, the latter of whom blocked a couple of layups after they broke our pressure. Trust me: 23–8 is an oh-shit deficit, and we were still down 31–25 at the half. Oklahoma State was a good team with a pair of brothers (Victor and Andre Williams) who played in the NBA and a great coach in Eddie Sutton. But it was early enough that we came back, again behind Edelin. Good thing, too, because both Carmelo and Gerry were flat, making only 10 of 29 shots between them. Edelin finished with 20 and we won going away, 68–56. It wasn't that easy.

It's a two-edged sword when a coach comes to the defense of a kid who constantly gets in trouble. That was Billy Edelin. Almost everything he did on the court was correct, but so many things he did off the court, particularly his dealings with women, got him in trouble, leading to his first suspension. Then he missed 12 more games because he'd played in a church recreation league during that suspension. He had played mostly against a bunch of ordinary 30- and 40-year-olds, but it didn't matter—he had violated an NCAA rule of which we weren't aware. So if I criticize the NCAA for that rule, it sounds like I'm excusing everything Billy did.

I'm not. He was responsible for his own behavior. He should've had a terrific four-year career here. His talent level and competitive personality were high. Instead, he's thought of as a troublemaker. I wish it had been different for him and maybe he could've caught a break or two along the way. But what happened to Billy is on Billy.

. . . .

OUR GOOD FORTUNE continued in the East Region in Albany. We drew Auburn, which was not a real strong team, and managed just a one-point victory. Again, it was the bench that made the difference, with Josh Pace contributing 15 points. Carmelo had an ordinary 18 points and I began to wonder, When is the real Carmelo going to emerge? In the Elite Eight, we met an Oklahoma team that just couldn't make a shot, particularly their best player, Hollis Price, who shot an ugly 3 for 17. We won 63–47 to qualify for my third Final Four. Now I'm beginning to think: Wait a minute, we're winning by double digits and Carmelo really hasn't gotten going yet?

While we were getting ready to play Oklahoma, I had one eye on the South Regional, which that year was in San Antonio, practically a home game for Texas, which was playing UConn. The Longhorns were good—they were led by T. J. Ford, the quick point guard—but they were absolutely not as good as UConn. And when Texas won that game 82–78, I breathed a sigh of relief that we would not be seeing the Huskies. To win a national championship, you always need one big break. For us it was UConn (which would win the national title the following year) drawing a Lone Star team in a Lone Star city.

WHEN WE GOT to New Orleans, the man from the local organizing committee who met us looked vaguely familiar.

"Coach, we're going to do better by you this time than we did in '87," he said. "We didn't get it right, but we'll get it right this time."

Then it dawned on me—he was the same guy who'd escorted us around when we lost to Indiana. Since we had not played that well in the regional and were not looking like a team that could go out and beat Texas or Marquette, never mind the juggernaut that was Kansas, I took that as a bad omen.

Then a funny thing happened before our semifinal game against Texas: A weird confidence settled over our team. I went to Carmelo and said, "Okay, this is your stage. I need you." He gave me a look that said "I know that. You don't even have to tell me." Before the game, Gerry told Mike Hopkins, "Hop, I'm not worried about this at all. We will smash these guys."

We did. Carmelo had 33 and 14 rebounds. Gerry had 19, Hakim 18, and we got nine strategic fouls out of Forth and McNeil. Pace and Edelin did exactly what they were supposed to do. In short, it was that almost perfect game out of my perfect team. We won 95–84. And I celebrated for all of about five minutes before I started to think: Can we possibly play any better against a Kansas team with All-Americans Kirk Hinrich and Nick Collison, a terrific little point guard in Aaron Miles, and a tough inside player in Jeff Graves? A team that in the other semifinal had absolutely sliced Dwyane Wade's Marquette into pieces?

We didn't even look at a tape of Kansas–Marquette. Why show it to them? That wasn't what our game was going to look like. If it did, we were in big trouble. The situation was somewhat analogous to what we'd faced in 1996 against Kentucky. This Kansas team wasn't quite as strong as that Kentucky bunch, and we were probably a little better, owing to the Carmelo Factor. But the Jayhawks were six-to-eight-point favorites, and though I scoffed at that publicly, I believed it to be pretty accurate.

A coach has to look at a big game both objectively and subjectively, the former so he can plot strategy, the latter so he can inspire confidence. One thing we absolutely needed to do was play tremendous transition defense, because Kansas loved to run. The corollary to that was: Take care of the ball so they don't get easy run-out baskets. Before the game, Carmelo even said to me, "Maybe I shouldn't go to the offensive boards as much as usual," and I said, "Good idea." That was a sacrifice, because, believe me, Carmelo loved to go to the offensive boards.

By the way, I didn't repeat my "We need you to be big" speech to Carmelo. He knew it.

What worried me most was getting off to a good start. Gerry took care of that. You could see in the locker room that he was ready to go, and he came out looking to shoot. He had six three-pointers in the first half, a couple of them from well beyond the line, real playground stuff. Several years later, I was an assistant coach on the national team that played in the World Championships in Turkey. Kevin Durant came out and silenced a noisy and hostile crowd by making three-pointer after three-pointer. That's who Gerry was in New Orleans against Kansas—he was Kevin Durant in Istanbul.

We led by as many as 20 points and were still up 53–42 at half-time. It had an unreal feeling. We played lights-out, and you don't often do that in a national championship game, when nerves are such a factor.

We talked about one thing in the locker room: They *will* come back. This *will* turn out to be a close game. That turned out to be the case, of course, and there is no doubt in my mind that we would've lost had we not gotten that flurry of threes from Gerry.

But he was emotionally and physically spent in the second half, when Hinrich, who is still an outstanding defensive player in the NBA, pretty much face-guarded him the whole way. We got very little from Gerry in those final 20 minutes, but that opened it up for Carmelo. He made one play in particular that sticks in my mind. With about seven minutes to go, our lead had shrunk to four points. But we got a steal, started out on the break, and Carmelo stopped right in front of our bench and took a three. Nothing but net. Four went to seven, and that's a nice cushion.

But it was tense. The last two minutes were played in 15 minutes of real time. Craig Forth fouled out with 2:55 left, when we were up 78–70. We moved Hakim to center, to go with Carmelo, McNamara, Edelin and Pace. Our lead was down to 80–77 with one minute left. Gerry was just about out on his feet. Carmelo missed the front end of a one-and-one. Graves, who never makes free throws, made one of two, and now it's 80–78 with 40 seconds left. Kueth Duany got fouled and missed the first. (Flashbacks to Indiana in 1987.) He made the second, and now it's 81–78 with 24 seconds left.

Hinrich's three-point attempt goes in and out. Hakim gets the rebound and gets fouled. But he misses both. (Flashbacks to Indiana in 1987, part two. Then again, we got the charity-stripe advantage in this one: Kansas missed 18 of its 30 free throws.) So a three-pointer will send it to overtime. Kansas works it around against our zone and gets it to Michael Lee in the left corner. Lee is not a starter, but he's a 50 percent shooter. Lee goes up . . . and out comes Hakim Warrick.

Early in the game, Hakim's responsibility is to just close out on the shooter, i.e., go toward him aggressively with hands up but also be prepared to defend a drive. In this case, though, his job was to go all out to block that shot. Which is what he did. As far as Kansas was concerned, Hakim came out of nowhere. One of Hakim's feet is in the paint when Lee receives the ball, yet he made it out there for a clean block. It was a play that few college players could've made.

And it stands as the biggest single play in Syracuse basketball history. Yes, there was Leo Rautins's tap-in to win the Big East tournament in 1981 and Pearl Washington's meet-the-freshman half-court shot against Boston College in 1984. But this won a national title. And if I ever need reminding of that moment, a photo of Hakim's block hangs ten feet away from my office chair, as beautiful as a Matisse.

And here's something else. Lee took the shot from the same spot in the Superdome where Keith Smart had beaten us in 1987.

Maybe that corner owed us something.

. . . .

THE LAST TWO minutes of that game took five years off my life. When I met Kansas coach Roy Williams, who, like me, had gone into the game as a two-time championship bridesmaid, I repeated the same thing that Bob Knight had told me 16 years earlier: "You're going to win one of these." I was right; Roy subsequently won two.

The feeling? Indescribable. John Thompson was doing radio, and he came over and gave me a big hug. All those battles over all those years, and it's guys like John, a title winner and a title loser himself, who truly understand how hard it is to win it all.

I know in my heart of hearts that I've coached better games than that 2003 championship game. Heck, maybe I coached a better *season* in 1996, when we got there with less talent. But a championship is what validates you. It's how the legacy makers keep score. If you don't win an NCAA championship, you will never get your due, which is the case for great coaches like Eddie Sutton, John Chaney, Gene Keady, Mike Montgomery, Rick Majerus and Ray Meyer, to name just a few.

Plus, a championship means so much not just to you and your team but also to your fans. And your family. I didn't break down after the game until I saw Elizabeth. I'm sure that the breakup between Elaine and me had taken an emotional toll on her, but there she was, as happy for me as anyone.

Juli and Elaine met after the game.

"I just want to congratulate you," Elaine said. And Juli told her, "This one is more for you."

The postgame memories rush together and become a blur. I got a call from Derrick Coleman, who was still playing in the NBA and couldn't be at the game.

"You're off the hook, D.C.," I say. "We won one in New Orleans."

We headed to the French Quarter and ate in the only steakhouse that was still open. We started out with a small group—family, a few close friends, Mike Tranghese, who was proud that a Big East team had won it all again—but soon we got recognized and were surrounded by a couple hundred people. It was raining. We ran into Mike Tirico, of ESPN, a Syracuse grad. You can't swing a cat without hitting a Syracuse media star.

Somebody handed me an orange cowboy hat. I have no idea where it came from. Maybe a Bourbon Street stripper had been wearing it ten minutes earlier. It couldn't have looked more ridiculous, but I kept it on . . . and was still wearing it when 25,000 people showed up for a delirious campus celebration in the Carrier Dome a few days later. I was introduced in a cloud of smoke. I felt like Springsteen. (Though I hardly sounded like him, much less the Temptations, when I serenaded Juli with "My Girl" at our gala a few weeks later.)

Those feelings of euphoria lasted about two days, maybe three. Then it was time, once again, for worry. Time, once again, for fear. But this time there was a little something positive tugging at me.

The kid from Lyons who had to beg for a locker had won the big one.

A COACH'S NOTES VII

On a cold night in the winter of 1992, I went to dinner in Syracuse with Jim Valvano, who was out of coaching by then and working as a commentator for ESPN.

"My back is killing me," he said, "and I don't know why."

It was just the two of us, and I didn't think much about it, but you could tell it was really bothering him.

A few months later he found out he had cancer, and a year after that he was dead. My first thought was how great it was that Jim had won that memorable national championship in 1983. Our game hasn't produced another Jimmy V. He cannot be replaced.

You can't fall prey to reminiscing when you're supposed to be game-planning. But I can take a minute, especially since I'm still trying to digest a Tyler Ennis buzzer beater that gave us a 58–56 victory at Pitt last night. It was a near-miraculous win. Jimmy V. was about miracles.

Yes, North Carolina State is coming to town, and it's impossible not to think about Jim. It's a dangerous game. We're 24–0 and ranked number one in the country, but we're living on borrowed time. We needed nine three-pointers from Trevor Cooney to beat Notre Dame 61–55 and that bomb from Tyler to beat Pitt. It's crazy. We're walking a very, very thin line.

MY RELATIONSHIP WITH Jimmy V. did not begin well. During the 1973–74 season, when I was an assistant to Roy Danforth, we drilled his Bucknell team 110–53. It might've been the worst defeat Valvano was ever involved in. In trying to energize the crowd at Manley, which was already nuts, Roy started leading cheers in the student section, about ten feet away from Valvano.

I walked by the Bucknell bench, and Jim was just seething. I didn't blame him. I'd be ready to punch something too. For 20 years Jimmy V. brought that up to me, even though I didn't have anything to do with it. We eventually became friends, of course, because almost everyone became friends with Jim Valvano.

One night, a bunch of coaches were in New Jersey at a summer camp. We're in a hotel suite about 11 at night and Jimmy announces, "I'm not going to bed." So we stayed there until 4:30, and I swear that no one else said two words. He talked for five hours. When you'd go to dinner with ten people, no one said anything except Jimmy.

There are lots of coaches who are good speakers—Lou Holtz is one—but it's always basically the same spiel. Jimmy was different. He was like a late-night host with a three-hour monologue. It was always fresh, always new, and if he ever got stuck he'd just make stuff up.

He used to poke gentle fun at Dean Smith, his chief ACC coaching rival. He did a great imitation of Dean insisting that he didn't want the University of North Carolina arena renamed in his honor.

So Jimmy would say, real innocently, "Well, Dean, why didn't you just *insist* that they name it something else? They would've listened to you, right?"

Before the name of the arena was to be changed officially from Carmichael Auditorium to the Dean Smith Center, Valvano grabbed a ball, dribbled onto the court, made a layup and said, "Ha! I just made the last shot before it became the Dean Dome."

Jim had a whole shtick about naming rights. He gave a speech on the Syracuse campus once and said, "I would've gladly named my baby *Carrier* Valvano, and it would've cost you a couple hundred thousand at most."

He was a physical comedian, too. He had us on the floor laughing one night when he did this slow-motion quarterback thing, hunching down behind an imaginary center, barking out signals, tucking the ball, turning to hand it off . . .

I guess you had to be there.

Had Jim lived, it's likely that he would still be broadcasting for ESPN. As famous as Dick Vitale has become—and few have done more than Dickie V. for college basketball—I think Jimmy V. would've been an even better ambassador for our sport.

THE N.C. STATE game starts fortuitously. Tip-off is pushed back from three to seven o'clock because N.C. State had a travel nightmare. They should be the tired ones, but we look half asleep. We're down 55–54 with 13 seconds left, N.C. State has the ball and I'm thinking our winning streak is definitely over. If they inbound, wait for the foul and make a couple, that will be that. But Trevor and Jerami trap in the corner, Rakeem Christmas makes a steal on a desperate pass and throws the ball to Tyler, who throws it to C.J., whose layup wins the game 56–55.

The likelihood of our winning the Pitt game when Tyler made the half-courter was about 5 percent. Same for this game, given the situation. The odds of winning both? Has to be around one in a hundred.

Somewhere, Jimmy V. is looking down, shaking his head, smiling and saying, "Those lucky bastards."

16

A CALL FROM THE HALL

A championship has its perks. An appearance on David Letterman. A trip to Augusta to play golf. A number of complimentary columns by pundits who previously thought that I wasn't fit to coach a junior high team. Best of all, a meeting with Hank Aaron, my boyhood hero. I was tongue-tied when we shook hands and managed to say, "You're the only guy I ever really wanted to meet." He couldn't have been more cordial, though he did not reciprocate by admitting to a lifelong ambition of meeting me.

Amid all that, the elephant in the room, of course, was Carmelo's decision on turning pro. Every place he went around campus, he heard shouts of "One more year!" and Carmelo just waved and went with it. But that didn't last long. One day in late April, he appeared in my office, sat down and tried to find a way to announce the inevitable. Before he even said anything, he had tears in his eyes. Then I had tears in my eyes.

"Coach, it's been a great year, but there's no way I can let this opp—"

"Carmelo," I interrupted him. "I understand all that. You *have* to go. You can't win a national championship and be almost guaranteed to be one of the top three picks in the draft and stay."

Carmelo cried at his farewell press conference on April 24,

too, and that might seem strange. He was on the Syracuse campus for exactly nine months and was subsequently picked third in the NBA draft, behind LeBron James and—permission to gag—Darko Miličić. But a team that wins a championship goes through so much together, collects so many memories in so short a time, that the experience is always vivid, always meaningful. That's one of the best things about sports.

IN 2005, I was elected to the Naismith Memorial Basketball Hall of Fame. There are no words to describe that honor, so I won't use many. You start out as a walk-on, you bust your ass for playing time, you're good but not great, you take a coaching job hoping to succeed, you hang around, you work at it 11 months a year . . . and one day something happens that seemed so unreachable that you never even thought about it.

They put you in the Hall of Fame.

Even better, I went in with Jim Calhoun, who by then had been a worthy foe for two decades. The "old" Big East was still alive. I got in one dig at Jim—"The only thing I can find wrong with the Hall of Fame," I said, "is that it's a little too close to Connecticut." And I got in another on my old friend P. J. Carlesimo. "Without P.J.," I joked, "I'd be another two years getting into the Hall of Fame." Some people didn't get the joke, but P.J. did. In actuality, every game against his Seton Hall teams was a struggle. (Even though we won most of the time.)

I turned 61 shortly after I got into the Hall of Fame. I had been through countless Big East battles, tournament battles, personal battles. I had won a national championship. The conference all around me was changing. I was getting ready to name Mike Hopkins as the official coach-in-waiting. The program was in great shape.

I've never been consumed by the idea of retiring, but I admit that it's passed through my mind. But then along came an opportunity that recharged my batteries.

At the suggestion of Mike Krzyzewski, Jerry Colangelo, the CEO of USA Basketball, inquired whether I wanted to be an assistant coach on the national team that would compete in the world championships and, two years later, in the Olympics in Beijing. Jerry had been the CEO who cut me from the Chicago Bulls 40 years earlier, so maybe I should . . . Just kidding. It took me about ten seconds to say yes.

The common thought was that Mike, who had been named head coach, wanted me because international play often involved zone defense. Untrue. The word "zone" never even came up in our initial conversations. We weren't going to pack our lineup with the best athletes in the world and stick them in a 2-3. Okay, there is one exception to that. In an exhibition game against Spain in Madrid in 2010, with the team that went on to win the world championship, I suggested to Mike that we go 2-3 out of a Spain timeout. We had a one-point lead with about 15 seconds to go. Spain was surprised, and Kevin Durant ended up blocking a shot to win the game.

But Mike wanted me for reasons other than the zone. Though there are similarities between us, there are also differences. Mike is a details guy, and I'm more of a big-picture guy. He wanted me to look at the games as a whole, spot trends and matchups that maybe he was missing. And there was this: The other assistants were pro guys, Mike D'Antoni and Nate McMillan. I think Mike wanted another college guy to make him feel comfortable.

I first met Mike at a charity golf event at Duke in the late '80s. He was a rising coach, but he wasn't yet MIKE KRZYZEWSKI in capital letters. The event demonstrated Mike's intelligence: He doesn't golf—ever—but he nevertheless recognizes that an outing is the best way to pry money out of otherwise sewn-in pockets. Then we coached the U.S. team at the 1990 Goodwill Games and World

Championships. That was right around the time that America was realizing that we couldn't send just anybody into international competition and expect to win. We faced a Yugoslavian team that included players like Dražen Petrović, Toni Kukoč and Vlade Divac, and they pounded us.

Mike and I didn't stay in close touch over the years, but I was his first call to be an Olympic assistant. He and P. J. Carlesimo were assistants on the 1992 Dream Team, and I'm sure P.J. spoke highly of me. (That must've been hard for him.)

Mike is the best motivational coach I've ever seen, largely because he's inclusive. The players and the other coaches all have a say. You give him a suggestion and chances are he'll implement it. That kind of thing inspires a team. In a career that has brought him four national championships and, soon, 1,000 wins, Mike's greatest attribute might be his willingness to listen. A lot of guys get to the top of the mountain and the only voice they hear is their own.

There was some question about a college coach doing the Olympic job because we are used to running the show, which is not the NBA way. But Mike is flexible. He understands that he can't coach superstars the way he coaches Duke. There are other outstanding college guys who could've handled the X's and O's, like Michigan State's Tom Izzo, but they might've been too rigid in their approach.

Getting back to Coach K's other assistants, Mike D'Antoni is an offensive innovator and Nate McMillan is a defensive specialist. My role was something else. I was the guy who gave Mike feedback on who was playing well, who should be out, who should be in. I was the one assessing the flow of the game.

Once in a while, Mike would say, "Okay, I'm going to come at them strong," and I'd say, "I don't think that's the way to do it." And Mike would say, "Well, I'm doing it anyway." And I'd say, "Well, you'll be wrong then." Most of the time he listened to me, because I picked my spots. No head coach wants an assistant in his ear all the time, so most of all you have to know when to shut the hell up.

It got me thinking again where good coaches come from. Who could've predicted that Krzyzewski would become maybe the greatest ever? Don Shula was a nobody before he became DON SHULA. Vince Lombardi was a high school coach and a college line coach—did anyone really believe that he would live an immortal life in bronze?

I'm sure the folks who hired Mike at Duke figured he would be good. They always had a strong program, with coaches like Vic Bubas, Bucky Waters and Bill Foster, but they never won an NCAA championship until Mike did it, and it took him 11 years. People forget that. They think you come in and win right away. John Wooden got the UCLA job in 1948 and didn't win it all until 1964. These days, the boosters and the press would've called for Wooden's head. And probably gotten it.

The Olympics represented a huge personal challenge, even in an assistant-coach role, but it was exactly what I needed at the time. Mike described how he had felt back in 1992 when Chuck Daly brought him on as an assistant on the Dream Team. He felt confident in his abilities as a coach but also understood that he was stepping up a level. That was how I felt.

I admit that I was nervous meeting these guys for the first time. Look, they're pros and you're a college guy, and you sense the distinction, even though you've been doing your job longer than they've been alive. And here's one of the first things that happened: LeBron James comes over and says to me, "Coach, tell me whatever you see that might help. You've been doing this a long time." LeBron was one of The Guys. Just as that 1992 team wanted Michael Jordan, Magic Johnson and Larry Bird, so did we pinpoint

LeBron and Kobe Bryant as our main targets. When they came aboard, everything else fell into place.

They showed all of us tremendous respect, and I suspect that I felt more relieved than anyone. After all, Mike D. and Nate were in the NBA, and Mike K. was the head coach, so I could've been just *this other guy*. But what I discovered was that players at that level have a sense of history. It went beyond the fact that I had been Carmelo's coach and he was on the team. They knew that I was Pearl's coach and Derrick's coach. They knew that I had won a national championship. They knew about the Big East.

And they know basketball. I'm sure many fans believe that LeBron gets by purely on natural talent, but that's not the case. (It might be the case with Dwight Howard.) We'd ask LeBron, "What play do you like here?" and he'd say, "The elbow." Sometimes you make the rules, but sometimes Coach K would say, "Do we need a longer practice or should we cut if off?" And LeBron would give an honest answer, even if that answer happened to be "More practice." They know their bodies.

The best word to describe the guys who signed on for the national team is "professional." They arrived early and went at it hard. They did the work, and some did extra work, like LeBron, who was polishing his post-up game all the time.

I took away something new every day. Like D'Antoni's offensive schemes, the way he replaces players when he runs the pick-and-roll, how he uses the roll guy to attract defenders so other shooters on other spots of the floor are open.

Or the way Coach K talks to his players. It's not so much that he's by nature a "people person," because I'm not sure that he is. It's more that he understands that players *want* to be talked to and *need* to be talked to.

But no competitive basketball experience, even with players like this, is without a crisis point. Maybe it was like that for the Dream

Team in Barcelona, but not in this day and age. If you recall, in the semifinals of the 2006 world championships in Japan, we got pick-and-rolled into oblivion by Greece, whose star guard, Theodoros Papaloukas, carved us up with his perimeter play in a 101–95 loss. I was tempted to say, "Well, maybe that wouldn't have happened if we had played a little more zone." But that wasn't the problem. We suffered from too little time together, which hurt our offensive cohesion, as well as too much confusion on how to defend the pick-and-roll.

And something else was missing: Kobe Bryant.

Kobe had been injured for the games in Japan but came aboard after that, determined to lead what was being called the Redeem Team, which vowed to make up for our disastrous bronze-medal showing in the 2004 Olympics in Athens. Everything changed when Kobe showed up. He had a dramatic effect on the younger players with his work ethic, how hard he brought it every day, his killer instinct at practice. During games, if we were up by 40, he wanted to be up 50. He lifted up our entire team by the pure force of his will. Mike Hopkins, who was with us as a workout coach, still talks about Kobe going one-on-one against him for a solid 90 minutes after a full practice.

Now, is there a flip side to that? Of course. The diplomatic way to put it is that Kobe can be *single-minded*. We'll be talking about matchups and Krzyzewski might say, "Okay, Kobe, you take him," and Kobe will say, "No, I'll take this guy instead," and Mike will say, "Okay, good idea."

Why not? That's how I'd handle it, too. The same thing happened to D'Antoni when he coached Kobe with the Lakers. Why fight him? During those 2008 Olympics, when we took back the gold, Kobe was just *that* good and *that* determined.

I'm not sure the average fan understands how difficult it was to have won it all in Beijing. It's a different game when international players compete for their own country. And there was so much pressure. Before the Olympics, Nike took us out on a boat with the Statue of Liberty in the background, and we felt like we were the last line of defense in the Revolutionary War.

When we finally won gold, beating a very good Spain team in the finals (which we had to do again in London in 2012), it was more relief than elation. Coach K and I definitely didn't want to be looked at as the college coaches who screwed this thing up.

When I got back in the late summer, I felt nothing resembling fatigue. I felt energized. I felt like I was smarter. I felt that while other coaches were taking the summer off, I had been working with some of the best basketball players in the world. When you get older, one of the things you tend to do is stop learning. You think that you know everything. I found out that I didn't.

As a result of my work with the Olympic team, we now use some different drills, run our shooting reps a different way. Mike Hopkins came back with a couple of little things that helped our zone, trapping on the wing more than we used to, for example. I just had this general feeling that I was more open to change, to trying new things.

Experiences are so important. You can start out and be a pretty good coach right away, but you should get *better*, and the way you get better is to listen, decide what needs to be changed and do it. To have been given that chance at my age was a blessing.

Now, on the other hand, the tendency when you get back from working with a professional national team is to see your own players and say, "Man, they're not very good." But of course they're good players. They're just not liable to be future superstars such as LeBron, Kobe, Durant and Carmelo.

The Olympic experience has gone on, beyond where I thought it would. There is no way I would've signed on for London in 2012 had Mike not accepted the job again, and it's almost unfathomable that we're going to be doing it again in Rio in 2016.

The team has transitioned from being Kobe's team to being LeBron's and Durant's and maybe a little bit of Chris Paul's team. I'm proud of the way Carmelo has handled himself. He understands that he's not the first option, and he's comfortable playing a subordinate role. And though there's not that adrenaline rush you get from a new experience, it's still an honor and a privilege to serve on the Olympic team.

Plus, Russell Westbrook makes me feel young. Inexplicably, he calls me "Jimmy."

But let me make one thing clear: For all the greatness of the Olympics, it doesn't top winning a national championship.

17

THE FOUR-DAY SHOW

The first call Gerry McNamara made when he got back to Syracuse the afternoon after the championship final was to his friends back in Scranton. They told him they were celebrating together and had, in fact, been going at it for quite a while.

"I'm coming home," Gerry said. So a few hours later, he was in a Scranton diner with his boys.

"Didn't I just see you on TV?" a waitress asked him.

Yes, he was the one shredding Kansas with three-pointers.

There has never been a hometown hero like G-Mac—the hero, really, of two towns: Scranton and Syracuse. He would get invited to kids' birthday parties up here, as if he was a magician hired to pull rabbits out of hats, which, in a basketball sense, is what he often did.

He was the best shooter under pressure I've ever seen. He wasn't the best player we ever had or even the best guard. Pearl and Sherman were better, and Adrian Autry, who coaches with him now, was a better all-around player. But I would guess that Gerry won more games for us with clutch shots than any player I ever had—maybe eight to ten games—partly because he was a four-year starter, of course, but mostly because he had a big heart and a big set of you-know-whats.

In the one season that Carmelo and Gerry played together, it was almost a toss-up deciding which one I would go to at the end of games. Gerry had that clutch gene, but Carmelo had more ways to score, so if we had enough time to get it inside, Carmelo was the first option.

But either one was capable, and here's a couple of examples from our championship season, Notre Dame being the victim both times. In a February game at the Carrier Dome, we're losing by ten points in the second half. The Scranton caravan was particularly large that night, since the town is filled with Irish people who worship Notre Dame football.

The Irish were ranked tenth and were really good. But Carmelo brings us back to within one with about 30 seconds left. We set up a play for Carmelo, but Gerry goes to the corner and no one picks him up. To that point he had made only two of his eight three-pointers, but he knew what to do when we found him. Up it went, in it went, we win 82–80, and that was when the legend of G-Mac began.

Flash-forward ten days and we're at Notre Dame in another close game. We go to Carmelo, he powers in and misses but tips in the rebound, and we win. He was—still is—one of the best ever at getting his own shot and putting it back, almost Moses Malone–like in that regard.

But after Carmelo left, we pretty much had one option in our endgame situation. What made Gerry more interesting was that he wasn't a great shooter. His percentages over four years were 35, 39, 34 and 33. What happened on many occasions was that he played so hard, so relentlessly, that he was simply exhausted at the ends of games. That's certainly what happened in the Kansas championship game, when he scored all of his points in the first half.

But Gerry's flair for the dramatic was on another level. In his sophomore year, the first season without Carmelo, he hit a buzzer beater to defeat Georgetown on the road, 57–54. In the first round of the NCAAs, we drew Brigham Young. Hakim Warrick, our leading scorer, got in foul trouble and Gerry had to take over. He made 9 of 13 three-pointers, and by the time the game was over he had the Brigham Young fans literally bowing to him. They must've thought they'd seen the second coming of Danny Ainge. We won 80–75, and Gerry finished with 43 points, his career high.

ONE COULD ARGUE that we never got as far as we should have in the three seasons that Gerry was here after Carmelo left. But no player in Syracuse history ever had a better four-day run than Gerry did in his senior year . . . and no player ever deserved it more.

The 2005–06 season had been up-and-down. I had managed to get thrown out of an exhibition game, the first time I had ever been tossed. It was nothing as dramatic as what happened this season, because it didn't happen against Duke on national television. It came early in November against the College of Saint Rose, a Division II school. Three straight times a Syracuse player went to the basket and got hit, and three straight times we got no whistle. I jawed about it, got hit with one T, kept jawing, got hit with the second and ejected.

Until that fateful night in Duke, that was the first and only time that I had gotten the thumb.

Gerry was fighting injuries the entire season, and we were not very deep anyway. As we entered the 2006 Big East tournament, six of our last seven losses had been by double digits, including a 108–69 drubbing at DePaul, the worst margin of defeat I ever suffered.

So heading into Madison Square Garden, we were close to toast. We had no shot at making the NCAA tournament unless we won at least two games, maybe three, in the Big East tournament. And though we played with great spirit against Cincinnati, we were still losing by two points when Gerry dribbled upcourt, split the defense and hit a three-pointer to give us a 74–73 win.

It was on that day that a story appeared in the Syracuse *Post-Standard* saying Gerry had been voted the most overrated player in the conference. The poll was taken among assistant coaches, none of whom was man enough to put his name behind the absurd opinion. In all likelihood, the same things that made Gerry a fan favorite—being undersized and a Caucasian in an African American game—were the things that counted against him, as if people thought, *He can't be that good.*

I took note of the poll after the Cincinnati game with these words, among others:

"Without Gerry McNamara, we wouldn't have won ten fucking games this year. Not ten!"

The quote still surfaces regularly as a see-how-much-of-a-jackass-Boeheim-is-with-the-press staple, but I regret not one word of it . . . although in retrospect I could've gone with "freakin'." Any coach who doesn't stand up for his player, particularly a player who did for his program what Gerry did for ours, is in the wrong profession.

(I have the feeling that when I get to the gates of heaven, the attendant is going to pull up a YouTube video of one of my press conference rants.)

Gerry's best was yet to come. In the next game, against top-ranked UConn, his three-pointer forced overtime. Then he hit three free throws in the extra session to give us an 86–84 win.

The anonymous assistant coaches looked more idiotic.

He wasn't done. In the semifinal against Georgetown, Gerry brought us back from a 15-point deficit with five threes in the second half and whipped a left-handed pass to Eric Devendorf for the game-winning layup in a 58–57 victory.

And the anonymous assistant coaches looked still stupider.

Gerry was exhausted by the final against Pitt. But the last three-point basket of his college career, his 400th, gave us a lead we never surrendered in a 65–61 win. He finished with 14 points and six assists, and an empty tank. Injuries and fatigue conspired to limit him in our first game of the tournament, against Texas A&M, and we lost 66–58.

Here's one more thing about Gerry: He played through more pain than anyone I ever saw and never missed a start. He had played much of his senior year with a stress fracture in his pelvic bone, which is located at the base of the spine. He couldn't put on his socks unless he was lying on the ground. It's one thing to play through injuries, quite another to play *well* through injuries.

As for the assistants who called him overrated, well, none of them ever identified themselves to me. I hope they read this and realize how moronic they were. It happened seven years ago, and I can still work up a good head of steam about it.

THERE'S A WORD you dread hearing when you're in this business as long as I have been. "Slippage."

Slippage seeps into a program in unremarkable ways at first. You have a bad year, then maybe you get back, but then you have two or three losing seasons in a row. Then it becomes "a thing" in the newspapers, and then the community can feel something bad happening. Coaches start using that feeling against you in recruiting and suddenly—or it seems like suddenly—your program has already slipped.

It happens. It happened to, in no particular order, DePaul, Houston, Georgia Tech, UNLV and Purdue, among others. One single factor doesn't cause slippage. It's a combination of things, and I'll tell you what exacerbates it more than anything: a fickle fan base. Nothing will wound a program quicker than a fan base that doesn't stay loyal. We have always had that here, and it's been a major factor in our success. You can have bad coaching years, bad recruiting years, bad playing years, but if your fan base stays behind you, there is almost no chance that you won't recover.

All that is a long way of saying that, while we have not had true slippage in this program over more than five decades, we did have two consecutive NIT years, which, by our standards, comes close. You can go to the NIT once every, say, ten years, but don't make it a habit.

I call for an asterisk here. Our 2006–07 team, which finished at 24–11 and 10–6 in the Big East, deserved to make the NCAA dance. Every other Big East team with that winning percentage in the conference had been selected to that point. The reason for our exclusion was that we didn't play a tough enough nonconference schedule. We lost to Drexel, which was very good that year, and we lost at home to Tulsa—both considered "bad losses." But we not only won at Marquette but also finished ahead of them in the league, and they got in. Georgetown won 20 of its last 21 games, we beat them by 14, and they got in. I could go on; never ask a bubble coach to deconstruct the reasons he didn't get in. And to be honest, I can't complain too much, because that was the only time since I've been around that I feel like we got jobbed.

But this is as good a time as any to talk about the NCAA selection process. To be blunt, I think they start off with a flawed philosophy, because each committee member seems to have his own set of criteria, which could vary from year to year. From some committee members I hear that what matters is how well you do in your league. Then I hear from others that it's how well you do against the *better* teams in your league. Then I hear that, no, it's how well you do *outside* your league. And while it's true that everyone factors all of these things into the equation, it's also true that they figure them in different proportions.

To me, the bottom-line goal should be this: Put the best 64 teams into the tournament.

Not the teams that play the hardest schedule. What good is it if you play six or seven hard games but lose four or five of them? It's really about whom you *beat*, not whom you *play*. And not the teams that seem to be playing best at the end of the year. If you're in a good league, coming down the stretch you might go 5–5 in your final ten games, and that's a helluva finish as opposed to someone going 9–1 in an inferior league.

No, the tournament field should consist of the 64 teams that played the best over the course of the season. All right, let's be honest—that's bound not to happen, because of automatic bids for the weaker conferences. Though I'm no sentimental softie, I understand; it's good for the tournament. But beyond that, let's do everything we can to get the best teams. The committee comes close, but there are always a couple of teams that don't belong. The third-place team from a mid-major might be more *interesting* than the eighth-place team from a power conference, but this isn't a curiosity shop.

Because for any program, it is *monumental* to get into the tournament. It's a big part of what you recruit on. So I would like established criteria. I'd like to know exactly what the committee is using to evaluate teams. I'd like it to be science, not part science and part *Oh what the hell*.

IF I EVER had worries about our fan base, they were assuaged in 2007–08, when we did deserve to be an NIT team. We went 21–14 and only 9–9 in the Big East, but we still drew an average of about 19,000 fans to our three home games in the NIT—two wins followed by a loss to UMass. Only in the Dome would that crowd look sparse; I remember it being a real nice scene, with people sitting wherever they wanted, much like a lazy afternoon baseball game.

I never felt like the program was in trouble, but we needed an upgrade in personnel. And we got one in Wesley Johnson, who transferred to us from Iowa State in 2008. Wes was as talented as any player in the country, and when he wasn't happy, he came to us.

I don't take many transfers, for one good reason: "Transfer" can be a code word for "underachieving," "unpredictable" and/or "malcontent." Wes was only our fifth transfer. (Since then I've taken a sixth, Michael Gbinije, from Duke.) You don't want to become known as a program saturated with transfers, just as years ago you didn't want to be a "juco program," a euphemism for "outlaw program." The juco situation has pretty much resolved itself with prep schools, which provide a preparation ground for those players who are in trouble academically or otherwise unprepared for four-year universities.

Wes also seemed to have another trait found in transfers: instability. He had attended three high schools and a couple of prep schools, and he was unhappy once he got to Iowa State.

But here's the thing about code words and generalizations: Sometimes they're wrong. Wes didn't get along with his coach Gregg McDermott, his coach at Iowa State, yet Gregg had nothing except good things to say about Wes's character.

Even though we needed a forward that year, I wasn't 100 percent sold on taking a transfer until we met Wes and saw both his talent and his personality. Then we kicked into high gear and convinced him to come before he took visits to other places, including Pitt. He came primarily because we fit the wide-open style he was looking for, although, counterintuitively, Wes's big problem was that he was too unselfish.

Wes had to sit out for a year, the 2008–09 season, and it was tough on him. The TV cameras and the cheerleaders aren't around at practice. But he also got in an unbelievable amount of work behind the scenes. At practice, he almost never came out. I played him most of the time with our second team, which was good for our first team, because he was better than almost anyone they were going to play, and slotted him in with the starters from time to time. On game days he would work out for an hour or 90 minutes on his own. (It was the same routine for Gbinije during the 2012–13 season after he had transferred from Duke.)

Wes lifted our team just by his presence. He was one of our leaders, even though he wasn't in uniform on game nights, that rare kid who had a sunny disposition and worlds of talent. Our backup center, Baye Moussa Keita, was like that for us this year . . . without that "worlds of talent" part.

Since we're on the subject, there is—always has been—much debate about the NCAA rule that mandates that a transfer sit out of games for a season. Why is it a good rule? Because if players could leave and play again right away, you would have *2,000* transfers instead of the 500 or so you have every year. I don't think people realize how many kids change programs every year, and the one-year sit-out rule is the main deterrent to mass player exodus.

And as for coaches not being penalized if *they* leave, well, here's the difference: Coaches can get fired. At any time. Yes, they will get paid, but they won't be working, and they might not get another job. If you give a coach a five-year contract and tell him that he won't be fired, that he's guaranteed to coach, then, okay, he should be barred from leaving without sitting out a year, too.

But that's not going to happen.

I do know this: If Wesley Johnson had been with us for the 2008–09 season, one of the most famous games in college basketball history would not have occurred. There's no way we would've gone six overtimes with Wes on the floor.

We would've needed only three overtimes—tops—to beat Connecticut.

All right, maybe four.

18

THE TWILIGHT ZONE

To reiterate, the Big East of the 2000s was not the Big East that we had come into, the league that had transformed college basketball in the 1980s and '90s. But that was as much a public relations issue as it was reality. The league didn't get as much attention, but we were still among the best conferences in the country, sometimes *the* best. We got a record 11 teams (out of 16) into the tournament in 2011, and, when you put us on the Madison Square Garden stage, we were still able to come up with a show like no one else.

Which is what happened on the evening of March 12, 2009 . . . and into the morning of March 13.

We were a solid team in the 2008–09 season, led by our backcourt, Jonny Flynn and Eric Devendorf. Jonny was like a comet passing through our program. He stayed for only two years, which is why people might forget how good he was. He wasn't exactly Pearl and he wasn't exactly Sherman, but when you look at his numbers (16.6 points per game and six assists) and the confident way he led us from his first moments in a Syracuse uniform, he wasn't that far behind either of them. Plus, though Jonny didn't physically resemble a marathon runner, he almost never got tired. He started every game in his two-year career and almost never came out, most notably during the game I'm about to describe.

There's possibly no name in Syracuse history that elicits as wide a variety of reactions as "Devendorf," which sounds like a villain in a melodrama. Some fans liked his devil-may-care attitude, his slashing moves to the basket, his unshakable confidence. Others despised his trash talking, his sometimes careless play and his penchant for getting into trouble off the court. In December of this 2008–09 season, he had been suspended for an incident involving a female student. The university judicial board recommended he be kicked out for the entire academic year, a penalty I thought was too harsh. He appealed, and it was eventually decided that he could be reinstated, to both the university and the team, after completing 40 hours of community service.

Once Eric completed that and was reinstated to school, I let him back on the team, a decision that was roundly criticized. A vocal minority thought that Eric should be barred from basketball permanently. I don't agree. I'm a coach, not an inquisition judge. If you go through the system, you go through the system, and I don't believe it's my place to impose an extra penalty on a kid. Anything that I punish a player for will stem from transgressions that happened within the program. And Eric, on a couple of occasions, did suffer penalties within our system.

What people didn't like about Eric was the whole *package*. He had the tattoos and the swaggering attitude, and when you threw in his off-court troubles, some people just concluded: *He's a bad guy.* He wasn't a bad guy. Yes, I wish he had kept his mouth shut from time to time, because sometimes he motivated the opponents, the flip side of the brash confidence that made him a clutch player. And I wish he had handled himself better in certain off-court situations. But Eric battled to become a better player and, more important, a better person. To this point, he's done that.

Another key player on this team was Paul Harris, who had been a high school teammate of Jonny's in Niagara Falls. Paul had a giant reputation and, no matter what I and the other coaches said to the contrary, some people were expecting Carmelo II. That comparison hurt Paul throughout his career and might have stunted his development a little bit. He was a double-figure scorer and a sometimes ferocious rebounder for us over three seasons, but he was no Carmelo, which didn't surprise us, even if it disappointed some of our fans.

Another starter, Andy Rautins, had been a bit of a gamble. Andy is the son of Leo Rautins, a beloved Syracuse player, and that was a lot to live up to. His mother definitely didn't want him to come here, and even Leo was hesitant. You know how they have legacies at colleges? Well, there aren't many legacies on athletic teams; the family connection in sports doesn't work as well.

When we visited with Andy, I told him there was no guarantee he would make it. Despite his obvious shooting ability, I saw a low-D1 prospect, not a Big East player. Providence had recruited him a little bit, but it was mostly schools like Siena and Niagara. But Andy wanted to come, and so we gave him a scholarship. He arrived in 2005–06, Gerry McNamara's senior year.

Andy is a good example of how it goes in the recruiting game. We're somewhat hesitant about signing a kid, but he wants to come. So we say, "Okay, but you're going to have to battle for playing time." He says, "I understand." Still, he sulks when he doesn't get enough playing time, which is what happened early in Andy's career.

Andy stayed with it, though, and became a reliable player for us, not only a good shooter but also a kid who could take it to the basket from time to time and someone who played a major role in the six-overtime classic. Andy is a good on-court model for Trevor Cooney.

WE CAME INTO the 2009 Big East tournament ranked 18th in the country—a very good, but not great, team. We beat Seton Hall easily to set up a quarterfinal game against UConn, which *was* a great team, ranked fourth in the country. By this time, Syracuse–UConn had become *the* rivalry in the Big East. Not that playing Georgetown wasn't a major deal, but UConn's program had reached the upper echelon of college basketball. The Huskies were clear favorites in this game, particularly since they had spanked us good in Storrs earlier that season, 63–49.

Still—and this should be obvious by now—few teams ever came into a Big East tournament thinking they were either a clear favorite or a definite underdog. Plus, we had had much tournament success against UConn in the Garden, having beaten them in 2005, 2006 and 2007.

When we tipped off at 9:36 P.M. on this March 12 night, there was nothing to indicate that this would be anything other than a typical hot-blooded Big East contest. It was a good game from the beginning, because it was close and competitive, but in truth, it wasn't extremely well played. Only flashes of regulation time come back to me, especially Arinze Onuaku making two free throws down the stretch. Arinze just might have been the worst free-throw shooter in the United States that year, with a percentage of about 30. He worked hard trying to improve, and you never know when the lessons of repetition will unexpectedly kick in.

The game was tied 71–71 with just seconds remaining, and everybody remembers what happened—or didn't happen—at the end of regulation. Devendorf let fly with a desperation three-pointer that settled into the basket after the buzzer sounded. But was it *released* before time expired?

I thought so. Eric thought so, too, since he jumped onto the scorer's table and started dancing, which is exactly what I would've expected him to do. (I was informed later that he was doing the Devo.) The refs conferred, and after a couple of minutes of staring at the replay, the verdict came back: Eric had released the shot a millisecond after the buzzer sounded.

"I take your word for it," I said to John Cahill, one of the referees, "but you better be right, because the whole country is going to be watching this." It turned out to be the correct decision, and in seven decades of watching basketball games I've never seen a closer call in that situation.

We had to battle back repeatedly in the subsequent overtimes. It looked hopeless in the third OT when UConn scored six points in a row to lead 93–87. But Jonny led us back, and Andy Rautins hit a huge three-pointer to tie it at 98 and send it to a fourth. Students of basketball history—and Leo Rautins, Andy's father, was one— surely remembered that it was in the third overtime that Leo had tipped in a missed shot to give us the Big East tournament title against Villanova in 1981.

We set up that play for Andy—a 2-Call, meaning a ball screen is set for the shooting guard, who comes off on a curl and looks to shoot. Pretty basic stuff. A player can usually get off the shot, so the main question is: Can he make it? Andy came off the screen, and the UConn defender was right in his face, but he just buried it.

We could've gotten a foul call in the final seconds of the fourth overtime when Paul Harris went up and got hammered, but there was no whistle. Maybe by then even the refs didn't want this thing to end.

Behind our bench, a couple of guys in suits, Wall Street types, said to me, "Coach, the last train out of Penn Station is leaving soon. Will you win this damn thing?"

"We're trying, guys, we're trying," I said.

Players and fans have subsequently described the game as having taken on a "surreal" or "fairy tale" quality by the third or fourth overtime. I don't remember it that way. As the overtimes kept piling up, the game seemed suddenly historic, but I only got more focused on trying to win. Our coaching staff grew more intense with concentration, trying to set an example for our tired guys on the floor.

If this game is going to be talked about for years, why not be the team that won it?

UConn had two good looks at the end of the fifth overtime, and when neither of those shots went in, I thought, *Okay, this is ours.* We had never led for one second of the first five overtimes, yet here we were, going out for the sixth. Their big man, Hasheem Thabeet, had fouled out, and we put a forward, Kris Joseph, at center. Kris actually got the tip in the sixth overtime, the first time we had the first possession. Who knows? Maybe that was the turning point. Andy hit a three-pointer that gave us the lead we never lost in the 127–117 win.

There were two crucial factors in our victory.

First, we had the best player on the floor that night, Jonny Flynn. He had 34 points, 11 rebounds and 6 steals. He was phenomenal when we put him in high pick-and-rolls. He got to the hoop, dished or got fouled. He made all 16 of his free throws, and many of them were in clutch situations. He played 67 minutes and had only two personal fouls.

Second, we won the foul-out game, managing to keep both Jonny and Paul Harris (29 points and 22 rebounds) on the floor. They were the only starters not to collect five fouls. We even got a couple of good defensive plays from a walk-on named Justin Thomas. He played seven minutes, about a quarter of his total minutes for the season. Justin, I thank you for your service, son.

The clock read 1:22 A.M. when the game was finally over. Another 14 minutes and we would've been out there for four full hours. I don't remember what I said to Jim Calhoun, but I saw a replay recently and it shows me stopping and trying to say something. Jim just nodded and kept on going toward the locker room, the same way I would've reacted. There wasn't much to say to the team, either. Everybody just wanted to get out of there. We had another game to play in 17 hours.

I wandered back onto the court while the custodians swept out the trash from a long evening and ESPN wrapped up its broadcast. "Are we still on the bubble now?" I yelled. The workers didn't even look up, but the ESPN guys heard me.

There was almost nothing open when we emerged from the Garden at about 2:45 A.M., and that was when it all seemed a little surreal, the streets of New York all but deserted and a basketball game not long concluded. Somebody said, "Hey, it's Friday the 13th." Our lucky day. Juli and I and a couple of friends found an all-night deli. As we waited for our food, we heard applause and shouts of "Great game, Coach." I looked over and did a double take—the guys were wearing UConn jackets. It was possibly then that I realized what a truly classic game this had been.

Some of our kids were so amped that they didn't get to bed until 8:00 A.M. And many people might forget what happened the next night: We had to go to overtime again to beat West Virginia 74–69. The next night we lost to Louisville 76–66 in the final. Louisville is a bad team to play when you're running on fumes.

A couple of final thoughts from the six-overtime game:

I hate when good players foul out, and a 70-minute game is a good argument for allowing a player to collect an extra personal foul if a game goes into overtime. They give you an extra timeout, right? Of course, I'm not sure that we shouldn't allow six fouls in the first place. We tried a six-foul experiment for three years in the Big East in the early 1990s and they concluded that it made the game too physical. Not true. What made the game so physical was that the Big East was physical.

Then again, part of me wants the five-foul rule to remain—now that we're playing all zone, we tend not to get into much foul trouble.

I can't call the six-overtime contest Syracuse's most *important win*. That had to have been in New Orleans in 2003. And both of the other championship final games, in 1987 and 1996, were more meaningful to the program. But I would have to call it our most *memorable* game. In a way, it's a hard game to talk about; the experience was one big, illogical spectacle—70 minutes of dramatic basketball in the world's greatest arena.

The six-overtime game was only one of several outstanding performances by Jonny Flynn in his sophomore season. He was great for us all year, especially in the NCAA tournament, where we handled both Stephen F. Austin and Arizona State, which had James Harden. We held Harden to eight points, and he's now one of the top scorers in the NBA.

Jonny decided to turn pro after that season, and—who knows?—maybe his heroic play in the six-overtime game spiked his draft stock a little higher than was merited. Still, I thought he would make it. He went sixth to the Minnesota Timberwolves, a team that didn't fit his style, then he hurt his hip and never seemed to regain his explosiveness. I feel bad about that. But when I need cheering up, I think about that March night (and morning) in Madison Square Garden, when Jonny Flynn became a Syracuse immortal.

YOU KNOW HOW coaches sometimes label terrible losses "learning experiences" or "an opportunity for growth"? Sometimes that's nonsense. But I can tell you all honestly that one of my worst losses resulted in a positive turning point for this program.

It happened early in the 2009–10 season, in an exhibition game against Le Moyne, a Division II school located about three miles from our campus, one of those early games you put on your schedule both as a tune-up and to help a neighbor put some cash into its athletic budget. I know people woke up the next morning thinking, *What? Syracuse lost to Le Moyne? On—ouch!—Jim Boeheim's Court?* But if you were there, it felt like a normal game, albeit an atrocious one from our perspective. Le Moyne shot jump shots and drove to the basket, we didn't stop them and they won the game 82–79. On that night, the Dolphins were clearly the better team, even though they were not even particularly successful that season, with ten losses. The defeat was comparable (on a much lower plane) to the U.S. team with LeBron, Wade and Carmelo losing to Greece in the World Championships. It made sense if you saw it unfold live.

It also conjured up a game in my distant past. During our junior year, 1964–65, we had beaten Colgate 91–52 at Manley Field House. The rematch in Colgate's bandbox Huntington Gym had a let's-get-this-over-with feel to it. But not for Colgate. Bing scored 45 points, but we needed triple overtime to beat them, 93–90. And we almost didn't get into the first overtime. With ten seconds left, Dave made a foul shot to put us ahead 74–72. But the old-fashioned scoreboard didn't add the point. So Colgate comes down and their star, George Dalzell, makes a shot. The place goes crazy when the scoreboard registers Colgate 74, Syracuse 73.

Fortunately, one of the referees, Johnny Gee, a giant of a guy who had been a major league pitcher, knew what the score was and got everybody back on the court. We almost lost it in the first overtime before somebody named Boeheim put back an offensive rebound. Then Dave took over in the second and third and we got out of there after what was probably the most memorable game in Colgate's history.

But I digress. The culprit on the night we lost to Le Moyne, as it had been on many nights, was our man-to-man defense. We had a meeting right after the game that lasted until 11:30. "Congratulations," I said to our guys, "we are now the second-best team in Syracuse, New York."

But I made a crucial decision on the spot: From that point forward, my Syracuse teams would never spend one more minute playing man-to-man defense.

We were already known for the 2-3 zone, but we often played

man-to-man in nonconference games and even in the league from time to time. That meant we had to spend practice time working on switching, defending the pick-and-roll, double-teaming, overplaying the passing lanes—all the rudiments of man-to-man defense. So I decided that we were a zone team and I was a zone coach. Period. It was probably the best basketball decision I ever made.

The season turned around immediately. The zone saved us prep time that could be better spent elsewhere, and during the game it saved us legs. Plus, we became more focused.

Less than three weeks after the loss, we pounded North Carolina 87–71 in the 2K Sports Classic, at Madison Square Garden, prompting Roy Williams to remark, "Man, that Le Moyne must be pretty good." A few weeks after that, we handled Florida easily in the SEC–Big East Challenge, in Tampa. It was then that the rest of the nation discovered something we had known for quite a while: Wesley Johnson might've been the best player in the country. Ohio State's Evan Turner won most of the player-of-the-year awards, but from my biased point of view, it was Wes.

Early in the Florida game, we ran an isolation for Wes, who was guarded by Chandler Parsons. Wes shoots a jumper right over him. Good. Next time down, we isolate, Wes fakes Chandler off his feet, goes around and dunks. I can still see Chandler, who's now a good defender in the NBA, shaking his head as he looks over at Billy Donovan on the bench, as if to say, "I can't guard this guy."

Wes had one of the single best seasons of any Syracuse player ever, comparable to Carmelo's 2002–03 year. Remember that Flynn, Devendorf and Harris had all left early, and we came into the season unranked. Wes carried us for much of the year until we found ourselves as a team.

We were number one in the country for a couple of weeks and came into the Big East tournament ranked number three. I thought we could make a deep run, but we desperately needed to stay healthy.

We didn't. Our center, Arinze Onuaku, who had developed into a solid post presence, injured his quadriceps in our first Big East tournament game, against Georgetown, and that took a lot out of us. We reached the Sweet Sixteen, where we lost 63–59 to the Butler team that made its Cinderella run to the final, finally losing to Duke.

When you've been coaching as long as I have, it's a fool's game to go back and remember all the could-have-beens. But this one is hard to get out of my head. With Arinze, I think we were as good as anybody in the country.

I won most of the major coaching awards that year, probably because we were better than anyone expected despite having lost so many key players and not having an experienced point guard. I'm not about to return any awards, but when you have a player like Wes, he sets the template for a team. He was unselfish and multi-talented, so the necessity of having a veteran quarterback to run the show was minimized. I owe a big debt to Wes . . . as well as to our Syracuse brothers, Le Moyne College.

I LIKE AN established starting five. If I were a football coach, I'd be the kind who decides on a quarterback—early—and sticks with him.

As we entered the 2010–11 season, I saw us as having four established starters: a backcourt of Scoop Jardine and Brandon Triche, both of whom had learned much by coming off the bench on the Wes Johnson team, and a forward combo of slasher Kris Joseph and solid post player Rick Jackson. The fifth spot was up for grabs, but what I didn't need was another swingman/forward-guard type.

Which brings me to the subject of Dion Waiters, an immensely talented player who was a freshman on this team. Was he good enough to start on most teams in the country? Yes. Was he good enough to start for us? Yes. But was he *better* than Scoop and Brandon as a tandem? No.

It is an ongoing debate and a difficult situation that comes up frequently in coaching: How do you handle talented freshmen who expect to start and who get impatient, even angry, on the bench when they do not?

You have to remember that, as tough as it might be for players who don't believe they're getting enough minutes, it used to be worse. Much worse. When I was playing, we had 20 scholarship players. You didn't play varsity as a freshman, and when you looked up you saw 15 guys on the varsity. If you think unhappy bench players are a creation of modern times, think again—it's just that young players didn't receive as much publicity back then, didn't come to campus with gaudy résumés and dreams of first-round futures, as Dion did.

We got through the 2010–11 season okay. Scoop and Brandon were solid, and we got a lot out of Dion as a sixth or seventh man. C. J. Fair, Fab Melo, Baye Moussa Keita and freshman James Southerland were all on that team. Handing out minutes in large packages was difficult.

But Dion made it clear that he intended to be a starter for the 2011–12 season. And I had to make it clear that he wouldn't be. When we talked in the spring, here's what I told him:

You will play a lot and even be in the game in key situations. Everyone will know about you, because we will have a very, very good team. You will probably go to the NBA after your sophomore year, because you're an NBA player, and you'll probably be drafted high. But you're not going to start, because I think we're better with Scoop and Brandon starting and you giving us a spark off the bench. That's the way it is. If you can't live with that, then you need to transfer.

Dion left the office and made it obvious that my logic was not his logic.

Understand that I didn't want him to transfer, but I also knew that I needed to communicate my message right away. The other way I could've done it was to leave the starting spots open, perhaps to inspire more competitiveness. I don't see it that way. It would undermine my credibility if I declared an open competition and then went with my first choice anyway.

In truth, I never thought that Dion would transfer, because his mother didn't want him to. She was an advocate for our point of view.

So what happened? Dion averaged 12.6 points (second most behind Kris Joseph) and played more minutes than Brandon and almost as many as Scoop without ever being announced as one of the starting five. He was the fourth pick in the draft, and Dion has thanked me several times for helping him to mature.

Most of all, Dion played a key role on a team that won 19 straight games to start the season and was ranked number one for over a month.

I wish that 2011–12 season could be remembered for things like that. But that's not reality.

A COACH'S NOTES VIII

This is what everybody is waiting for, right? The Boeheim Sport Coat Shuffle. Cameron Indoor Stadium, February 22, 2014. Oh, what a night. (The Dells, original release 1956.)

Let's begin at the end. I'm on the bus after the game when my cell phone rings. It's been buzzing for a while, but I've ignored it. What I don't need now is long conversations, which I don't indulge in during the best of times, and this is clearly not the best of times. The caller ID reads KRZYZEWSKI.

"I'm sorry, Mike," I say by way of greeting. "I got a little crazy."

"No need to be," says Mike. "I understand completely."

"I hope this didn't mess up the game too badly," I say.

"Are you kidding?" says Mike. "People will remember this one for a long time."

We exchange a few more pleasantries before we hang up. I look around. The bus is almost silent. Outside of our own little bubble, though, the basketball world is buzzing.

. . . .

BY THE TIME of the Duke game at Cameron, which was our 14th in the conference, Syracuse had become, for all intents and purposes, an ACC team. Certainly the change in conference didn't matter much to our players—it's all just basketball to them. I didn't know whether the average fan could identify UConn as a member of the American Athletic Conference or rattle off every member of the reconfigured Big East, but we had planted our flag squarely in the belly of our new league with that February 1 overtime classic against Duke at the Dome.

As a longtime Big Easterner, though, I couldn't help but feel some pangs for the old league. And certainly there were those in the ACC who weren't thrilled with me, the Boeheim sarcasm sometimes falling flat below the Mason–Dixon Line.

I had fired the first verbal shot across the ACC's bow the previous season, during a game at Providence. I wasn't trying to start anything; mostly I was feeling sentimental about Dave Gavitt (Providence had been his home) and the old days and started reminiscing about the great restaurants in that town. "Now, I go down to Clemson, South Carolina," I said. "I'm sure there's a couple Denny's down there." After that, a joke I made about Waffle Houses in the ACC made it into the public record.

Suddenly Boeheim was a jerk or, at best, a northern snob. Columns were written about it, and I heard it from fans on road trips. But you have to understand where I was coming from. Though we might've been culinary rubes when we started—at least I was—we thrived on a restaurant culture built around the Big East cities. P. J. Carlesimo knows more maître d's and chefs around the country than Bobby Flay.

It became important for us to get a good meal on the road, a way to cut through the tension. Restaurants became a way of life for all of us eastern coaches. Take Mike Fratello, who, though he never coached in the Big East—a long time ago, I did interview him for an assistant's position but didn't hire him, because he already had a job—was a friend to several of us and around our crowd a lot. Fratello would find out where we were going to dinner that evening, go there in the afternoon, lay down his credit card and pay in advance. Eating a good meal and arguing about who was going to pay was a way we showed respect, even if we did nothing but insult one another from salad through dessert.

The insult was indeed the very essence of our language in the Big East, the fulcrum of our communication. When somebody asked me why Pitino had not attended the 2013 ACC spring meeting on Amelia Island, I referenced Rick's being a racehorse baron and said, "He's still at the Kentucky Derby waiting for his horse to come in." Compared with the way we slung around insults in the Big East, Denny's and Waffle House references were nothing. What if I suddenly start referring to Buzz Williams, the new coach at Virginia Tech, as Wacko, like we used to call Gary Williams?

I have no doubt that the Syracuse bean counters are happier with us in the ACC. Our pregame meal at the hotel, which was nothing sumptuous, would cost as much as $110 per person during the Big East tournament. Four of us went out to an Italian restaurant in Clemson and it cost $150; it would've been $350 at almost any Big East stop (except Syracuse) and probably $500 in New York.

And, yes, the food in the ACC was very good. And, yes, we stayed at some excellent hotels, particularly one in Blacksburg, Virginia. I was always careful to provide any positive restaurant and hotel reviews to the locals.

Still, there are subtle differences between the Big East and the ACC, little things that make an impression on you, particularly off the court.

ACC luncheons, dinners and press get-togethers, for example, attract all sorts of sponsors and business people. They're more of an "event" than a basketball gathering, business people looking to mingle and press the flesh. Big East functions, on the other hand, tended to include just the coaches, league officials and sometimes wives, with the main business being basketball and insults. They weren't community-oriented. You're getting together over cracked crab in New York? Big deal. I'll wait for the games.

At root, the ACC is a club, formal, official and proper, but not without backroom feuds and nastiness. The Big East, by contrast, was a fraternity, complete with the spirit of brotherhood that bound each coach to the other, even if our civility would occasionally crumble and we'd have ourselves a good food fight.

Jim Valvano had a little routine he did about the difference between the Big East and the ACC. He would broadcast a Syracuse–UConn game and he'd describe Calhoun and me going at each other, the referees snarling, the fans F-you-ing each other—and that was all before the opening tip. Then he'd go down to the ACC and everything would be nice and gentlemanly and outwardly civil . . . until the cameras were off. (None of that civil stuff, by the way, applies to Cameron.)

Krzyzewski has accurately observed that the leagues reflected their respective geographies. The fan base of the Big East was urban, more professional sports, more Yankees–Red Sox, Celtics–Sixers bitterness, more overt hostility, while the ACC has a collegiate, let's-cheer-for-all-the-kids ambience—some of it, to be sure, contrived. The Big East celebrated a cult of in-your-face coaches, while the ACC was about "leaders of programs." Coach K gets more than his share of publicity, of course, but that's because he's won so much, and such a large percentage of the rest of the country hates Duke.

For my part, I didn't feel that much like the classic, feeling-my-way-in-a-new-conference underdog. I've been around too long, and it was obvious that I came in at relatively the same level as the esteemed ACC coaches like Mike and Roy Williams. Syracuse was an overdog, not an underdog, and people wanted to kick our butt from the beginning. They didn't need to get to *know* us; they knew us and didn't particularly like us.

Overall, I feel nothing but optimistic about the direction of the ACC, which it can be argued has been the best basketball conference over the past 50 years. That's because teams like the now departed Maryland, North Carolina State, Virginia and Wake Forest all had their glory moments to go along with the perennials, Duke and North Carolina. Even with UCLA's dominance of college basketball from the mid-'60s through the mid-'70s, the Pac-10 was never nearly as good as the ACC from top to bottom.

Over the past few decades, though, I wouldn't say the ACC has been on top; after all, Duke and North Carolina have been responsible for 95 percent of the conference's success. I'm prejudiced, but over that period, I think that the Big East has been the best.

But there's no doubt that John Swofford pulled off one of the all-time commissioner moves by adding us, Pitt, Notre Dame and incoming Louisville, and I think the ACC will be dominant for a long time going forward. Plus, it's a great conference for restaurants. The ACC tournament is due to come north, to the Barclays Center, in Brooklyn, in 2017. The eating will be terrific, but four words of warning: Bring lots of cash.

BEFORE OUR TRIP to Durham, C. J. Fair is concerned, and so is most of Syracuse Nation. After 25 straight wins, we finally lost, and it was an ugly one, a home defeat to lowly Boston College, 62–59. The only positive spin is that, if Duke beats us, the Cameron Crazies won't have the thrill of knocking off the unbeaten number one.

C.J. is in a bit of a shooting slump, and I can read his mind. *What are the pro scouts thinking about this?* He returned for his senior year to better his chances of being a high draft pick, and now he feels that slipping away. He hopes to make pro ball his livelihood, and it's understandable that he's worried.

"C.J.," I tell him. "It honestly doesn't matter whether you score two points or 20 points. You know what you can do, and teams know what you can do, because you showed it in the first Duke game, never mind your whole career. A team is going to watch you work out and decide then whether they like you. And it only takes one team. Forget about everything and just go out and play."

I have to say that I'm not overly impressed with Cameron Indoor Arena. Obviously it's been great for Duke, and now, 90 minutes before the game, the crowd is already at what seems like full-throated roar. But the Syracuse fans tell me later that the first-floor bathroom situation is disastrous. There's only one. You would think they'd be able to have as many bathrooms as national championships, which means four.

I like to wander out onto visiting arena floors before games, just stand around and soak it all in. Sometimes fans notice me, sometimes they don't. At Pitt this season, I must've posed for 30 photos. I've heard fans yell, "Boeheim sucks!" and then request a photo.

The Cameron fans see me, and that riles them up. A few point to the signs in the arena, two of which have no effect on me:

BOEHEIM USES INTERNET EXPLORER
BOEHEIM LIKES NICKELBACK.

I don't have a personal computer and I don't know who Nickelback is. People tell me I should be complimented for the latter.

As for the third sign—WEGMANS IS OVERRATED—it's just plain wrong. Wegmans is the treasure in our little corner of the world, the best grocery store ever. So don't start comparing Wegmans with Piggly Wiggly, because you're going to lose that battle.

At any rate, for whatever reason, despite the noise, the clamor and Duke's thirst for revenge from that overtime classic in the Dome, I believe that we're going to play a good game.

AND WE DO. It's a homecoming of sorts for Michael Gbinije, who transferred from Duke. He gives us eight points and a solid 20 minutes off the bench, and we need all of it. Our backcourt can't do anything (Tyler is 2 of 13 and Trevor is 1 of 5), but they play solid defense, take good care of the ball against the Duke pressure and make the Blue Devils work for everything. C.J. and Jerami are terrific throughout, and Baye gives us nine rebounds in split time with Rakeem Christmas. We limit their three-point shooting, something we didn't do in the game at Syracuse, and, after Rasheed Sulaimon (the guard who threw it into overtime at the Dome) makes one of two free throws, we have a chance to tie or win the game on a final possession. There are 24 seconds left and we trail 60–58.

I don't always call for a set play in that situation, so I decide to just work something out of the offense, with Tyler making decisions. We want to get a shot fairly quick, so we'll have a chance for an offensive rebound on a miss. Our offensive rebounding has been terrific, though our ability to convert second-chance points has been awful.

Duke closely defends Trevor coming off of screens, and as the clock ticks down, we get the ball in an opportune spot—C.J. isolated with one defender in the left corner. He sees an opening, drives baseline and goes up to shoot an acrobatic right-handed layup as Duke's Rodney Hood slides over from the middle and . . .*

---

* Remember all that I've said in these pages about referees. Home teams tend to get a few more calls. On that night, we would end up with 14 free-throw attempts, Duke with 25. A few ticks earlier, Christmas was slapped on the head on a follow shot and got no call. In the first half, Gbinije tried to take a charge and was called for a block in a play that seemed more charge-y than this one. Most of all, keep in mind that the emphasis all season long has been on giving the advantage to the offensive player on a block/charge. If the driver even *begins* his move before the defender slides over, he gets the whistle. It's a block.

So C.J.'s shot goes in, Tony Greene blows the whistle, makes some kind of hand gesture (C.J. will later say he thought it was *basket good and one free throw*) and . . . Offensive foul. No basket.

Subsequent commentaries and news stories will theorize that I should've known better, that my brain should've been able to run through all of the potential consequences and remain calm, figuring that we could still turn around a two-point deficit with 10 seconds left. Okay, I hear all that.

But life isn't made out of "should'ves." What ran through my brain was that it was a clear block, particularly given the new rule interpretation, and that we had gotten jobbed. So I reacted instinctively, in a way that I had never reacted before.

I charged onto the court, all the while tearing off my sport coat and managing to land a solid elbow to the chin of our head manager, Pete Corasaniti, supplying him with years of YouTube replays. Tony Greene was waiting for me. He T'd me up right away and, when I kept arguing, he gave me my second and thumbed me out of the game, the remainder of which consisted mostly of Duke free throws.

We lose 66–60.

OKAY, WHAT HAPPENED? There is a simple explanation: the heat of the moment. And there's a complicated one: the collective frustration of playing in the Cameron madhouse against a perennial over-dog, with a close friend on the opposing bench whom I really want to beat . . .

Trust me—it was the heat of the moment. It happened, I reacted, the one subconscious thought being that those kinds of calls are supposed to go to the offensive player. That's not my policy—that's college basketball's policy. In the hushed locker room, I'm immediately due for the postgame press conference. I make a decision: It's time for diplomacy. Diplomacy with a little Big East seasoning, anyway.

The first thing I do in the postgame press conference is describe the game as "extremely well officiated," which breaks up everyone.

"Don't laugh," I say. "I do make jokes, but that's not a joke."

I make it clear that I thought it was an obvious block, particularly given the new rule emphasis. "C.J. was into his motion," I say.

Then I joke that my dash onto the court was deliberate. "I wanted to see if I still had it in me to get out there," I say. "And I did. I was quick. I stayed down. Most of all, I didn't get injured."

A little humor will keep the jackals at bay.

I am asked if the technicals sealed the game. From the press perspective, that is the big question: Did I blow the game by giving Duke technical free throws?

"Well, I kind of thought the game was over," I say. "I guess we still could've won the game. But that play decided the game. I thought it was the worst call of the year. I hated to see the game decided on that call. No, I don't have any regrets. And I won't have any today, tomorrow or the next day."

The *cha-cha-cha* with the media goes on. My reputation for being a smartass has been firmly established, and something inside me wants to let that out. I had said something in past weeks about the Syracuse–Duke games and the Syracuse–Pitt games having a "Big East feel" to them, and some people felt I was slighting the ACC. Look, a man cannot forget where he came from. "They got mad at me down here," I tell the press. "They're always mad at me down here."

The subject of our next game, less than 48 hours hence at Maryland, comes up. "Maryland's off today, which is quite strange," I say. "I guess they do those things down here." And in conclusion: "These were two great games we played with Duke. And they'll remember this one for 30 years, because the old coach went out there and got a little excited."

At his later press conference, Mike Krzyzewski talks about "our phenomenal celebration of basketball" and says he "applauds me" for showing that I still care that much about the game. By the time he calls my cell, he has already seen my press conference. "It was just the right tone," he tells me. I'm sure not everyone agrees.

BACK AT THE hotel, sitting in front of a 1:00 A.M. steak, there is time to think. Regrets do seep in, but it's mostly frustration about losing a game we could've won. I do wonder if I'll be fined by the conference. Early in January, the Big Ten had suspended Iowa coach Fran McCaffery for one game and fined the school $10,000 for violating the sportsmanship policy after Fran got ejected during a loss to Wisconsin. There is no set policy on fining and suspending coaches. It happens rarely in college basketball.

I also concede that I thought there was less time on the clock than 10 seconds. I thought we were at about three or four seconds. But I still hold that the charge call cost us the game.

Should Tony have run me? Well, I think he was looking to do it after I charged off the bench, but I suppose I would've been thumbed in the old Big East, too. Upon reflection, I guess it's amazing that a single call never propelled me off the bench like that in all those years. If anything, it made me realize, as Mike said, how much I still want to win.

Conventional wisdom says that games like this help you become a better team. There could be something to that, I suppose, but my natural pessimism tends to dismiss that notion. This year so far we've probably had a dozen battles, games that could've gone either way. We won the first ten, and now we've lost two in a row, Boston College and this one. So who knows what the effect will be? I did tell the team that they should be proud of their effort. We walked into one of the toughest places in the country and almost walked out with a win.

If possible, the Boeheim family back in Syracuse had a worse evening than I did, as I discover when I talk to Juli. First, they all believed that the ESPN announcers were biased toward Duke—not the first time that opinion has been offered. Then the power went out in the neighborhood. They had to go to a neighbor's house and then over to Adrian Autry's house to watch the game. There was a backlog on pizza orders. Then Dad goes bananas on national TV and gets thrown out.

Meanwhile, the scene has gone viral. I know this because seemingly every single person in the Syracuse party except me has fired up his or her personal device to read the responses to Duke–Syracuse II, a.k.a Boeheim–Sport Coat I. Everyone is a little afraid to let me know, but finally there's so much buzz that even I—a man without a computer—have to pay attention.

It's as a result of this game that I first learn about the word "meme." The photo of me tearing off my jacket with my mouth wide open in protest has been photoshopped everywhere, proving if nothing else that a lot of people have a lot of free time. There I am with a crowd of movie stars at the Academy Awards. There I am with Leonardo DiCaprio at the helm of the *Titanic*. There I am with Michael Jackson. I have a feeling that at my funeral, all of the photos will be of me tearing off my sport coat. Boeheim in *Ghostbusters*, Boeheim in *Breaking Bad*, Boeheim running with the bulls . . .

Dave Gavitt once gave me a piece of advice: Don't watch sports talk shows or read the paper if you know you're going to be the subject. I've gotten better at it, but, back in my hotel room, I've already seen myself tearing off my sport coat a half dozen times on TV, and I suspect that image will be run into the ground until somebody else does something crazy.

Bob Knight had a lot of great moments as a coach, but you know the first thing people remember about him? When he threw a chair across the court. At the NCAA championship this year in Dallas, I ran into Phil Knight, the chairman of Nike. "Wow, Jim," he said, "I didn't know you had those moves left in you."

Sometime early the next morning, Daryl Gross, our athletic director, gets a call from Swofford, the ACC commissioner.

"I'm not fining or suspending Jim," says Swofford. "I have too much respect for him."

The best compliment I can give John is that Dave Gavitt would've handled it exactly the same way.

P.S. In April, a longtime Syracuse fan, Neil Gold, will pay $14,000 for the sport coat as part of the charity auction for the Jim and Juli Boeheim Foundation.

P.P.S. It was a block, not a charge.

19

THE BERNIE FINE SAGA

On November 17, 2011, my 67th birthday and three games into the season, a story broke nationally that Bernie Fine, my top assistant, had been accused of molesting two kids who had been Syracuse ball boys. The incidents, which had allegedly happened almost ten years earlier, had been dismissed as groundless by Syracuse police.

Before going any further, you have to remember what else was going on at around this time. Two weeks before the story broke about Bernie, Jerry Sandusky, Joe Paterno's top football assistant at Penn State, had been indicted on 40 counts of sex crimes against young boys. He had been arrested on November 5, and the video of him being hauled away by police rolled on a continuous loop throughout our 24-hour news culture.

There is positively, absolutely no connection between Fine and Sandusky other than this: The national outrage that understandably followed in the wake of the Sandusky incidents—outrage that included the presumption that Joe Paterno knew about Sandusky's behavior and didn't do enough—leaked into the allegations against Bernie.

I would not go so far as to describe the atmosphere around college sports at that time as a "witch hunt." After all, Sandusky was eventually adjudged guilty in a court of law, and, to the best of anyone's knowledge, the incidents at Penn State happened and were horrific. But there is little doubt that what happened—or didn't happen—at Syracuse was put into the same blender and mixed around with all the ingredients at Penn State.

I first met Bernie in my sophomore year on the Hill. He had graduated from Erasmus Hall High School, in Brooklyn, the same school that sent Barbra Streisand, Bobby Fischer and Neil Diamond into the world (though none of them graduated from there), as well as Billy Cunningham, the Kangaroo Kid, who was a fantastic player and coached the Philadelphia 76ers to the 1983 NBA title (and who did graduate). Bernie loved basketball and wanted to coach, so he became our student manager. After graduating from Syracuse, he coached junior high and high school basketball and had great success. I brought him in as an assistant with Rick Pitino when I got the job in 1976, and I knew he would be a real asset to the program.

As for a coach succeeding without having been a good player, which was the case with Bernie, it's certainly not unprecedented. Lou Carnesecca, to name one, didn't play at all, and he knew enough basketball to coach in both the NBA and college. True, the majority of coaches did play the game at a fairly high level, but it's not a prerequisite for doing the job—there are only two men who are in the Hall of Fame as both players and coaches: John Wooden and Lenny Wilkens.

Bernie instantly gravitated to coaching our big men. He understood the technical parts of the game, particularly footwork and positioning, but he was also a great motivator. Working with big men takes patience above all, because it is the little things that make the biggest difference. Mike Hopkins never played a minute under the basket, but he handles our bigs now, and I'd stack Mike's coaching up against anyone's.

In addition, Bernie became a terrific recruiter, and that's something you really can't be sure of until somebody goes out and does it. He was the same no-nonsense, here-are-the-facts, leave-out-the-bullshit kind of recruiter that I was. He was a salesman for our program because he didn't come across as a bullshit artist, and he still has great relationships with many of the guys he helped bring to the program.

I'm sure there were times when Bernie thought he should be a head coach, which is a perfectly normal aspiration for an assistant. I think he could've gotten a head job years ago, but he was kind of fussy about where he wanted to go, and then it got too late for him to move on.

The allegations against Bernie were first made in 2002, by a man named Bobby Davis, who took them to the police and then to ESPN. The local newspaper found out about them, too. Bernie and I talked briefly about the allegations, which he denied. Not the police, ESPN, the local newspaper, nor Syracuse University, which launched its own investigation, could find proof or any kind of corroboration, so the story went away.

Then it came back with a vengeance nine years later. Another former ball boy, Michael Lang, also claimed that Bernie had molested him, and this time ESPN went with the story. Lang and Davis are stepbrothers. If it hadn't been for what was going on at Penn State, I don't think ESPN would've done it. That's just my opinion. Bernie was put on administrative leave and eventually fired.

No matter how long you've been doing what I do, nothing can prepare you for dealing with a media onslaught like that. Nothing. You can say to yourself, "Just shut up about it," and you can hear the advice of lawyers, public relations people, family and friends saying, "Don't say anything." But it's hard not to say anything. Anyone who is being honest understands that if you issue a "No comment," it is tantamount to saying, "He's guilty." That's just the way it is.

So despite the fact that everyone was urging me not to comment, I just couldn't keep quiet. I stand by that decision, but I did make an error. In retrospect, here's what I should've said:

"I've known Bernie Fine for 50 years and worked with him for 40. I trust him. I believe him. My owns sons stayed at his house, and I know other boys who have gone over there."

That should've been the end of the statement.

But in my initial response to the story, I said all that but, alas, went on to suggest that Bernie's accusers were only looking for money. Considering all that had happened at Penn State, my comments seemed callous. I should not have said what I did about the alleged victims' motivation, and I apologized for it because it was—however unintentional—insulting to victims of abuse.

The outcry was swift. Advocacy groups condemned me, and there were calls for my resignation. To this day, I have little doubt that many people were disappointed when I wasn't fired. But at this writing, it is important to clarify a number of facts:

- The biggest misconception to come out of the story is that Bernie knew Bobby Davis because Bobby was a Syracuse ball boy. Absolutely untrue. Bernie knew Bobby from his neighborhood. Bobby even lived with Bernie and his wife from time to time. They took him in when Bobby had some real family problems. Bobby became a ball boy only after moving in with Bernie and his wife. Davis did go on the road with us, but only because he was babysitting Bernie's kids. He was part of *their* family, not Syracuse's. Ball boys never travel with us on the road. We've probably had 500 of them over the years, including my sons and a lot of other friends' sons, and ball boys are *never* alone with a coach. There was a history between Bernie and Bobby that had nothing to do with the university and our program. Let me emphasize that I don't know every detail of that history.
- Eventually, two other boys came forward to claim that Bernie had molested them, which obviously only added to the charged

atmosphere. However, both have recanted and admitted that they made the story up out of whole cloth. So that leaves only two accusers: stepbrothers Davis and Lang.

- The investigation against Bernie is over. Had there been grounds to charge Bernie, the statute of limitations had expired, and—to repeat—nothing was ever discovered in the initial investigation. However, a lawsuit against me for slander, filed by the accusers, remains alive in the courts.

- Though I was taken to task for my comments about the accusers, no one ever suggested that I was hiding anything. Even Lang said, "I don't blame Jim Boeheim." Had Bobby said that I *did* know something, I suppose I could've been out of a job, because—in the fraught atmosphere at that time—it would've been extremely difficult to combat a he-said, he-said situation.

- I don't know why Bernie was fired. That wasn't my decision, and I had nothing to do with it. That is between him and the university.

- I don't talk to Bernie, even though he and his wife live across the street from our family. A reason for that, I concede, is because the situation is awkward. Too many unfortunate events have transpired to make a continuing relationship between us seem natural. But another reason we don't communicate is that we were never close friends. Juli and I never socialized with Bernie and his wife. People who don't know me find it strange that I am not close to someone with whom I worked for that long, but those in my circle understand completely. I never get that close to my assistants. It's just the way I conduct the program. Al McGuire told me a long time ago that he never became friends with his assistant coaches, and I feel the same way. It's nothing against Bernie, or my guys now, Hop, Adrian and Gerry.

- No one can say with absolute, 100 percent certainty—except for Bernie, Davis and Lang—that nothing happened. I know that now. But I came to Bernie's defense, a decision I still stand behind, for two reasons:

First, loyalty, which I think is one of the most important qualities you can possess. That's partly why I've been at Syracuse for 50 years.

Second, because I have yet to see anything that has convinced me that anything untoward happened between Bernie and those men. I understand that there is a difference between loyalty and blind stupidity, but I'm simply saying that from everything I've observed, Bernie is innocent of what he was accused of. I base this not on our close personal friendship, which did not exist, but on our close *professional* relationship, which did exist. We were together for 300 days a year for four decades. Practices, games, meetings and recruiting—I'd say that provides a good sample size to get to know someone.

DESPITE ALL OF this swirling around, there was still a season to play. And if there is one word to describe how I dealt with the Bernie situation among the team members, it would be "expeditiously."

Here's what I told them:

"These allegations have been made against a coach you respect. It shouldn't change what you think of Bernie. Whatever happened, if something did happen, happened long before any of you knew anything about Syracuse University. What you have to be concerned about is your season, what it means for you and what it means for the program. Questions about Bernie are not for you to answer; your job is to get better as a player to help yourself and help our program."

That was it. I didn't bring it up again. I did not consider it, as many would, "a teachable moment." We moved on. We tell our kids all the time that obstacles will appear in their lives and, at those times, they just have to get through them. But this was not their obstacle. It was, in part, mine, and the university's—but not the players'.

We told them not to discuss it with the media, because no good could come of that. One warning was enough; the players didn't *want* to talk about it.

Plus, it had become a legal issue, with all of those binding prohibitions against commenting. There was still heightened interest in the Bernie Fine story, which I understand, but I simply couldn't say anything. To several interviewers, on and off the record, I said, "I can't talk about it. Can't you see I've already gotten myself in trouble?" Most understood. Andy Katz, of ESPN, though, corralled me for an interview, heard me say that I couldn't talk about Bernie, then asked me about it anyway—on camera. It made me feel like one of those CEOs getting sweated out by Mike Wallace on *60 Minutes*. I didn't forget it, as evidenced by my refusal to answer a postgame question Andy asked me a year later. (We've since mended fences.)

Still, with us barely mentioning Bernie and the players putting it out of their minds, an us-against-the-world mentality started to form. It wasn't something we talked about; it was just in the air, something that happens on teams without anyone saying anything about it. Was that the main reason that we won our first 19 games, finished at 34–3 and never dipped below fourth in the national rankings after early December? No. The main reason was that we were a very good team. But there's little doubt that the feeling of unity, of forging ahead together under a burden, was there.

Needless to say, I'm always happy when we're winning, but it was especially crucial in that 2011–12 season. Because if we had lost a bunch of games, there is no doubt what the reason would've been: that we were "distracted" by the Bernie Fine story.

That would not have been true. The players liked and respected Bernie, but he was not at the center of their lives—nor should he have been. In most cases, we overstate this "distraction" issue with players. Young men are focused on their own lives, and here's what 19-, 20-, and 21-year-old basketball players are focused on: finishing their schoolwork so they can stay eligible, impressing NBA scouts and getting along with their girlfriends.

THE BERNIE FINE story wasn't all we had to deal with in 2011–12. An eligibility issue engulfed one of our sophomores, Fab Melo.

Fab had arrived in 2010 as an athletic phenom but a basketball question mark. He had played only one year of high school ball, and he wasn't in the kind of shape to play Syracuse basketball, on offense or defense. Plus, in front of him were a bunch of good frontcourt players such as Kris Joseph, Rick Jackson, Baye Moussa Keita, C.J. and James Southerland.

Fab wasn't happy about his limited minutes as a freshman, but I'll tell you this: I've never had a player make as big a change between his freshman and sophomore years as Fab Melo. He worked hard right after the season was over in the spring, he worked hard in the summer and he worked hard in the fall before the 2011–12 season began. Mike Hopkins was right there with him; his development of Melo stands as one of his greatest achievements as an assistant.

Fab was having a great 2011–12 season—he blocked ten shots against Seton Hall—when he was declared academically ineligible after the first semester. We suspended him for three games. After that, we were under the impression that he could appeal and do some academic work to get himself eligible. He did that work. But then there arose a question about *how* he had gotten eligible, and he was declared ineligible again, right before the NCAA tournament.

The issue is extremely complicated, and at any rate I can't really go into it, because it is part of an ongoing NCAA investigation. The NCAA does not even want you to acknowledge that you are being investigated. I wish that these issues with the NCAA had been resolved by the time this book came out, so I would be free to comment, but that is not the case. Suffice it to say that we thought we had done things the right way, but the NCAA thought differently. We will see.

OUR BEST PLAYER that season was Kris Joseph, kind of a Wes Johnson Lite. But our leader was Antonio "Scoop" Jardine, an interesting kid out of Philadelphia. Scoop, a teammate of Rick Jackson's at Neumann-Goretti High School, had arrived in 2007 and played more than expected early in that season because of injuries. But Scoop struggled on the court, where he was trying to transition from 2 guard to point. And he had an issue off the court, too—he was involved in the theft of another student's dining card. I suspended him for two games, and he stayed on the bench after that.

Then he took a medical redshirt in 2008–09 because of a stress fracture. At that point it looked as though a career at Syracuse just wasn't in the cards for Scoop.

But you can't give up on kids who make mistakes—not the ones worth saving, anyway. And over the next three years, Scoop Jardine turned into a terrific leader, a dependable player and a fine young man.

How do you "coach" leadership? How do you turn someone like Scoop into a leader? The answer is, the raw materials have to be there, and I saw them in Scoop. He just had a way of getting people to follow him, a bravado that wasn't forced. We work on leadership as a team, try to nudge the freshmen a little bit with the understanding that they will do more as sophomores and even more as juniors. But if a kid isn't a born leader, it's difficult to turn him into one.

It's fortunate, too, when the point guard is your vocal leader, which was the case with Scoop. And he was an important ingredient in one key dynamic on this team: getting Dion Waiters to accept his off-the-bench role. They are cousins and had grown up together, and while Scoop wasn't nearly as talented as his cousin, Dion came to understand Scoop's value and also accepted his counsel.

So, behind Scoop's leadership, the occasional brilliance of Dion and Kris, the steady play of Brandon Triche and an atypically deep bench (our tenth player in the rotation was a freshman named Michael Carter-Williams), we earned a number-one seed in the East Region going into the tournament, despite having no Fab Melo. We played an indifferent game in a 72–65 win against UNC-Asheville, a solid game in a 75–59 win over Kansas State and a superb game in a 64–63 win over a tough Wisconsin team. But one win from the Final Four, we lost to Ohio State 77–70.

So the year ended on a down note, as every year does except for one team—the national champion. Fab, Dion and Kris moved on, but I knew we would be good the following season, when the Bernie Fine story would be behind us.

To an extent, of course, it never is. The slander suit against me, which was first thrown out, has been revived. That happened despite the fact that, after the suit was tossed out the first time, Lang told the newspaper, "I'm kind of glad [Boeheim] won," and that he, Lang, "didn't even want to pursue the lawsuit." Not sure how that statement can be reconciled with the refiling, but I'm no lawyer.

Through it all, though, I reject the notion that the 2011–12 season was "difficult" or "trying." Life is tough. It's not supposed to be easy. Problems occur. Good people get sick. Good people die too young. You still have to go to work, you still have to do your job and you still have to coach your team.

Maybe that ethic came from being the son of a man who dealt with death. And you know what would've been tougher in 2011–12? Going 3–34 instead of 34–3.

20

THE END OF THE EAST

Dave Gavitt was laid to rest on a drizzly morning in Providence in September of 2011. The funeral followed hard upon the announcement that Syracuse, along with Pitt and Notre Dame, would be leaving the Big East for the ACC in the 2013–14 season.

Dave had been sick for a while, so his death wasn't unexpected, but it was still the saddest of days, the end of the line for so many things. The basketball world wouldn't be the same without Dave, and the world of the Big East wouldn't be the same without us, one of the charter members.

All of us were there—Big John, P.J., Rick Pitino, Louie Carnesecca, Rick Barnes, Jim Calhoun—and we all felt like we had lost a best friend, which in a way we had. Dan Gavitt, Dave's son, who's now running the NCAA tournament, was among the speakers. No coaches were asked to take the podium, which was smart. We would've all wanted to say something, and it would've turned into a giant blubberfest. Except maybe for John Thompson, who would've reached back into the Old Testament for some bit of wisdom.

No one felt sadder than Mike Tranghese, who had worked under Dave for so long, and who'd had to watch in agony as the behemothification of college football slowly pulled the conference apart.

Mike was a very good commissioner. He just faced too many long odds. He always told me how uncomfortable it was for him when he found himself having to answer questions about Boston College's defection to the ACC, right after our national championship in 2003. B.C. was the first to go, and Mike never forgave them for it.

In truth? We could've been right there with B.C. We would've been the other team to go to the ACC ten years ago, if not for the fact that the governor of Virginia insisted that Virginia Tech was going in. I'm so happy that happened, and not just because we were spared the dubious distinction of being among the first Big East defectors. We also got almost another decade of great play in the Big East.

Dave's death hit me hard (I'm not alone in that), because he played so many roles in my life. Dave was a great coach when I was younger. After he got out of coaching, he'd be one of the few guys I would ask, "Hey, take a look at my team. Let me know what you see." He would always come up with something. "Your team is more active when so-and-so's in the game." Or "I think your zone is more effective in this situation." I took a lot of his advice, and I never took much of anybody else's.

Dave had vision, and I haven't met many people with that gift. I can't imagine how frustrating it must've been for him sometimes—trying to move us to the bright lights of Madison Square Garden while some of his athletic directors are griping about spending an extra hundred bucks to heat their gyms, for example. But Dave always kept his cool. I often wonder what would've happened to our program had Dave not come along. We would've eventually left the ECAC, I suppose, but I don't know where we would've landed. Hard to imagine any alternate histories so lucky as the one Syracuse basketball has written.

I understood the significance of Syracuse's leaving the conference. "Syracuse's departure is basically the end of the Big East as we know it," Tranghese told a reporter. "It's going to be rebuilt.

It's going to be different. It can have success. But it will never be what it was."

I heard all the comments about how *Jim Boeheim could've stopped Syracuse from leaving the Big East if he had wanted to* . . . On the ESPN documentary *Requiem for the Big East*, Rick Pitino said, "I never thought Syracuse would leave because of Jim Boeheim." And John Thompson reached into Shakespeare and said: "*Et tu*, Brute?" as if Syracuse, and Syracuse alone, had plunged the dagger into the belly of the Big East.

Let me assure you of one thing: Jim Boeheim could *not* have stopped it. I have the power to recruit players, figure out a playing rotation and make a schedule. (There are even limitations on that.) But I do not control the purse strings of the university or even the athletic department. Sure, our basketball program makes about $15 million, and when you think Syracuse, you think first—I hope—about basketball, not football. But football has been driving intercollegiate athletics for a long time now. We went to the ACC because of pigskin. End of story.

Despite the inevitability of the whole thing, it is sad to see the Big East in tatters. In December of 2012, the Big East's Catholic, non-football schools became a conference unto themselves. They would retain the Big East name and continue to play the tournament at the Garden. The remaining football-playing schools joined the American Athletic Conference, further complicating the national picture—*AAC? ACC?* And Louisville and Rutgers were aboard for just one season before the former joined us in the ACC and the latter joined the Big Ten.

The school I feel the worst about is Connecticut. Who wants to be an eastern power and have to plan trips to SMU and Houston, two members of the AAC? The ACC didn't invite UConn because it had enough strong basketball programs, and UConn's football profile wasn't elevated enough to make a difference. Plus, Boston

College didn't want the Huskies, and they had more influence with the ACC than UConn did.

But UConn didn't exactly pine over it, did they? They went out and won the 2014 national championship. If the Huskies can sustain that kind of dominance in the AAC, more power to them.

My final word about the "old" Big East is this: What's most remarkable is not that such a successful league broke up; it's that it stayed together for so long.

WHEN THE SUBJECT of my retirement comes up, I say all of the predictable things. But it was around the time of Dave's death—the period right before it and the period right after it—that I really did think about hanging it up. We had gone through consecutive NIT years in '07 and '08. I had designated Mike Hopkins to be the next coach of Syracuse so a smooth transition would be assured. The Big East was hemorrhaging. Several weeks after Dave's death, the Bernie Fine story broke.

I can't describe this whole time as "gloomy," because I always tend to be a little gloomy, but it did make me wonder how long I should hang around. There were a couple of days, in fact, when I was pretty close to walking away. That indecision remained throughout the 2011–12 season, when we had a terrific team.

In the end, a few factors convinced me to stay. We continued to be competitive at the highest level. That always makes it easier. Then again, had we faltered, I might've rationalized that it was not fair to leave Mike with limited personnel. That decision might've been taken out of my hands by the Syracuse administration. *Okay, Boeheim's program is going down. Time for a change. New conference, new leadership.* And who knows if the new coach would've been Hop? Mike is part of our program, and assistants sometimes don't get promoted when a program isn't winning.

A few key people wanted me to take Syracuse into the ACC, and that helped, too. They included Mike Krzyzewski, Mike Tranghese and Dave Odom, the former Wake Forest and South Carolina coach who is now chairman of the Maui Invitational (nice work if you can get it). Dave was one of the first to know that I wasn't going to retire, since I made a commitment to go to Maui at the beginning of the 2013–14 season.

I don't want to make it sound like there was a nationwide Make Boeheim Stay crusade. But I've been identified with the Syracuse program for so long that it only seemed right that I should be the one to take on the ACC challenge. Maybe Coach K read the tea leaves and saw something in the future . . . saw a crazed man in glasses leaping off the bench . . . saw him ripping off his sport coat . . .

Above all, my family doesn't mind my continuing to coach. When they do, I'll stop. I'm sure there are times when my disposition after a tough loss is trying, but my family is part of the Syracuse program. People recognize Juli throughout the community; as I said before, they're usually more eager to talk to her than they are to me.

I don't build miniature ships in a bottle. I'm not a stamp collector. I'm a reader, but there's lots of time to read on airplanes and in hotel rooms, even during the season. I don't miss nearly as many of my kids' school- and sports-related events as one might think. I've just now learned that there's a diagram that will help you correctly insert the batteries into the TV remote, which should give you a gauge for how interested I am in—and how capable at—home improvement projects. And how interested Juli is in having me around to perform them.

ON DECEMBER 17, 2013, we beat the University of Detroit 72–68 for my 900th win. Dave Bing came down for the ceremony, and that made me very happy. Almost 50 years ago, when I visited him in

Detroit during his rookie year, I heard this whispered more than once: "Who's that gawky white guy with Bing?" When Dave came to celebrate with me, he heard this more than once: "Who's that handsome black guy with Boeheim?"

The victory came three days after 20 kids and six adults died in the massacre at the Sandy Hook Elementary School, in Newtown, Connecticut. After the game, I couldn't stop thinking about it, couldn't help but wonder how I would feel if one of my four kids had been among the victims. It seemed wrong to be celebrating a basketball victory when this was all going on, and at the postgame press conference I felt I had to address it. Here's what I said:

"If we cannot get the people who represent us to do something about firearms, we are a sad, sad society. If one person in this world—the NRA president, anybody—can tell me why we need assault weapons with 30 shots . . . This is our fault if we don't go out there and do something about this. If we can't get this thing done, I don't know what kind of country we have."

I didn't plan it, I didn't write it down. But I would've felt I was being untrue to myself if I didn't say anything. Over the next few days, I got mostly support, although a couple of e-mails expressed the view that politics and basketball don't mix, and, anyway, who cares what a coach has to say?

Well, questioning the excess of assault weapons isn't political, the way I see it. And as a coach, you're engaged daily in the lives of young people. They are your *life's work*. I don't think I'm nearly important enough that the world at large needed to pay attention to what I said, but in my little corner of the world, I wanted to be heard.

Understand that this wasn't a sweeping antigun statement; it was about the excess of assault weapons. Guns were part of my upbringing. My father liked to hunt, and though I admit I never wanted to shoot a deer, I did go pheasant hunting. I was a pretty good shot, and I understand the pleasure of being out in the field with a dog. The fact that I don't hunt these days has nothing to do with having any anti-hunting views.

Since we're on the subject of politics, let me just say that I'm not a highly political person; I'm more of an interested citizen. If I'm in the car, I'm probably listening to sports radio or talk radio, preferably not from the extreme right or the extreme left. If I'm in my office, I have on ESPN or one of the newschannels, more to keep up with events, not to hear pundits. I could never envision myself as a politician, because I don't have the temperament for it. Somebody would ask me a question that required a diplomatic answer and I'd say, "Are you crazy? What is wrong with you?"

For most of my life, I was basically centrist, possibly leaning more toward Republican. I did campaign for Bill Bradley, but I told you about my personal history with him. Clinton changed me, I guess. When we lost to Kentucky in 1996, he got me on the phone and would not get off. He talked to me for, like, 15 minutes and knew everything about the game. I finally had to say, "Mr. President, I really, really appreciate this, but I have to go talk to my team."

It wasn't just the fact that Clinton was a basketball fan. It's the charisma. Clinton enters the room, shakes your hand, and you say, "Here's my wallet." Aside from the personal appeal, I believe he wanted to get things done, really desired to help people. And while I understand that his personal indiscretions were wrong, the effort to impeach Clinton was when I came over to his side. You shouldn't try to get rid of someone who is doing that much good for the country as a whole.

The extreme elements are really hurting our country today, the Tea Party in particular, which really doesn't want to get anything done, only bring down Obama, who has done a pretty fair job overall.

As far as local politics goes, I stay out of them completely. The district attorney and a county executive are friends of mine, but that's bound to happen when you've been around the same place for as long as I have. If I were to get associated with one side or the other, I would just draw everyone who wasn't on that side away from our program, and I have enough people who don't like me as it is.

But I'll say this about the gun control message: I desperately wanted to win the NCAA championship that year so I could repeat it on a national stage.

WHEN THE 2012–13 season began, I don't think anyone saw us as having a chance at the title. Our best player turned out to be Michael Carter-Williams, who had come off the bench the previous year. Michael was a unique player, a real talent, long-armed and highly effective both driving to the basket and playing outside on our 2-3. I know he chafed on the bench from time to time when he was a freshman, but he had a great player to model himself after in Brandon Triche.

I *knew* we would be good after we beat Arkansas early in the season, 91-82, after being up by as much as 20 points. We were the only team to beat them at home the entire season. Still, we were up and down, mostly because our big guys weren't that effective offensively. We wanted to get more out of DaJuan Coleman, but he got hurt, had surgery and was out for the year, a foreshadowing of what would happen again in the 2013–14 season.

In the back of my mind, of course, was the Big East coming to an end, which is why some of our defeats were particularly disappointing, like losing to Villanova, Pitt and UConn on the road. They were all NCAA tournament teams, but it would've been nice to get a *W* in our final battles within the league.

And then there was Georgetown. They had a terrific forward in Otto Porter, the consensus player of the year in the Big East, but I thought we were the better team. They beat us in the Dome 57–46 and then, to top off a late-season losing streak, just buried us 61–39 in the final regular-season game at the Verizon Center, in Washington, D.C. That point total, by the way, was the lowest Syracuse had scored in a single game since the 1962–63 season. (Don't blame Bing and me—we were on the freshman team.)

It's over. Doomsday. Tapped out. Forget about it. That was the overwhelming sentiment after the Georgetown debacle.

Big John Thompson, no longer the coach but never far from the picture, was in rare form after the 61–39 blowout. First he called the football-playing schools that had left the Big East "pimps." Then, referencing Georgetown's 22-point win, he couldn't resist harking back to the "Manley Is Closed" game, saying, "We officially closed Syracuse, and now we kiss them good-bye."

You have to understand what our relationship was by that time. We were like two retired generals from the Cold War: not close friends, but generally respectful of each other. I had been on John's radio show several times, and in 2010 I had introduced him when he came to Syracuse to accept the Citizen of the Year award from Temple Adath Yeshurun. (They were honoring John for his charitable work and contributions to the game, but I suspect that someone had a sense of humor when they decided on the choice, too.) We even shared a man hug before this game.

But when it came time to get a dig in on Syracuse, he just had a Pavlovian response. He couldn't help himself. As you might have noticed, I have a sharp tongue, but I wouldn't have said what John did, particularly since there was still a Big East tournament to be played.

I understand that our fans were deeply concerned about our late-season swoon, which left us with a 23–8 overall record. But while I can't claim that I was full-out optimistic, I had also been around long enough to understand that it takes only one half—20 good minutes of basketball—to turn around a team. Now, if you're not a good team, that isn't going to happen; but that wasn't the case with us. We just got into a slump and, with the road loss to Georgetown, we bottomed out.

The day after the Georgetown loss, the players, on their own, organized a four-on-four game, while the coaches were upstairs trying to figure out what the hell had happened. We felt really encouraged when we came down and saw them going at each other full tilt. Plus, if there's one lesson I've learned over the years, it's that anything can happen when you get to the Garden. West Virginia coach Bob Huggins once said that it was harder to win the Big East tournament than it is to get to the Final Four. In many years, that is true, as we were about to demonstrate.

THERE WAS AN unmistakable air of melancholy surrounding that 2013 Big East tournament. So many of the old legends were on hand, and you could conjure up a hundred memories just by taking one step into the Garden. I've spent so much time talking about us, Georgetown and UConn that it's easy to forget the other great players who graced this conference. Mark Jackson and Malik Sealy, from St. John's. Otis Thorpe, from Providence. Michael Adams, Dana Barros and Troy Bell, from Boston College. Kerry Kittles and Eddie Pinckney, from Villanova. Charles Smith, from Pitt. Troy Murphy, from Notre Dame. Terry Dehere and Dan Callandrillo, from Seton Hall.

Still, I don't think your players feel the weight of history. All Big East players have this osmotic understanding of the tradition, but their motivation is to beat *this year's* Georgetown team, not to avenge some loss from 30 years ago.

I was worried when we fell behind Seton Hall in our first game. I started looking down the bench for Pearl and Derrick. But we recovered, began to find our shooting eye and pulled away 75–63.

It was against Pitt in the quarterfinals that I knew we were back. We converted 12 of 19 three-pointers, and our defense was really solid. We won 62–59 to set up a semifinal matchup with Georgetown, the one that every Big East historian wanted to see.

John Thompson III had warned his dad, after he made his incendiary comments in Washington, "We could play these guys again." Predictably, it turned into an overtime classic with strange plot twists. One of our most unreliable offensive players, Baye Moussa Keita, hit all seven of his free throws and made a key basket in overtime to help us win 58–55.

After the game, I passed John Thompson III in the hallway. Our relationship had never been as rich, deep and complex as the one I shared with his father, which is to be expected.

"You've been doing this for how long?" John III asked me.

"Too long," I told him. "You'll never make it."

"I know," said John III. "I'll never make it."

Funny, but I didn't run into Big John.

That put us into a final against a strong Louisville team. I say this now only because I also said it before that game: It was more important to win that last game against Georgetown than it was to win the tournament.

The story line for the final against Rick Pitino's Louisville team was, of course, my wedding-weekend job interview. Rick did most of the talking. On the day I die, this story is going to have become so embellished that they'll have me charging into the church to interrupt the ceremony, like Dustin Hoffman in *The Graduate*.

In truth, Louisville, the eventual national champion, was better than us and beat us 78–61, although the game was closer than that. I was asked if I would've preferred to play Georgetown or St. John's or one of the other "historic" Big East teams in the final. It didn't matter, I said. We had played them all so many times, and in this tournament we had beaten Seton Hall, Pitt and Georgetown. It was enough. It was time to bid adieu to the Big East.

And I'll tell you this: I was extremely proud to be the last man standing. I walked among giants in that conference. We all did.

YOU NEVER KNOW what you're going to get in the NCAA tournament. First-round opponents are sometimes as tough as Final Four opponents. That didn't happen in 2013. We blew out Montana 81–34 and beat Cal 66–60 in a game that really wasn't that close.

That put us in the Sweet Sixteen in, of all places, Washington, D.C., the site of our 61–39 loss to Georgetown three weeks earlier. It was almost scary how well we were playing, particularly on defense. We picked apart both Indiana (61–50) and Big East rival Marquette (55–39) to reach my fourth Final Four and the fifth overall for Syracuse. The 39 points Marquette scored? That had been our total when we had lost to Georgetown at the Verizon Center three weeks earlier.

I didn't get a chance to talk to Big John, who was at the game doing color commentary. I looked for him as I gleefully snipped down the final cord of net but didn't see him.

The composition of the 2013 Final Four in Atlanta tells you all you need to know about predictions—nobody had us, Michigan or Wichita State in it. (Just as no one had UConn to win it all in 2014.) I honestly felt we could win the title, even though Louisville was on an incredible roll. We drew Michigan in the semis. They were a terrific shooting team, led by All-American guard Trey Burke, but that was not my concern—our defense had really tightened and we knew how to stop shooters. In our first four tournament wins, teams had shot just 29 percent against us and 15 percent on threes.

The question would be: Could we score enough to win? And would we get dominated inside?

The answers were, in order: Not quite and sort of.

We had a chance to send the game into overtime, but Trevor Cooney missed a shot with six seconds left. It wasn't Trevor's fault. The play was to go to James Southerland, but Michigan switched on him and Trevor did the best he could. Both Michael Carter-Williams and Brandon Triche had fouled out by then. Michael's came on an illegal screen with 1:15 left, and Brandon's came on a charging call with 25 seconds left. Both of those are tough calls to get down the stretch. After Trevor's miss, Michigan scored a meaningless dunk as time ran out on a 61–56 defeat.

We did a good job on their shooters but couldn't contain their center, Mitch McGary, inside. That was probably the difference.

All in all, it was an excruciating loss, made even worse by all the questions about retirement after the game. In fact, it was the first question thrown at me. Right after a loss like that, I wasn't in the mood to answer it and said to the reporter, "Why would you ask that question? Are you going to ask [Michigan coach] John Beilein that question?"

I wasn't thinking about my retirement at that moment. I was thinking how we had just lost a game that we could've won. But we continued to spar around the subject, just because I kind of like sparring.

In truth, though, I had made up my mind by that time.

Let's see what this ACC is like.

21

ONE AND DONE

N ice shooting, huh?"

I am sitting in the TNT blue room, outside our locker room at the First Niagara Center, in Buffalo, talking mainly to myself. My 14-year-old son, Jack, is next to me. He can't stop crying. Nobody takes losses tougher than Jack. If I were 14, I'd be crying, too.

Our season is over after a 55–53 loss to Dayton in a game that could've sent us to the Sweet Sixteen. We couldn't make a shot all game. We went 0 for 10 on three-pointers, compared with 7 of 16 for the Flyers, a 21-point differential right there. One of their three-point shots in crunch time hit the back rim, stopped, died as if the air had gone out of the ball, seemed to be falling off, then dropped in. Nobody could believe it went in, including the shooter.

Our two best scorers, C. J. Fair and Tyler Ennis, were a combined 11 of 35. We made exactly one perimeter jumper. The closest we came to actually making a three-pointer was Tyler's desperation shot just before the buzzer, and even that was a decent look.

Had it gone in, we would be celebrating right now and making plans to go to the South Regional in Memphis. Had it gone in, everyone would've said, "Watch out for Syracuse. They can shoot *that* badly and still win a game."

But it didn't go in. And what I feel now is that the 2013–14 season was one of the most disappointing finishes I've ever experienced, considering our 25–0 start.

You could theorize, I suppose, that our play against Dayton was a hangover from the last part of our season, when we lost four of our last five ACC games, including that heartbreaker at Duke. But in our final regular-season game, we torched Florida State on the road, 74–58, one of our best wins of the year.

You could also theorize that it was a hangover from the ACC tournament, where we couldn't stop North Carolina State's big gun, T. J. Warren, who scored 28 points on us and we lost 66–63. But in our first NCAA game in Buffalo, we rolled over a Western Michigan team that some thought would give us trouble, 77–53. There was nothing wrong with our shooting in that game. Tyler, C.J., Trevor and Jerami all shot over 50 percent.

The truth is, there is no clear answer other than this: Our shooting was tenuous all season. We were tenth in the league in field goal percentage; overall, we had the offensive statistics of an eighth-place team. It was our defense that held us together, and I'm proud of that. Who knows—maybe we needed the bright lights of New York to get reenergized for the postseason.

Using normal metrics, it was a terrific season. With a young team, one that lost three starters from a Final Four team and had a freshman at point guard, we went 28–6 and finished second in our debut year in the ACC. We were number one or two in the country for two full months. We won the early-season tournament in Maui. We won a highlight game against Duke that people will be talking about for years. (We also lost a highlight game against Duke that people will be talking about for years.) We routed both Indiana and North Carolina and handled Pitt twice. But I've said this before: I can't pretend that the NCAA tournament isn't incredibly important, and we needed to get at least one, if not two, steps further to call the season a success.

WE NEED A day to replay all the frustrations of the Dayton game. That's a bad, bad day. I keep envisioning Tyler driving down the court in transition, no one around, and losing the ball. It just flies out of his hand. That never happened to him before.

I think about whether I should've put Trevor back in after lifting him for Michael Gbinije. Yes, Mike was playing well and Trevor was missing shots, but at a key point in the game, Mike lost his sneaker and tried to put it back on while the action continued. I've had guys who, if their foot got cut off, they'd keep on playing.

I think about how we would've game-planned Stanford, which would've been our Sweet Sixteen opponent. But that's nothing but wasted energy.

Then a new day comes and it's back to some semblance of normality and time for individual meetings with the players. It's my time to talk. It's not an exchange of ideas, except with the seniors, who are now out from under my thumb and free to talk, though nobody has too much to say.

It's an unusual postseason, in that I am hearing nothing about transferring. Jumping to the NBA, yes, there's plenty of that, but not transferring, which is unusual, given the fact that we had three freshmen who didn't see much action—Tyler Roberson, Ron Patterson and B. J. Johnson. When you have a few guys who don't play, usually one of them leaves.

Over the past few years, we've been able to develop a system whereby kids who sat as freshmen have big sophomore years. Sherman Douglas is an early example, and Michael Carter-Williams is the latest. But even Michael talked seriously about transferring, as did James Southerland, who averaged 3.2 points a game as a freshman . . . and over 13 as a senior.

During my meeting with C.J., I tell him what I told him before. "If an NBA team needs your skill set and you play well for them in tryouts, you will be drafted. Over four years, you were a credit to this program. You won a lot of games for us, and I know that Syracuse fans will remember you fondly."

I tell Baye Moussa Keita that he was one of the greatest kids ever to go through our program, something he already knew. At the basketball banquet, I had given him the first postseason award that I ever presented. It was for being a consummate teammate. Baye played hard, he played without complaint and he lifted everybody up every day. The award will not necessarily be given every year, only when it is deserved, but it will be named after him. I hate to see him go.

My talk with Michael Gbinije was a little different. "Mike," I say, "right now you are a player who stops to put on a sneaker while we give up a three-point shot. That's who you are. But we don't want you to be that guy, and you don't have to be that guy. You need to play hard and you need to play tougher." I think he will.

I went through the predictable things with Trevor Cooney (get stronger, learn to take it to the hole) and Rakeem Christmas (keep working on offense and you can be dominant at both ends), but I had entirely different discussions with Jerami Grant and Tyler Ennis. There was already talk that both would jump to the NBA. This wasn't the time for me to hear them plead their case or beg them to stay. It was the time for me to be frank.

I wasn't sure what Jerami's decision was going to be, and I don't think he knew either. I'm certain he didn't want to hear what I told him, which was: "You're not ready. You don't have a dependable jump shot and you get stripped too much when you go to the hole. You're athletic and talented and a great kid, but if you come back for your junior year you will get drafted even higher, and someday you will be a terrific NBA player."

With Tyler, the tone was more different still, because I was almost certain he would be leaving. Consider how quickly his basketball career had changed. Eight months ago, when he was installed as our starting point guard, the conversations about him were cautious. "He takes care of the ball." "He's mature." "Nothing flashy about his game." "Good college player."

Then we started to win, and it developed that Tyler had a terrific assist-to-turnover ratio, particularly for a freshman. Then he scored 14 points, had nine assists and made all eight of his free throws in our much-watched win over Duke. Eleven days later, Tyler calmly dribbled upcourt with time running out and made a 35-footer at the buzzer to beat Pitt.

The conversation kept changing, and the superlatives kept growing. Tyler Ennis is the surprise of the college basketball season. Tyler Ennis is the best freshman point guard in the country. Tyler Ennis is ready for the NBA.

I tell Tyler that he did a terrific job as our floor leader. He took care of the ball, and, when I needed him to, he became more of a scorer. He has every chance to be a star in the NBA. But I also tell him: "I think another year would help you physically. You know that because I've said it before. You have to get together with your father and figure out what is best for you. You never know where you're going to get drafted. One mock draft will have you at 10th, another at 16th and another at 20th. Do you want to take the chance of going 20th? Is that high enough? Or do you want to come back, try to win a national championship, have a great, great feeling about your college career and be a surefire top-ten pick next year?"

We shake hands. There is nothing at all bitter about our conversation.

There's little doubt that in the Tyler Ennis discussions I've been cast as the bad guy, the stubborn NCAA "loyal soldier," the obstructionist standing in the way of a kid's future. That ignores the fact that many of our players have left early for the NBA with my blessing. There is nothing hidden about my agenda. I think Tyler might be skills-ready but could use another year physically. As for Jerami, I don't think he's skills-ready or physically ready to play forward in the NBA.

It's the NBA that says you cannot jump directly out of high school and must stay in college for at least one year. I don't care all that much when players leave our program or, for that matter, if a potential recruit wants to make the jump to the NBA right out of high school. It doesn't make a profound difference to our program. We will have players, our fans will support us, and most seasons we'll have a chance to contend for a national championship.

If the rule were changed tomorrow and players were once again allowed to turn pro right after high school, I don't think you would see a run on it. A lot was made about the 2013–14 freshman class—Jabari Parker, Andrew Wiggins, Joel Embiid—and I don't think any of them would've skipped that one year of college. Look how good Carmelo Anthony was and, though there was no prohibition against his going pro in 2002, he still came to school for one year.

Cynics may disagree, but kids *do* get a lot out of coming for even one year—the travel, being on your own, classes and, of course, competition. There is no comparison between the level of play in high school and college, just as there isn't between college and the pros. Jabari Parker had a seven-point and an eight-point game this year; that didn't happen in high school.

Which brings me to this point: Yes, I would rather have kids stay for two years than one year, and that feeling didn't begin with Tyler Ennis. It is rare for a kid to be ready after one year. If he is, then he would go with my blessing, as was the case with Carmelo.

Is part of this selfish? Yes, I think it's better for the image of college basketball when a kid stays for two years—and college basketball is my business. But in most cases, it's also better for the kids, physically, mentally and competitively. And here's one other thing: If a kid stays for two years, he is probably more than halfway toward getting his degree, considering summer school sessions. He has a better-than-even chance of getting it—which will be the case with Michael Carter-Williams—as opposed to a one-year player, who has almost no chance. No big deal in most cases, you say? That's your opinion. I think it is a big deal.

We are moving in the direction of a two-year minimum. Well, maybe that's optimistic on my part. The NBA wants it and college basketball wants it, but it's anyone's guess if the NBA Player's Association will want it.

But one thing is certain right now—you can't *tell* your player what to do. Tyler's father is a knowledgeable AAU coach, and Jerami's dad, Harvey, played in the NBA, as did his uncle Horace. Now, do I think they necessarily know more than I do? No, I don't. But they know a lot, and I will respect their opinions.

There is usually no absolute right or wrong answer about whether a player should leave early. It worked out for Carter-Williams, who was the 11th pick in the 2013 draft. He got to the right team and, though his 76ers lost 26 straight games, that's why they pay you the big money. Michael made the right decision, though I would remind everyone that he was here for two years.

I hope Tyler makes the right decision for him; I suspect I already know what that decision is.

A COACH'S NOTES IX

As I look down from my office window onto the courts at Melo, the "circus" I described in an earlier chapter looks quieter but still gratifyingly busy. There is Trevor Cooney dribbling his way through cones and practicing jump shots. There is Mike Hopkins feeding Rakeem Christmas so he can attempt short jumpers in the lane, shot after shot after shot. There is Mike Gbinije making his way around a circuit set up by our conditioning guys.

Our final loss of the season is several days behind us, an eternity in college basketball. In fact, it feels almost like a new season.

In many ways, today's game is much more efficient than it used to be, the kids more knowledgeable about strength and conditioning, the preparation and contact with coaches more contiguous than it was in my day, when you drifted apart after the season and came together only to play pickup once in a while. Strict NCAA rules monitor how much off-season work the players can do—six hours in the weight room and two hours on the court per week—but this year-round contact is enormously helpful to players' basketball growth, like having a 12-month school year.

A KNOCK ON the door, and there's Tyler Ennis. He has made his decision. As we make the arrangements to get his father on speakerphone, Tyler tells me, "Coach, I'm going to leave. I'm going to enter the draft."

"I figured that's the direction you were going, Tyler," I say. "Good luck to you. I hope it works out."

When Tony McIntyre, Tyler's dad, gets on the phone, he says that he is comfortable with Tyler's decision. It's something they decided to do when their research suggested he would get picked between 7th and 15th.

"There are only two pure point guards rated that high," Tony says. "Tyler and Marcus Smart [from Oklahoma State]. Plus, you can't be sure whether Tyler would necessarily move up next year if he stayed. Maybe he is still in that same range. Now is the right time to go."

Both of them know how I feel. "I wish Tyler nothing but the best," I say, "and he'll be a good pro eventually. But I don't believe he will go that high in the draft this year. I hope he does, and I'll be happy if he does. But he's more likely to go 10th to 20th than 7th. And I believe if he came back, he'd go between 4th and 10th, which is a big jump, and he'd also have a chance to play for a national championship."

In the wake of Tyler leaving, I was asked by ESPN to comment. Here is the entirety of what I said:

"[Tyler] is a great college player. I think physically he could've used another year. It's a little different than Dion Waiters, who left early a couple years ago. I think Dion was physically ready. [And even that, by the way, was after Dion spent two seasons at Syracuse.]

"When you go to the NBA, you need to be as physically ready as you can be. I think Tyler could've benefited from another year. But certainly he's a tremendous player, and a very, very smart point guard.

"The one thing I think is that point guard is probably the hardest position to break into in the NBA. It's a very difficult position, but he's got the skill set to be able to do that. It's just a question of landing in the right place."

The backlash to what I thought were fairly predictable remarks was strong in some quarters, even vicious on one website. Look, would we be a better team next year if Tyler were to come back? Of course. So if you want to call me selfish, go ahead. But my position on Tyler hasn't changed since last September. He's a great kid who was terrific for our program and who would've been even better after one more season, during which he'd grow and mature. And as for my trying to undermine him with the NBA, here are two factors to consider:

If I'm not honest about evaluating my players, I lose credibility. Almost every year, I have a player who wants to leave early, and if I'm not sincere in what I say, I'm doing everyone a disservice.

Plus, my saying that Tyler is not physically ready should make no difference to NBA personnel people. They will make that judgment themselves. Having an opinion on a player's physical readiness is not like making vague references about his character, which I would not do.

But beyond the questions about Tyler's physical readiness is the question of where he'll be picked. Will he go to a team where he can play right away? To a good organization where he can develop? Or will he get picked back in the pack and end up in the NBA's Developmental League? I would argue that a year at Syracuse would be better than that. It's the uncertainty of the whole thing. I've seen guys projected in the top 10 who go 20, and we've had kids who weren't projected in the top 20 who end up going in the top 10. You just don't know.

And as for the idea that Tyler staying for more than one year is crazy, consider his competition when he gets to the NBA. True, John Wall, Mike Conley, Kyrie Irving and Derrick Rose all jumped to the NBA after one year in college. It took a couple of them a while to adjust, but they're all doing quite well, Rose's injury problems notwithstanding. But Damian Lillard of Portland stayed for four years at Weber State. Steph Curry (Davidson) and Ty Lawson (North Carolina) stayed for three years. Chris Paul (Wake Forest) and Russell Westbrook (UCLA) stayed for two years. If I'm not mistaken, these guys are all pretty good, too. And there's another two-year guy named Michael Carter-Williams, who was the NBA's 2014 rookie of the year.

About ten days after Tyler's visit, Jerami Grant calls from home.

"Coach, I'm leaving," he tells me. By this time I'm not surprised at that decision, either. Jerami had gone home to Maryland to consult one more time with Harvey, his father.

I tell him basically the same thing I told Tyler: Good luck, and you'll always be welcome here.

Six weeks later, the draft results came in: Tyler went 18th to the Phoenix Suns, and Jerami went 39th to the Philadelphia 76ers. That is close to what I expected but certainly a little lower than Jerami expected. C. J. Fair was not drafted. That's not a surprise, and I do think C.J. has a chance to make a team as a complementary piece.

THERE SHOULD BE a better system to take some of the mystery out of where kids are going to get drafted. I'm tempted to say that the solution is "simple," but nothing is simple when it involves the cooperation of the NBA and the players' union.

Right now kids can put their names up for the NBA draft until

April 27. But if they decide not to declare, they have to pull out by April 15, which is much earlier than in the past. The earlier date actually was put in to help college basketball, the thought being that coaches need more time to fill their rosters if kids leave. But in actuality, the earlier date doesn't matter, because 95 percent of the best recruits have committed by that time anyway.

Beyond the minimum of two years in college, I'd like to see a combine, much like the NFL runs, that would take place in May. Invite the 60 best players, work them out for all the NBA teams, and let the kids get an idea of where they would be drafted. If a player doesn't like the sound of "We think you're a late-first-rounder," he can come back to school.

Look, the entire NCAA system is at a crisis point. The executives keep making more money, the schools keep making more money, and we coaches keep making more money. The 2014 Final Four was held in a *football stadium* that holds 80,000 fans, for heaven's sake. So it's becoming increasingly difficult not to listen to the calls for some kind of trickle-down revenue to go to the players.

The endemic flaw is the NCAA structure. About 1,000 schools huddle under the NCAA umbrella, and there are vast differences in the goals of their athletic programs. Even Division I schools have divergent M.O.'s, never mind the operating gulf between a university that makes $100 million on its football program and a D3 program that crams its athletes into minivans for road trips. The NCAA's one-size-fits-all system, controlled by college presidents, is clearly outdated and has been for quite a while.

But things are changing. In April, the NCAA made a major alteration to its structure by creating another advisory level, this one composed chiefly of athletic directors, conference commissioners and student-athletes. The NCAA also granted more autonomy to the major conferences, more leeway in deciding our own rules and regs. There is still a lot to figure out in terms of providing the athlete with what is known as "total cost of attendance," i.e., money needed for after-hours food, emergency travel, etc., that goes beyond the scholarship. This is just a hypothetical, but let's say Syracuse decides that number is $2,200, but Louisville decides it's $6,000. That represents a distinct recruiting advantage. But I'm confident it can be worked out equitably among the conferences, which is perhaps where it should've been done years ago. By adhering to an outmoded system for so long, the NCAA has found itself on the defensive, responding to legitimate calls for change.

Speaking of being on the defensive, that's the position in which you are put when the NCAA investigates your program, the present state of affairs at Syracuse. You're not allowed to say anything, but meanwhile details about the investigation, some of them misinformed, make their way into the newspapers. You can't defend yourself, and the investigation drags on and on. It's wearing. Sometimes the wrongdoing involves things out of your control, but as the NCAA sees it, *nothing* should be out of the control of a head coach. Okay, I accept that, the price of being in charge. And I like being in charge.

"HOW'S MY FAVORITE player?"

I'm on the phone with Chris McCullough, a six-foot-nine high school junior who has committed to us.

"You're getting strong, right? They're making you lift down there? You'll be the surprise player in the country next year, I'm telling you that right now."

It sounds like a sales job, right? Like I had to psych myself up to say all that to an 18-year-old kid?

Well, at that moment, Chris McCullough, who in all likelihood will be starting at power forward for us in the 2014–15 season, was my favorite player in the country.

"Did you see that Kaleb won the MVP in the prep champion-ship?" I ask Chris.

I'm talking about Kaleb Joseph, our second prime recruit, the point guard who will likely take Tyler's place next season. Kaleb is both a little flashier and a little more turnover-prone than Tyler. Right now Kaleb Joseph is my second-favorite player, and if Kaleb were on the phone instead of McCullough, he would be my favorite.

"We need a go-to guy, and you're going to be it," I say to Chris. "Keep working hard."

I'm sure my critics believe that, after I heard from Tyler and Jerami, I sat around my office griping about today's younger genera-tion, throwing darts into a wall and wondering why the whole world was going to hell.

I didn't. I had moved on by the time they made their decisions. If you don't move on, you might as well get out, because college sports, and basketball in particular, is a game of constant loss and replen-ishment. My assistants and I are not unlike personnel managers at a corporation—people leave all the time, and you have to be ready to fill their spots.

The recruiting game is not just about getting the splashy guys, the McDonald's All-Americans whose names appear in the paper after you sign them. You also have to find players like Trevor Cooney and Andy Rautins. Even C. J. Fair, who turned out to be an All-American, was that kind of athlete, a player with an obvious upside but not a big-time recruit. Everyone knows about the super-stars, but what you have to do is home in on the secondary players and try to decide this all-important question:

Can they become an All-ACC player, or almost an All-ACC player? Because if they can't, you're not going to beat Duke and North Carolina.

It continues to be a fascinating, inexact science, but we have a pretty good track record. What makes you *want* a guy? What are you looking for? The best way I can summarize it is: You think about all the good players you've seen at this stage in their basketball lives and try to figure out if the kid you're recruiting can become like one of them. Hakim Warrick: Can he be another Louis Orr? C. J. Fair: Can he be Josh Pace with a better shot? Trevor Cooney: Can he be a little bit like Gerry McNamara, not as good a ballhandler but a big-time shooter? Tyler Ennis: Can he be another Adrian Autry, maybe not as strong but just as smart? (When Adrian was recruiting Tyler, he admitted, sheepishly, that the kid reminded him of himself.)

What you must *not* do is see a kid and immediately stack him up against, say, Derrick Coleman or Carmelo Anthony. Then all you're doing is sabotaging your own judgments. You want once-in-a-decade players, but you have to recruit as if you're not going to get them. Because you usually don't.

Adrian says that, as a recruiter, I don't "drool much." That's true. I've been in a lot of gyms in a lot of places and salivated only four or five times in my life—over Derrick and Carmelo, Billy Owens, Pearl and maybe Gerry McNamara a little bit, because I saw the fire in his eyes. Recruiting isn't about going head over heels. It's about trying to make sober decisions. And you'd better be right more than you're wrong.

ON AN OVERCAST April afternoon, I'm driving east along Interstate 90, heading back to Syracuse from a solo recruiting trip. I won't even tell you whom I was visiting, for fear that I would be breaking some kind of NCAA rule. The kid is a high school junior, but he wasn't home. It was his mother I went to see, and we spent a good hour together. She walked me to my car and offered me cheesecake for the road.

My assistants thought that the trip would be a good idea. I'm a decent closer on recruiting deals, and mothers, particularly African

American mothers, tend to like me and trust me. I suppose the biggest advantage the schoolmaster glasses have given me is that it's impossible for me to look slick. Mothers and grandmothers generally don't like slick.

It strikes me that I'm driving along the same road that I took with my parents from Lyons to Syracuse in September of 1962. The Boeheim family car was quiet, because we were all nervous. Like most parents, mine were probably thinking, *I hope the kid just makes it through the semester.* That was over a hundred semesters ago.

I noticed a small item in a newspaper before the beginning of the NCAA tournament this year. It read, "Jim Boeheim was hired as head coach of Syracuse in 1976. Players from that team will turn 60 this year." I don't usually think about things like that, but I'm one of the few guys who have been around long enough to have coached the sons of my former players. I doubt I'll be around to coach grandsons, although, let's see, if Andy Rautins has a son right now . . . No, not possible.

But I suppose it's inevitable that I end this with my thoughts about retirement, which are not—and I'm not kidding—fully formed. I want to leave the cupboard full for Mike Hopkins, but I don't want to get out while I still have something to give.

I don't ever feel "old" in my job, never feel like the game has passed me by. But there are moments when I realize that I'm still doing the same job I was doing in the 1960s and many others I once knew are gone from the face of the earth. Like Jimmy Valvano. Or Al McGuire, a true original as a coach and broadcaster. Al would come to town to do a game and call me from the Greyhound bus terminal. That's right—he took a bus to Syracuse. "I need a ride, Jim," and after I picked him up, he'd have me drop him off on South Salina Street, where he wandered among the people, barbershop, bookstore, luncheonette, whatever. They don't make characters like that anymore.

But you can't wallow in the past, and right now I have no desire to sit in the stands and talk about the old days. Neither do I have a desire to sit in a TV studio and, with the benefit of hindsight, pick apart mistakes that other coaches have made.

No, it's not quite time yet. Soon, maybe. But there is so much I would miss if I left.

I would miss my many little superstitions. Driving from my home to the Dome the exact same way every time—same back roads, same impatient honking if someone in front of me is driving too slowly. Wearing the same shoes and the same T-shirt at practice during winning streaks. (They both got a lot of use when we won 25 in a row this season. Regarding the T-shirt, I don't really sweat that much.)

I would miss the weekly radio show I do with Matt Park, the voice of Syracuse sports. We share a good meal as Syracuse Nation phones in its complaints. Actually, it's rarely combative. Though I sense an urge to second-guess among my listenership, the calls are almost never negative, perhaps because my penchant for wanting to win arguments has been well documented.

"Coach, are you planning on playing more than seven players?"

"Well, for now," I'll answer, "I'm thinking about keeping it like this."

"Good idea."

More typical is the type of caller who will tell me he's phoning about somebody else.

"Coach, I understand what you're doing, but my brother thinks your rotation is too short."

"You tell your brother I'm pretty happy with our system right now."

"Okay," he'll say, "I'll do that."

I would miss walking into a half-filled arena before games, feeling the tension and the excitement. After the second Duke game, whenever I did that I'd hear a chorus of "Hey, Coach. Block or charge?" I didn't lose many fans after the double technical, incidentally—a lot of people don't like Duke.

I would miss the daily ritual of filling out my practice card. We don't change much from day to day, but the feel of ritual, tradition and organization is compelling.

I would miss putting my arms around my sons, my daughter and my wife after games, sometimes in celebration, sometimes in sadness.

I would miss sitting in an almost silent room with my assistants as video of the next opponent rolls on the screen, all of us making our calculations about strategy.

I would miss the opportunities that come along with being the de facto CEO of a great university athletic team. As I write this, I haven't been back long from Washington, D.C., where, with several other college coaches, I was part of a leadership seminar hosted by the Pentagon. The visit included a brief stop in the Oval Office, where we met the president. When celebrated Syracuse College of Law graduate/Orange fan Joe Biden wandered in, Mr. Obama commented, "Biden's only here to see Boeheim." Those moments don't happen when you're sitting on the sidelines.

So . . . I feel the excitement, but I also feel something else. The little tightness in the stomach, the looking ahead to next season, the dread. It's my old friend, Fear.

If McCullough and Joseph aren't ready to make the jump from high school; if Trevor can't knock down three-pointers; if Rakeem Christmas can't be a force inside; if we don't find someone to replace Jerami Grant; if, if, if . . .

I'll be honest with you: Right now I'm not sure we can win a game.

ACKNOWLEDGMENTS

I doubt that I would've been gainfully employed for this long without Dick Blackwell, my high school coach, who demonstrated, on a daily basis, what great coaches are supposed to do. Ditto for two great leaders at Syracuse, Fred Lewis and Morris Osborne, who showed me how to coach and recruit at the college level.

There are lots of people to thank at USA Basketball, which has given me a second career and renewed energy. Sean Ford, who makes it happen at all levels. Jim Tooley, for his leadership. And Craig Miller, Caroline Williams and B. J. Johnson, who work hard every day to make this a great organization.

I'd also like to thank the two guys at the top of the program: CEO Jerry Colangelo, who resurrected USA Basketball, and Mike Krzyzewski, for being a great coach and a better friend.

During my 38 years at Syracuse I've worked with two terrific athletic directors—Jake Crouthamel and the current boss, Daryl Gross, who helped get the Carmelo K. Anthony Center built. Which brings me to the obvious—thanking Carmelo for the $3 million gift that jump-started the facility, which has been a major factor in our recent success.

Besides Carmelo, I could take the next ten pages to thank all of the players who have passed through here and made Syracuse basketball what it was and what it remains. There isn't room to do that, but their names, stories and collective impact pass through the pages of this book.

I've had many great assistants over the years, but I have to single out my top guy, Mike Hopkins, a future head coach and the driving force behind our recruiting success for the last 18 years.

Two other formidable forces of energy around Syracuse basketball have been Pete Moore, the sports information director, and my assistant, Kelly L. Seubert, who drives the ship on a daily basis. And thanks to all the supporters, financial and otherwise, of Orange Nation. Long and loud may you root. One of the most loyal members of that group is my sister, Barbara; I thank her for her unwavering support.

My first wife, Elaine, helped me through the first 18 years of this coaching life, as did our beautiful daughter, Elizabeth. I was 41 years old when Lizzie changed my life, so it was about time. And my "younger generation" of children, Jimmy, Jamie and Jack, are what make this journey fun and worthwhile these days.

Most of all, I have to thank my wife, Juli, who has helped me become a better coach and, more important, a better person. I don't know if I would've made it through these last two decades without her love and support.

The enthusiasm and encouragement of the folks at HarperCollins are a major reason that, at long last, I decided to get my memories down on paper. Thanks to ace editors David Hirshey and Barry Harbaugh, as well as editorial assistant Sydney Pierce. Scott Waxman of the Waxman Leavell Agency also helped me to get this going.

Finally, thanks to my collaborator and friend, Jack McCallum. Please direct all your complaints to him.

—Jim Boeheim
Syracuse, New York
July 2014

ABOUT THE AUTHORS

JIM BOEHEIM is the second-winningest coach in college basket-ball history behind Mike Krzyzewski. In 2005, he was elected to the coaches' wing of the Naismith Memorial Basketball Hall of Fame. The 2014–15 season will be his 39th as head coach of the Syracuse Orangemen. He lives in Fayetteville, New York, with his wife and three children.

JACK McCALLUM is the author of ten books, including the 2012 *New York Times* best-seller *Dream Team*. In 2005, he was presented with the Curt Gowdy Media Award from the Naismith Memorial Basketball Hall of Fame for excellence in basketball writing. He lives in Bethlehem, Pennsylvania, with his wife.